D1083865

THE ANALYSIS OF BEHAVIOR

A Program for Self-Instruction

THE ANALYSIS
OF BEHAVIOR

68417

JAMES G. HOLLAND and B. F. SKINNER

Harvard University

BF77
.H73

McGRAW-HILL *Book Company, Inc.* 1961
New York *Toronto* *London*

Library of Congress Catalog Card Number: 61-11128

TO THE INSTRUCTOR

Edward Thorndike and Arthur Gates in their *Elementary Principles of Education,* published in 1929, wrote, "If, by a miracle of mechanical ingenuity, a book could be so arranged that only to him who had done what was directed on page one would page two become visible, and so on, much that now requires personal instruction could be managed by print." The present volume is perhaps the beginning of the fulfillment of this dream. Nothing miraculous was required. A simple type of teaching machine achieves the result by taking the student through a carefully prepared sequence of steps (generally items to be completed) so designed that he usually takes each step successfully. Early steps in the sequence prepare him for later, more advanced material.

Simple as this may seem, efforts to produce effective teaching machines were for a long time unsuccessful. Patents go back well into the nineteenth century. The wish of Thorndike and Gates was not fulfilled in their day, even though Sidney Pressey saw the need for instrumentation. What was lacking in early efforts was a set of techniques for analyzing and controlling behavior. Such techniques have gradually emerged from an experimental analysis of behavior and from its extension to the verbal field. What appears to be a revolution in education, beginning only six years ago, is now under way as scholars prepare programs in areas ranging from beginning arithmetic to calculus, from modern behaviorism to the Old Testament, from spelling and English grammar to many modern languages, from biology and physics to medical-school courses, and in hundreds of fields of industrial education.

Machine programs share with the individual tutor many advantages over other techniques of teaching: (1) Each student advances at his own rate, the fast learner moving ahead rapidly while the slower learner moves at a speed convenient for him. (2) The student moves on to advanced material only after he has thoroughly mastered earlier stages. (3) Because of this gradual progression and with the help of certain techniques of hinting and prompting, the student is almost always right. (4) The student is continuously active and receives immediate confirmation of his success. (5) Items are so constructed that the student must comprehend the critical point in order to supply the answer. (6) "Concept" is represented in the program by many examples and syntactical arrangements, in an effort to maximize generalization to other situations. (7) A record of students' responses furnishes the programmer with valuable information for future revisions. [The present program has been thoroughly revised twice, and minor changes have been made from time to time. The number of errors made by students was halved (reduced to about 10 per cent) as a result of the first revision.]

Earlier versions of this material have been widely used as models for programming other subject matter. The authors would like to believe that it has been helpful not only as a model but in teaching some elementary aspects of the science from which this type of programming emerged. This program is offered, however, mainly as a teaching instrument to be used in an introductory course in psychology emphasizing the analysis of behavior. The material has been thoroughly tested on more than seven hundred undergraduates at Harvard and Radcliffe, and the authors have profited from comments by many psychologists who have used the material in other institutions.

TO THE STUDENT

With this book the student should be able to instruct himself in that substantial part of psychology which deals with the analysis of behavior—in particular the explicit prediction and control of the behavior of people. The practical importance of such a science scarcely needs to be pointed out, but understanding and effective use of the science require fairly detailed knowledge. This program is designed to present the basic terms and principles of the science. It is also designed to reveal the inadequacy of popular explanations of behavior and to prepare the student for rapidly expanding extensions into such diverse fields as social behavior and psychopharmacology, space flight and child care, education and psychotherapy. This book is itself one application of the science.

How to Use the Book

The material was designed for use in a teaching machine. The teaching machine presents each item automatically. The student writes his response on a strip of paper revealed through a window in the machine. He then operates the machine to make his written response inaccessible, though visible, and to uncover the correct response for comparison.

Where machines are not available, a programmed textbook such as this may be used. The correct response to each item appears on the following page, along with the next item in the sequence. Read each item, write your response on a separate sheet of paper, and then turn the page to see whether your answer is correct. If it is incorrect, mark an "x" beside it. Then read and answer the next question, and turn the page again to check your answer.

Writing out the answer is essential. It is also essential to write it *before* looking at the correct answer. When the student, though well-intentioned, glances ahead without first putting down an answer of his own, he commits himself to only a vague and poorly formulated guess. This is not effective and in the long run makes the total task more difficult.

It is important to do each item in its proper turn. The sequence has been carefully designed, and occasional apparent repetitions or redundancies are there for good reason. Do not skip. If you have undue difficulty with a set, repeat it before going on to the next. A good rule is to repeat any set in which you answer more than 10 per cent of the items incorrectly. Avoid careless answers. If you begin to make mistakes because you are tired or not looking at the material carefully, take a break. If you are not able to work on the material for a period of several days, it may be advisable to review the last set completed.

The review sets will help you to find your weaknesses. When you miss an item in a review set, jot down the set number given in the answer space and review that set after you have completed the review set.

Conventions

Observe the following conventions:

1. The number of words needed to complete an item is indicated by the number of blanks. Thus "___" indicates a one-word response, whereas "___ ___" indicates a two-word response. When asterisks (* * *) are used in place of blanks, fill in as many words as you think necessary to respond to the item.

2. The abbreviation TT calls for a technical term. When it is used, a nontechnical word is incorrect.

3. There are often several reasonably equivalent responses, and it would be a waste of time to list them all. This is particularly true when the response is nontechnical. Use reasonable judgment in deciding whether your response is synonymous with the printed form. Score it **correct if it is.**

JAMES G. HOLLAND

B. F. SKINNER

ACKNOWLEDGMENTS

Unlike conventional textbooks, this program omits detailed citations of data within the textual material itself. This is because the program includes only material which the student is taught. We are nonetheless indebted to the many scientists who have contributed to this analysis of behavior. Quantitative data have been used from the following sources:

Anliker, J., and Mayer, J. Operant conditioning technique for studying feeding patterns in normal and obese mice. *J. appl. Psychol.*, 1956, 8, 667–670. (Set 28.)

Azrin, N. H. Effects of punishment intensity. *J. exp. Anal. Behav.*, 1960, 3, 123–142. (Set 40.)

Brady, J. V. Assessment of drug effects on emotional behavior. *Science*, 1956, *123*, 1033–1034. (Set 35.)

Ferster, C. B., and Skinner, B. F. *Schedules of reinforcement.* New York: Appleton-Century-Crofts, Inc., 1957. (Sets 18, 19.)

Guttman, N. The pigeon and the spectrum and other perplexities. *Psychol. Rep.*, 1956, 2, 449–460. (Set 22.)

Morse, W. H. An analysis of responding in the presence of a stimulus. Unpublished Ph.D. dissertation, Harvard Univer., 1955. (Set 21.)

Morse, W. H., and Herrnstein, R. J. Unpublished data. (Sets 19, 34.)

Sidman, M. Avoidance conditioning with brief shock and no exteroceptive warning signal. *Science*, 1953, *118*, 157–158. (Set 34.)

Sidman, M. By-products of aversive control. *J. exp. Anal. Behav.*, 1958, *1*, 276. (Set 35.)

Skinner, B. F. *The behavior of organisms.* New York: Appleton-Century-Crofts, Inc., 1938. (Sets 13, 26, 38.)

Pavlov, I. P. *Conditioned reflexes.* London: Oxford University Press, 1946. (Set 4.)

We are indebted to the students of Harvard's course entitled "Natural Sciences 114, Human Behavior," who gave valuable data which made possible the development of this program, and to the many persons who aided in supervision of the self-instruction room, tabulation of data, and typing of material. Particularly outstanding has been the diligent assistance of Beverly Meeker, Stella Kramer, and Dorothy Schneider.

CONTENTS

THE ANALYSIS OF BEHAVIOR

stimulus (tap on the knee) 1-7	Technically speaking, a reflex involves an eliciting stimulus in a process called elicitation. A stimulus _____ a response. 1-8
threshold 1-15	The fraction of a second which elapses between "brushing the eye" and "blink" is the _____ of the reflex. 1-16
threshold 1-23	The greater the concentration of onion juice (stimulus), the _____ the *magnitude* of the response. 1-24
elicit 1-31	In the pupillary reflex, a very bright flash of light elicits a response of greater _____ than a weak flash of light. 1-32
latency 1-39	A solution of lemon juice will not elicit salivation if the stimulus is _____ the threshold. 1-40
(1) magnitude (2) latency 1-47	Presentation of a stimulus is the "cause" of a response. The two form a(n) _____. 1-48

A doctor taps your knee (patellar tendon) with a rubber hammer to test your ____.

1-1

---

elicits

1-8

To avoid unwanted nuances of meaning in popular words, we do not say that a stimulus "triggers," "stimulates," or "causes" a response, but that it ____ a response.

1-9

---

latency

1-16

In the patellar-tendon reflex, a forceful tap elicits a strong kick; a tap barely above the threshold elicits a weak kick. Magnitude of response thus depends on the intensity of the ____.

1-17

---

greater
(higher,
larger)

1-24

Onion juice elicits the secretion of tears by the lachrymal gland. This causal sequence of events is a(n) ____.

1-25

---

magnitude
(intensity)

1-32

A response and its eliciting stimulus comprise a(n) ____.

1-33

---

below
(less than,
sub-)

1-40

The latency of a reflex is the (1) ____ between on-set of (2) ____ and ____.

1-41

---

reflex

1-48

The layman frequently explains behavior as the operation of "mind" or "free will." He seldom does this for reflex behavior, however, because the ____ is an adequate explanation of the response.

1-49

eflexes (reflex) **1-1**	If your reflexes are normal, your leg _____ to the tap on the knee with a slight kick (the so-called knee jerk). **1-2**
licits **1-9**	In a reflex, the stimulus and the elicited response occur in a given temporal order; first the (1) _____, then the (2) _____. **1-10**
timulus (tap) **1-17**	The magnitude of a response corresponds to (is a function of) the _____ of the stimulus which elicits it. **1-18**
eflex lachrymal eflex) **1-25**	When speaking technically, instead of saying onion juice "stimulates" tears; we say onion juice "_____" tears. **1-26**
eflex **1-33**	In a warm room, your sweat glands rapidly excrete sweat. The response is (1) _____; the stimulus is (2) _____; and the two together form a(n) (3) _____. **1-34**
time (interval) stimulus (and) response **1-41**	A very hot surface brought into contact with the hand, elicits arm flexion with a(n) _____ latency than a less hot surface. **1-42**
stimulus **1-49**	Because the stimulus is sufficient in accounting for the reflex response, there * * * a need to explain reflex behavior with concepts of "mind" or "free will." **1-50**

sponds
eacts)

1-2

In the knee jerk or patellar-tendon reflex, the kick of the leg is the ____ to the tap on the knee.

1-3

---

1) stimulus
2) response

1-10

A kick of the leg is ____ by a tap on the patellar tendon.

1-11

---

ntensity
magnitude,
strength)

1-18

A reflex consists of *both* a(n) (1) ____ and a(n) (2) ____, occurring in that order. The term "reflex" (3) * * * synonymous with the single term "response."

1-19

---

licits

1-26

A child touching a hot surface withdraws his hand quickly. The word "quickly" suggests that the response has a short ____.

1-27

---

sweating
cretion of sweat)
heat
aperature,
nth)
reflex   1-34

The softest touch on the surface of the eye needed to elicit a blink, marks the ____ of the stimulus.

1-35

---

horter
smaller)

1-42

A very hot room causes (1) ____ sweating than a merely warm room (i.e., the response has a(n) (2) ____ magnitude).

1-43

---

s not

1-50

Latency is the ____ between the onset of an energy change and the onset of a response which it elicits.

1-51

esponse
eaction)

1-3

The stimulating *object* used by the doctor to elicit a knee jerk is a(n) _____.

1-4

---

licited

1-11

The time which elapses between the onset of the stimulus and the onset of the response is called the *latency.* Thus the time between tap and kick is the _____ of the knee-jerk reflex.

1-12

---

1) stimulus
2) response
3) is not

1-19

When a person is startled by a loud noise, his sudden movement is his (1) _____ to the noise which has acted as a (2) _____. The two together are called a(n) (3) _____.

1-20

---

atency

1-27

In withdrawing the hand from a hot surface, arm movement is a(n) (1) _____ which is elicited by a painful (2) _____ to the hand.

1-28

---

areshold

1-35

A cat held upside down and dropped will land on its feet. In this "righting reflex," acceleration due to gravity is the main _____ for righting.

1-36

---

1) more
   (greater)
2) greater
   (larger)

1-43

The greater the concentration of onion vapor reaching the surface of the eye, the (1) _____ the magnitude of the response, and the (2) _____ the latency.

1-44

---

me
nterval,
eriod)

1-51

The (1) _____ of a stimulus is the intensity which is barely sufficient to (2) _____ a(n) (3) _____.

1-52

ammer
nallet)

1-4

The *stimulus* which elicits a knee jerk is the ____ delivered by the so-called stimulus object or hammer.

1-5

---

tency

1-12

The weakest stimulus sufficient to elicit a response marks the *threshold* of the reflex. A tap on the knee will not elicit a kick if it is below the ____.

1-13

) response
) stimulus
) reflex

1-20

If a sip of very weak lemonade does not cause salivation, the stimulus is said to be below the ____.

1-21

) response
) stimulus

1-28

In the hand-withdrawal reflex, the stimulus must be intense enough to exceed the ____ or no response will occur.

1-29

---

imulus

1-36

In any (1) ____ , there is a stimulus which (2) ____ the response.

1-37

) greater
) shorter
(less,
smaller)

1-44

The greater the concentration of lemon juice sipped, the (1) ____ the flow of saliva, and the (2) ____ the interval of time between onsets of stimulus and response.

1-45

) threshold
) elicit
) response

1-52

In a reflex, a(n) (1) ____ always precedes a(n) (2) ____ .

1-53

ap (blow)

1-5

In the knee-jerk reflex, we call the rubber hammer the (1) ____ ____ and the tap or blow, the (2) ____ .

1-6

---

hreshold

1-13

If you blink when something brushes your eye, the ____ is a response.

1-14

---

hreshold

1-21

In the salivary reflex, the (1) ____ (food) precedes the response (secretion of saliva) by an interval of time called the (2) ____ .

1-22

---

hreshold

1-29

A light flashed into the eye elicits constriction of the pupil. This sequence is called the pupillary ____ .

1-30

---

1) reflex
2) elicits

1-37

Sticking a finger in your throat may (1) ____ vomiting. (2) ____ is the response. The (3) ____ is tactual (touch).

1-38

---

1) greater
2) shorter
   (smaller)

1-45

A very bright light flashed into the eye elicits a pupillary response with a short ____ .

1-46

---

1) stimulus
2) response

1-53

In a reflex, the magnitude of response varies with the ____ of the stimulus.

1-54

(1) stimulus object (2) stimulus 1-6	An event is explained when its cause is identified. The "cause" or explanation of the knee jerk is, technically, the ____ which elicits it. 1-7 ←To p. 1
blink 1-14	A puff of air striking the eye will elicit a blink only if the force exerted by the air exceeds the ____ value. 1-15 ←To p. 1
(1) stimulus (2) latency 1-22	If an actress uses onion juice on her handkerchief to elicit tears during an emotional scene, she must use enough to exceed the ____. 1-23 ←To p. 1
reflex 1-30	In the pupillary reflex, a flash of light is said to ____ the response. 1-31 ←To p. 1
(1) elicit (2) Vomiting (3) stimulus 1-38	If vomiting began 0.1 second after the onset of the stimulus, the reflex had a(n) ____ of 0.1 second. 1-39 ←To p. 1
latency 1-46	The more intense the stimulus, the greater the (1) ____ of the response, and the shorter the (2) ____ of the reflex. 1-47 ←To p. 1
ntensity (magnitude) 1-54	End of Set

Set 2

Conditioned Reflexes

Estimated time: 14 minutes   **Turn to next page and begin** ▶

---

cannot	On the *first* occasion when a young child simply hears the word "candy," his mouth * * * water.
2-4	2-5

---

conditioning	Technically speaking, when the word "candy" is repeatedly paired with eating candy, ____ takes place.
2-9	2-10

---

unconditioned	After conditioning, the word "candy" is a conditioned stimulus which elicits salivation. In this case, salivating is the (1) ____ response in a(n) (2) ____ reflex.
2-14	2-15

---

extinguished	A conditioned reflex is extinguished when the conditioned stimulus is repeatedly presented * * * the unconditioned stimulus.
2-19	2-20

---

unconditioned reflex	In this unconditioned hand-withdrawal reflex, heat is the ____-ed ____.
2-24	2-25

---

extinction	In reflex behavior, the process by which a new stimulus comes to elicit a response is called (1) ____. A process by which a stimulus loses the power to elicit a response is called (2) ____.
2-29	2-30

In a reflex, a sufficient explanation of the response is a description of the preceding _____.

2-1

will not

No learning (or conditioning) is necessary in order that candy in the mouth elicit salivation, but the word "candy" will make a child's mouth water only after some _____ has taken place.

2-5

2-6

onditioning

After conditioning, the word "candy" alone will elicit salivation in a conditioned reflex. The word "candy" is a learned or _____ stimulus.

2-10

2-11

1) conditioned
2) conditioned

Candy in the mouth is an unconditioned stimulus which elicits salivation. In this case, salivating is the (1) _____ response in a(n) (2) _____ reflex.

2-15

2-16

ithout
n the
osence of)

In extinction, the word "candy" is repeatedly presented * * * the unconditioned stimulus.

2-20

2-21

ncondition (-ed)
imulus

In the unconditioned hand-withdrawal reflex, the movement of the arm is the _____ _____.

2-25

2-26

) conditioning
) extinction

End of Set

2-30

stimulus 2-1	When food in the mouth elicits the secretion of saliva, the whole series of events is called a(n) ____. 2-2
conditioning (learning, experience) 2-6	When a child has often had candy in his mouth after hearing the word "candy," the word alone may cause ____. 2-7
conditioned 2-11	The word "candy" is a learned or (1) ____ stimulus. Candy in the mouth is an *un*learned or (2) ____ stimulus. 2-12
unconditioned unconditioned 2-16	After conditioning, the word "candy" will ____ the response of salivating. (TT) 2-17
without 2-21	In conditioning, the word "candy" is repeatedly presented * * * the unconditioned stimulus. 2-22
unconditioned response 2-26	If a bell sounds 30 seconds before a hot object touches the hand (and the procedure is repeated several times), ____ will take place. 2-27

eflex salivary eflex) 2-2	Candy put in the mouth of a child for the first time _____ salivation. 2-3
alivation the response) 2-7	If the child is to learn to salivate to the word "candy," "candy" and eating candy must occur nearly _____. 2-8
:onditioned ınconditioned 2-12	Salivation elicited by the word "candy" is a conditioned response, whereas salivation elicited by candy in the mouth is a(n) _____ response. 2-13
licit 2-17	Conditioned stimuli presented repeatedly but not paired with unconditioned stimuli cease to elicit the response. If the word "candy" is often repeated without pairing with candy in the mouth, it * * * elicit(s) salivation. 2-18
ith ust before, t the same me as) 2-22	The process by which a conditioned stimulus loses its power to elicit the conditioned response is called *extinction*. When the word "candy" is presented alone, the conditioned reflex undergoes _____. 2-23
ɔnditioning 2-27	After conditioning, the bell will elicit movement of the arm. The conditioned stimulus is the _____. 2-28

et 51   53-3

D_s (stimuli)
ncompatible

et 51   53-3

When a person cannot recall some previously punished behavior, we say he has _____ it.

53-4
← To p. 333

---

controll-)ed
einforcing
or
.versive
EITHER ORDER)

et 47   53-8

In the laboratory, it (1) * * * possible to isolate
simple functional relations; but in interpreting most
events outside of the laboratory, we must be alert
to the possibility of (2) _____ effects in complex
situations.

53-9
← To p. 333

L) respondent
(reflex)
2) operant

et 46   53-13

The goal of a science of behavior is to be able to
(1) _____, (2) _____, and (3) _____ the behavior of
living organisms.

53-14
← To p. 333

---

ounter-
ggression

et 51   53-18

When we admit, even to ourselves, only the least
punishable reasons for our behavior, we are _____.

53-19
← To p. 333

---

s not

et 45   53-23

We sometimes speak of cause and effect. A cause
is a(n) (1) _____ variable, and an effect is a(n) (2)
_____ variable. The relation is a(n) (3) _____ _____
or a(n) (4) _____.

53-24
← To p. 333

licits

2-3

Since the young child salivates the very first time candy is put in his mouth, we _____ (can or cannot ?) attribute this reflex to learning.

← To p.9 **2-4**

---

ltaneously
ther)

2-8

The technical term for one kind of learning is conditioning. The word "candy" comes to elicit salivation after _____.

← To p.9 **2-9**

---

conditioned

2-13

Salivation elicited by candy in the mouth is a(n) _____ response.

← To p.9 **2-14**

---

ases to
o longer,
es not)

2-18

When the conditioned stimulus can no longer elicit the response, the conditioned reflex is said to have been extinguished. If the word "candy" is repeatedly presented alone, the conditioned salivary reflex is _____.

← To p.9 **2-19**

---

tinction

2-23

When a man's hand is touched by a hot surface or receives an electric shock, the hand is immediately withdrawn. Since this reflex was not established by previous conditioning, it is a(n) _____ _____.

← To p.9 **2-24**

---

ll

2-28

If the bell sounds many times without being paired with contact with a hot object, _____ will take place.

← To p.9 **2-29**

) algebraic
  summation
) oscillation
et 44   53-2

Reaction formation may be interpreted as behavior which removes (1) _____ which make the punishable behavior more probable; it may also be interpreted as behavior which is (2) * * * with punishable behavior.

53-3

---

any
multiple, more
an one)
et 44   53-7

In self-control, the (1) controll-_____ response usually has both (2) _____ and (3) _____ consequences.

53-8

---

ecreased
owered,
duced)
equently (more
equently, often)
et 50   53-12

Sneezing which clears the upper respiratory passages is (1) _____ behavior. However, the "imitative" sneezing by the little boy who "only does it to annoy" is (2) _____ behavior.

53-13

---

on-punishing
audience
extinguished
et 52   53-17

A man who strikes his adversary shows _____.

53-18

---

vithdrawal
ymptoms
versive stimuli
aversive
onditions)
et 50   53-22

To eliminate undesired behavior, such as a dog's scratching a door, it * * * necessary to use aversive control.

53-23

---

multiple
(several,
different)
multiple
(several,
different)   53-27
et 44

End of Set

(A) The conditioned reflex was discovered by Pavlov, a Russian physiologist.

(B) A dog is placed in a special room, free of extraneous stimuli.

(C) Under anesthesia, a small opening has been made in the dog's cheek and the duct of a salivary gland brought to the surface where it remains after healing. A tube fastened to the cheek leads to the next room where the experimenter can count the drops of saliva secreted.

(D) In a typical experiment, a tone is sounded several times. After an early slight disturbance has passed, the dog does not salivate in response to the tone. The tone is called a *neutral stimulus* because it is ineffective in eliciting salivation.

(E) When food powder is dropped nearby, the dog eats the powder and salivation occurs. Food powder in the dog's mouth is an *unconditioned stimulus*, and the salivation it elicits an *unconditioned response*.

(F) The sequence of food-in-mouth and salivation is called an *unconditioned reflex*.

(G) Next, a new stimulus, a tone (neutral stimulus), is presented either simultaneously with the food (unconditioned stimulus) or just before the food.

(H) The two stimuli are presented together, or paired, this way many times.

(I) When the tone is then presented alone, it elicits salivation.

(J) *Conditioning* is said to have taken place. The tone is no longer a neutral stimulus, it is a *conditioned stimulus*.

(K) In this *conditioned reflex*, salivation is the *conditioned response*, and the tone the *conditioned stimulus*.

(L) If the tone is now repeatedly presented but no longer paired with food, it loses its power to elicit salivation. The conditioned reflex is said to have been *extinguished*. The process is called *extinction*.

The letters in parentheses in the accompanying set refer to the letters above.

independent (and a) dependent variable	When a dog stands "not too close and not too far" from a strange object, its behavior shows (1) _____ _____ . When it approaches, jumps back, approaches, jumps back, approaches, etc., it shows (2) _____ .
Set 42 53-1	53-2

(1) conditioned (2) incompatible with	A word which "expresses multiple meanings" is controlled by * * * stimuli.
Set 48 53-6	53-7

transference	The effects of conditioned aversive stimuli are (1) _____ by drinking alcohol. This is shown when behavior which automatically generates aversive stimuli occurs (2) * * * under alcohol.
Set 52 53-11	53-12

isolate (analyze, study)	A therapist frequently tries to change his patient's behavior by acting as a(n) (1) * * * and thereby the aversive properties generated by previously punished behavior can become (2) _____ .
Set 43 53-16	53-17

stimulus generalization	A man is said to be addicted to a drug if withholding the drug produces (1) _____ _____ which furnish (2) _____ _____ .
Set 52 53-21	53-22

multiple (several)	A single event may have (1) _____ effects on behavior, and (2) _____ events may have a common effect.
Set 43 53-26	53-27

Set 3

PART I Reflex Behavior

Conditioned Reflexes (continued)

See exhibit on preceding page

Estimated time: 15 minutes

Turn to next page and begin ▷

neutral stimulus 3-4	In (E), the food powder is an unconditioned stimulus in the sense that conditioning * * * necessary to make it an eliciting stimulus. 3-5
together (nearly simultaneously) 3-9	If, instead of the procedure described in (G), the tone had *followed* the food, the conditions required for ____ would not have been present. 3-10
not be (be not, is not) 3-14	In (J), conditioning is said to have taken place because a previously neutral stimulus is now capable of ____ salivation. 3-15
conditioned 3-19	The conditioned response, salivation, is elicited by the conditioned stimulus, a tone. The tone and the salivation elicited comprise a(n) ____ salivary ____. 3-20
(1) conditioning (2) extinction 3-24	In Pavlov's famous experiments on conditioning, ____ was the unconditioned response. 3-25

▷

In a functional relation, there is an observed systematic relation between a(n) * * * and a(n) * * *.

53-1

---

(1) does not
   (cannot)
(2) is not
Set 49   53-5

Inadequate self-knowledge may result because we have not yet been (1) _____ to notice some aspect of our behavior, or because we engage in behavior which is (2) * * * noticing this behavior.

53-6

---

reinforcement
(conditioning)
aversive stimuli
conditioned
(aversive stimuli)
Set 47   53-10

In psychotherapy, a patient often manifests strong love or hate toward his therapist. This is sometimes called _____.

53-11

---

activation
syndrome

Set 51   53-15

By using simple organisms with controlled histories in simple environments, we hold many variables constant in order to _____ one effective variable at a time.

53-16

---

1) respondent
2) operant

Set 46   53-20

Transference during psychotherapy can be interpreted as an example of _____ _____.

53-21

---

1) controlling
2) controlled

Set 47   53-25

A single aversive stimulus used in punishment elicits respondents, conditions other stimuli to elicit these respondents, and makes possible the conditioning of avoidance behavior. The single aversive stimulus has _____ effects.

53-26

The room in (B) is designed to _____ uncontrolled factors which might affect the experimental result.

3-1

---

s not
'is un-,
las not been)

3-5

In (E), salivation elicited by food powder is an unconditioned response because food powder elicits salivation even though no _____ has taken place.

3-6

---

conditioning

3-10

As described in (G), the procedure for conditioning a reflex is to pair an initially (1) _____ stimulus with a(n) (2) _____ stimulus repeatedly.

3-11

---

eliciting

3-15

A previously neutral stimulus acquires the power to elicit a response in the process called _____.

3-16

---

conditioned
(salivary)
reflex

3-20

In (L), the conditioned stimulus is frequently presented * * * the unconditioned stimulus.

3-21

---

salivation

3-25

The process of conditioning was discovered by _____.

3-26

---

repressed

Set 48   **53-4**

In rationalization, a person (1) "* * * tell the whole truth" even to himself. Rationalization (2) * * * the same as lying.

53-5

(1) is
(2) multiple
(many, various)

Set 43   **53-9**

In so-called self-control, the controlling response is established through (1)_____. Usually this takes place through the reduction of the (2) * * * associated with the controlled response.

53-10

edict, control,
nd) interpret
NY ORDER)

Set 42   **53-14**

The bodily malfunctions called "psychosomatic" result from prolonged elicitation of the responses characteristic of the * * *.

53-15

rationalizing

Set 49   **53-19**

By tickling his throat with a feather, a man can regurgitate poisonous food. The controlled response is a(n) (1) _____ (TT) and the controlling response is a(n) (2) _____. (TT)

53-20

(1) independent
(2) dependent
(3) functional
relation
(4) law

Set 42   **53-24**

In self-control, the (1) _____ response affects variables in such a way as to change the probability of the (2) _____ response.

53-25

liminate emove, avoid, ontrol) 3-1	(C) is used to obtain a measurement of the _____ of the response. 3-2
onditioning 3-6	In (F), the unconditioned reflex has (1) _____ components; an unconditioned (2) _____ and an unconditioned (3) _____ 3-7
eutral nconditioned 1ER ORDER) 3-11	In (G), little or no conditioning would have occurred if the tone had preceded the food by more than a few seconds. The interval between the stimulus-to-be-conditioned and the unconditioned stimulus must be rather _____. 3-12
onditioning 3-16	In (K), the tone is called a *conditioned* stimulus because it elicits the response only after some _____ has taken place. 3-17
ithout n the osence of) 3-21	In (L), the conditioned reflex has been extinguished in the sense that the stimulus has frequently been presented without being _____ with the unconditioned stimulus and has, therefore, lost its ability to elicit the response. 3-22
avlov 3-26	A stimulus able to elicit a response without previous conditioning is called a(n) (1) _____ _____; a stimulus able to elicit a response only after conditioning is called a(n) (2) _____ _____. 3-27

unish **52-3**	A person may be unable to remember past punished behavior if a reduction in the conditioned aversive stimuli generated by covert forms of this behavior has reinforced behavior (1) _____ with it. This phenomenon is called (2) _____. **52-4** ← To p. 328
extinction **52-8**	Early in psychotherapy, the patient cannot recall aversive situations. He is said to _____ memories of them. **52-9** ← To p. 328
unished **52-13**	A patient "blocks" or shows "resistance" when he suddenly (1) _____ talking because he is about to emit (2) _____ verbal behavior. **52-14** ← To p. 328
s **52-18**	One possibility is that the responses which appear to be the recalling of childhood experiences are, in part, conditioned by the therapist's attentive interest in such responses. The therapist may accidentally _____ descriptions of a particular kind of experience. **52-19** ← To p. 328
stimulus generalization **52-23**	A patient may manifest strong "love" or "hate" toward his therapist. In so far as this is due to the therapist resembling a parent, sibling, or other person, it is an example of generalization. It is sometimes called _____. **52-24** ← To p. 328
non-punishing audience environment (world) body (physiology) **52-28**	**End of Set**

agnitude amount) 3-2	In (D), "neutral stimulus" means a tone which * * * effect on salivation before conditioning. 3-3
1) two 2) stimulus 3) response 3-7	When a response is elicited by a stimulus without previous conditioning, the sequence is called a(n) ____ ____. 3-8
hort brief) 3-12	An important aspect of the conditioning procedure is the ____ between presentation of the initially neutral stimulus and of the unconditioned stimulus. 3-13
onditioning 3-17	Before conditioning, the tone was a(n) (1) ____ stimulus; after conditioning, the tone has become a(n) (2) ____ stimulus. 3-18
aired presented) 3-22	In the extinction process, the ____ ____ is presented alone. 3-23
unconditioned stimulus conditioned stimulus 3-27	A response elicited by a conditioned stimulus is a(n) (1) ____ ____; a response elicited by an unconditioned stimulus is a(n) (2) ____ ____. 3-28

conditioned aversive 52-2	Most listeners _____ verbal responses which they describe as immoral, unjust, etc. 52-3
(non-)punishing 52-7	As a non-punishing audience, the therapist arranges conditions under which the stimuli generated by talking about punished behavior lose their aversive properties through _____. 52-8
extinguished 52-12	The patient may suddenly stop talking and show signs of anxiety (that is, he may "block" or show "resistance"). This probably occurs when a response is about to occur which has been severely _____ and, therefore, strongly repressed. 52-13
reinforce 52-17	Many responses became repressed in very early childhood. When these are recalled by the patient, the accuracy of his account * * * difficult to check. 52-18
generalization 52-22	Strong emotional behavior may be evoked by a therapist if he resembles in any way people with respect to whom these emotions have been conditioned. This is sometimes called transference. It illustrates _____ _____. 52-23
changing manipulating, controlling) 52-27	A therapist frequently tries to change his patient's behavior by acting as a(n) (1) * * * . He may also change the (2) _____ in which the patient is to live, and he may change the person's (3) _____ as with drugs, surgery, or shock treatment. 52-28

has no 3-3	Since the tone has no effect on salivation before conditioning, it is a(n) * * *. 3-4 ← To p. 15
unconditioned reflex 3-8	According to (G), conditioning will occur only if the two stimuli occur * * * in time. 3-9 ← To p. 15
time (interval, temporal relation) 3-13	The presence of a conditioned reflex is occasionally tested as in (I). It is essential that the unconditioned stimulus, food, * * * presented on these test trials. 3-14 ← To p. 15
(1) neutral (2) conditioned 3-18	A tone elicits salivation as a(n) ____ response. 3-19 ← To p. 15
conditioned stimulus 3-23	A new neutral stimulus is able to elicit a response after (1) ____ has taken place. It ceases to do so after (2) ____ has taken place. 3-24 ← To p. 15
conditioned response unconditioned response 3-28	To condition a reflex, a neutral stimulus is (1) ____ with a(n) (2) ____ ____ . 3-29 ← To p. 15

ɔunish 52-1	If a child is severely punished for sex play, stimuli associated with the behavior become ____ ____ stimuli. 52-2
punishment (aversive stimuli) 52-6	The psychoanalyst may listen to the "free associations" of his patient for hours and never show displeasure or shock at anything the patient says. The therapist is acting as a non-____ audience. 52-7
non-punishing 52-11	As more and more punishable behavior is emitted and not punished, conditioned aversive stimuli are ____. 52-12
repressed 52-16	The therapist may show particular interest when his patient speaks of emotional experiences. This is likely to ____ (TT) talking to the therapist about emotional experiences. 52-17
generalization 52-21	We may immediately like or dislike a stranger because he resembles someone we have known. This is stimulus ____. 52-22
change (manipulate, control, alter) 52-26	Some therapists may use drugs, electroconvulsive shock, or surgery. These therapists attempt to change behavior by ____ the body. 52-27

Read exhibit now and refer to it as needed.

EXPERIMENT 1.

Pavlov placed a dog in a standard experimental situation. On repeated *conditioning* trials a tone was sounded for 5 seconds, and approximately 2 seconds later the dog was given powdered food. This pairing of tone and food powder was repeated, with trials spaced from 5 to 35 minutes apart at random intervals, for fifty trials. Trials 1, 10, 20, 30, 40, and 50 were *test* trials, that is, the tone was sounded for 30 seconds and *no* food powder was given.

I Trial Number (tone alone)	II Drops of Saliva	III Time Between Onset of Tone and Salivation (in seconds)
1	0	—
10	6	18
20	20	9
30	60	2
40	62	1
50	59	2

EXPERIMENT 2. (Do not read Experiment 2 until instructed to do so.)

A dog had been conditioned to salivate to a metronome beating at 104 ticks per minute. Several interspersed test trials (metronome ticking for 30 seconds but not followed by food powder) provided approximately 10 drops of saliva on each trial. The ticking metronome was then presented on every trial for 30 seconds without being paired with food powder. (Sufficient time was allowed between trials to avoid appreciable fatigue.) The results for this series of consecutive trials without food are presented on the following table.

I Trial Number	II Drops of Saliva	III Time Between Onset of Metronome and Salivation (in seconds)
1	10	3
2	7	7
3	8	5
4	5	4
5	7	5
6	4	9
7	3	13
8	0	—
9	0	—

If a person publicly says he hates his father, many persons are "shocked" or otherwise _____ (TT) his response.

52-1

---

cannot
(do not)

52-5

If incompletely repressed punished behavior is emitted, it will again be followed by _____ if the same or a similar punishing audience is present.

52-6

---

little

52-10

As free association continues, the patient may say punishable things or act in punishable ways (e.g., exhibit strong emotions). To extinguish responses to the aversive stimuli generated by this behavior, the therapist remains a(n) _____ audience.

52-11

---

extinguished
resistance

52-15

When the patient shows resistance, the therapist may use the various procedures designed to induce the patient to emit the behavior which continues to be _____ and which causes resistance.

52-16

---

reinforce
(condition)

52-20

Emitting the same response to two different but similar stimuli, only one of which was present during earlier reinforcement, is an example of stimulus _____.

52-21

---

conditioned
aversive
stimuli

52-25

In addition to providing a non-punishing audience, the therapist may recommend changing jobs, getting a divorce, etc. He is attempting to _____ environmental contingencies.

52-26

Set 4

---

followed by (paired with, presented 2 seconds before) 4-4	On Trial 10 (a "test" trial), the tone * * * followed by food powder. 4-5

---

(1) tone (2) conditioned response 4-9	Experiment 1. The magnitudes of the conditioned response are found in Column ____. 4-10

---

conditioned response 4-14	If the experiment had continued to Trial 60, the magnitude of the conditioned response would probably be in the vicinity of ____ drops. (IN ROUND NUMBERS) 4-15

---

minimum 4-19	Experiment 1. Conclusion: As the number of pairings of the conditioned and unconditioned stimuli increases, the latency of the conditioned reflex (1) ____ and the magnitude of the conditioned response (2) ____ until both reach a limit. 4-20

---

conditioned 4-24	When a conditioned stimulus is repeatedly presented alone, the magnitude of the conditioned response (1) ____ and the latency of the conditioned reflex (2) ____. 4-25

---

(1) conditioning (2) extinction 4-29	**End of Set**

Set 52

Psychotherapy

Estimated time: 11 minutes   **Turn to next page and begin** ▶

---

incompatible
repression

52-4

Since repressed behavior is not often emitted, the conditioned aversive stimuli * * * undergo extinction.

52-5

---

repress

52-9

From the patient's point of view, the therapist is at first much like any other audience. The patient therefore emits very _____ punishable behavior.

52-10

---

(1) stops
(2) punishable
   (repressed)

52-14

When repressed behavior is emitted, in therapy, conditioned aversive stimuli may be (1) _____; but when a particularly punishable response is about to occur, the patient may "block" or show (2) _____ (i.e., be unable to continue to recall experiences).

52-15

---

reinforce

52-19

A therapist who has a theory that incestuous tendencies are the basis of many neuroses may show special interest in any emotional reference to parents, children, or siblings and thereby inadvertently _____ that class of verbal responses.

52-20

---

transference

52-24

Many different forms of psychotherapy have in common, the creation of a non-punishing audience which extinguishes _____ _____ _____ generated by the early stages of behavior which have been punished.

52-25

In Experiment 1, the food powder is a(n) ___ ___ for salivation.

4-1

4-5

as not
s not)

On Trial 10, the initially ___ ___ is presented alone.

4-6

Experiment 1. Column III lists the ___ of the conditioned reflex. (TT)

4-10

4-11

0 (59-62)

In the early conditioning trials, while magnitudes of the conditioned responses are increasing, the latencies of the conditioned reflex are ___.

4-15

4-16

1) decreases
2) increases

READ EXPERIMENT 2 AND REFER TO IT AS NEEDED. Experiment 2. The technical term for the data in Column II is the (1) ___ of the conditioned response and for Column III, the (2) ___.

4-20

4-21

1) decreases
   (declines)
2) increases

Experiment 2. After repeated presentations of the conditioned stimulus alone, the ___ ___ no longer occurs. (TT)

4-25

4-26

does not (will not, fails to) **51-3**	When ordinary conversation generates conditioned aversive stimuli, withdrawing is ____ by a reduction in these stimuli. **51-4** ← To p. 323
avoidance **51-8**	Overthrowing a harsh dictator is similar to slapping a mosquito in that both are forms of ____-aggression. **51-9** ← To p. 323
counter-aggression **51-13**	A criticizes B. B criticizes A in return (counter-aggression). A in defending himself stops criticizing B. B's criticism of A has received ____ reinforcement. **51-14** ← To p. 323
has little (has no, loses) **51-18**	Many so-called "psychosomatic" disorders are bodily malfunctions resulting from prolonged elicitation of the responses characteristic of the * * *. **51-19** ← To p. 323
reaction formation **51-23**	While preoccupied with fighting a certain type of sinful behavior, a person is * * * likely to emit that type of behavior. **51-24** ← To p. 323
incompatible s^{D}s (stimuli) **51-28**	In a play, a young man is persecuted as a homosexual by a college coach who is eventually shown to be a latent homosexual. The coach's persecution of the young man may illustrate * * *. **51-29** ← To p. 323

nconditioned timulus 4-1	Experiment 1. Technically speaking, Column II reports the _____ of the response in each test trial. 4-2
eutral timulus 4-6	Experiment 1. Column II shows that on Trial 10 there were (1) _____ drops of saliva. This is evidence that the tone is already a(n) (2) _____ _____ . 4-7
atencies (-y) 4-11	The magnitude of the conditioned response _____ appreciably as the number of conditioning trials increases until about Trial 30. 4-12
ecreasing becoming horter) 4-16	On Trials 30, 40, and 50, the latency of the conditioned response remains essentially constant, fluctuating slightly between _____ and _____ seconds. 4-17
1) magnitude 2) latency 4-21	Experiment 2. Before these data were collected, _____ had already taken place. 4-22
onditioned esponse 4-26	Experiment 2. When the conditioned stimulus is repeatedly presented alone, the conditioned reflex undergoes _____ . (TT) 4-27

avoidance 51-2	We sometimes describe someone as "withdrawn" if he * * * take an active part in social interactions. 51-3
avoid 51-7	Spraying a room to kill mosquitoes might be called a form of counteraggression. Aversive stimuli are prevented by attacking the organism which may generate them. In that case, counteraggression is an example of _____ behavior. 51-8
aggressively (aggressive) 51-12	A person who, when criticized, criticizes in return shows _____. 51-13
is 51-17	An individual in a state of anxiety * * * interest in sex, food, art, etc. 51-18
withdrawal symptoms 51-22	In so-called "reaction formation," a person engages in behavior which is incompatible with or otherwise displaces or weakens behavior which has both aversive and reinforcing consequences. The action of a former libertine in crusading against sin may exemplify _____ _____. 51-23
(1) eliminates (avoids) (2) reduces (decreases, lowers) 51-27	Reaction formation may be interpreted both as behavior which is (1) * * * with punishable behavior, and as behavior which removes (2) _____ which make the punishable behavior more probable. 51-28

magnitude 4-2	Experiment 1. The zero in Column II for Trial 1 is evidence that the tone is a(n) ____ ____ on this trial. 4-3
1) six 2) conditioned stimulus 4-7	Between Trials 1 and 10, the neutral stimulus must have begun to elicit salivation. It was becoming a(n) ____ stimulus. 4-8
increases 4-12	On Trials 30, 40, and 50, the magnitude of the conditioned response remains essentially constant, fluctuating slightly between a low of (1) ____ and a high of (2) ____ drops. 4-13
(and) 2 4-17	If the experiment had continued to Trial 60, the best guess is that the latency would have remained between ____ and ____ seconds. 4-18
conditioning 4-22	Experiment 2. The 10 drops of saliva recorded for Trial 1 in the table demonstrate that the tick of the metronome is a(n) ____ ____ . 4-23
extinction 4-27	As the number of trials in which a conditioned stimulus is presented alone increases, the latency of a conditioned reflex (1) ____, and the magnitude of a conditioned response (2) ____ until (3) ____ is complete. 4-28

interpreted	We interpret a neurotic symptom when we say that the hermit's behavior is a form of ____ in that it reduces aversive stimuli administered by society.
51-1	51-2

reinforced (conditioned)	A man sprays a room to kill mosquitoes in order to ____ getting stung.
51-6	51-7

(1) positive (2) negative	The aggressive person, though often reinforced, generates conditions in which others are reinforced for acting ____ toward him.
51-11	51-12

incompatible	Extensive use of aversive control results in a chronic (i.e., more or less continuous) activation syndrome with the result that the normal functioning of the body * * * continuously disrupted.
51-16	51-17

reinforced	Reduction in the aversive stimulation of "guilt" may contribute to the early use of alcohol or other drugs, but after frequent use, the drug continues to be taken because of the * * * which otherwise occur.
51-21	51-22

1) not likely 2) stimuli (S^{D}s)	A person may control his own tendency to drink by righteously boycotting magazines which publish liquor ads. In so doing, he (1) ____ S^{D}s for his own drinking and (2) ____ the probability that he will engage in behavior from which he receives aversive stimuli.
51-26	51-27

aversive (punishing)	**End of Set**
51-31	

eutral timulus 4-3	On Trials 2 through 9, the tone is * * * food. 4-4 ← To p. 21
onditioned 4-8	Experiment 1. On Trials 10, 20, 30, 40, and 50, the (1) * * * is a conditioned stimulus eliciting salivation; on these trials, salivation is termed the (2) * * *. 4-9 ← To p. 21
) 59) 62 4-13	After Trial 30, there is no further appreciable increase in magnitude of the ____ ____. (TT) 4-14 ← To p. 21
(and) 2 4-18	When the response magnitude has reached a maximum, the latency has essentially reached a(n) ____ . 4-19 ← To p. 21
onditioned imulus 4-23	Experiment 2. When the data in the table were collected, only the ____ stimulus was presented. 4-24 ← To p. 21
) increases) decreases) extinction 4-28	*Experiment 1* follows the course of the (1) ____ process, and *Experiment 2* follows the course of the (2) ____ process. 4-29 ← To p. 21

Even though conditions may be too complex for precise control or prediction, a variety of everyday behaviors can to some extent be _____ in terms of their possible causes.

51-1

---

nore

51-5

One who gives up a belief in hell escapes from the aversive stimuli of a "fear of damnation," and skeptical behavior is thereby _____.

51-6

---

counter-
aggression
(aggression)

51-10

An aggressive person is often reinforced when he coerces others, either to produce (1) _____ reinforcers or to cease using (2) _____ reinforcers.

51-11

---

activation
syndrome

51-15

The activation syndrome may be useful when extreme exertion is required, but the responses are often _____ with the normal, relaxed functioning of the body.

51-16

---

aversive

51-20

In a person who has been punished severely, any return of the resulting repressed behavior will generate conditioned aversive stimuli often called "guilt." Drinking alcohol may be _____ (TT) by a reduction in these aversive stimuli.

51-21

---

stimuli (S^D s)

51-25

In reaction formation, a person controls a tendency to drink by campaigning for prohibition with great zeal. While so doing, he is (1) * * * to drink and if his campaign succeeds, he will have eliminated (2) _____ for drinking.

51-26

---

avoids

51-30

In general, many types of behavior which in their extreme forms characterize neurosis are conditioned as unfortunate by-products of _____ contingencies.

51-31

nconditioned sponse 5-8	A person can sometimes be "cured" of drinking alcoholic beverages by adding to beverages a chemical which elicits vomiting. After conditioning, liquor is a(n) ____ ____ for vomiting. 5-9
xtinguished 5-17	When the tone elicits salivation, *salivating* is then a(n) ____ ____. 5-18
ame (painful) 5-26	Blood pressure is increased by a painful or "frightening" stimulus. In "fear," there is a(n) ____ in blood pressure. 5-27
onditioned sponses 5-35	If you are punished for telling lies, stimuli generated by lying may become ____ stimuli for responses similar to those in fear and anxiety. 5-36
xtinction 5-44	A child who stutters may be laughed at by other children or scolded by a thoughtless adult. Hearing oneself stutter then becomes a(n) ____ stimulus which elicits anxiety. 5-45
) conditioned stimuli) conditioned responses 5-53	One way to avoid undesirable conditioned responses is to condition an incompatible response to the same stimulus. A funny picturebook in a dentist's office may elicit responses ____ with fear. 5-54

einforced

51-4

Military desertion is prevented mainly by making the consequences of desertion * * * aversive than the consequences of serving.

51-5

ounter

51-9

The harsh dictator puts down a revolt if he can. In doing so, he shows _____ against revolutionaries.

51-10

egative

51-14

Aversive stimuli are not only a condition for the reinforcement of escape and avoidance behavior; they elicit a group of respondents comprising the

_____ _____.

51-15

ctivation
yndrome

51-19

Alcohol, morphine, cocaine, and certain other drugs reduce the effects of _____ stimuli.

51-20

ess (not)

51-24

In reaction formation, a person who has stopped smoking may insist that others around him not smoke. This is self-control through the elimination of _____ which increase the probability that he himself will smoke.

51-25

eaction
ormation

51-29

The extremely restrained behavior of the meticulous or "inhibited" person may be the result of aversive control. The meticulous person _____ the consequences of certain kinds of punishable behavior.

51-30

An object brushing the eye is a(n) (1) _____ stimulus which will (2) _____ the unconditioned response of blinking.

5-1

onditioned timulus

5-9

In Pavlov's experiment, a tone did not normally elicit salivation when first presented. The tone was a(n) _____ _____ prior to conditioning.

5-10

onditioned sponse

5-18

Electric shock, sudden loud noises, and other painful or "frightening" stimuli elicit perspiration. The very "frightened" person may break out in a "cold _____."

5-19

se (increase)

5-27

Many different reflexes are observed in "fear" or "anger." In emotional states, many responses are _____ by a common stimulus.

5-28

onditioned

5-36

Stimuli for responses which occur in fear or anxiety are paired with lying when it is punished. Lying generates stimuli which acquire the power to elicit the conditioned responses which occur in _____.

5-37

nditioned

5-45

When the previously scolded stutterer is no longer scolded, his anxiety * * *.

5-46

compatible

5-54

The dentist's office provides conditioned stimuli for fear. This office can also come to provide conditioned and unconditioned _____ for more favorable emotional responses.

5-55

← To p. 318

1) aversive 2) emotional (anxious, sorrowful) **50-3**	When a truck driver keeps himself from falling asleep and running off the road by drinking strong coffee, his coffee drinking exemplifies ____ behavior. **50-4** ← To p. 318
ncreased greater, heightened) **50-8**	Obscene and blasphemous verbal responses are common in the behavior of intoxicated people. Under the influence of alcohol, a man is more likely to engage in forms of behavior commonly ____ (TT) by society. **50-9** ← To p. 318
negative(-ly) positive(-ly) **50-13**	A man who frequently engages in positively reinforced behavior is commonly said to have a habit. Thus, a man who watches television a great deal is said to have the television ____. **50-14** ← To p. 318
withdrawal symptoms **50-18**	A drug is called habit-forming not because it is so highly reinforcing that it is repeatedly used, but because its withdrawal after continued use generates (1) ____ ____ which, as (2) ____ ____ function as negative reinforcers for taking the drug. **50-19** ← To p. 318
cannot (would not) **50-23**	In giving up tobacco, some people space their smoking, allowing longer and longer periods between cigarettes. This is effective in avoiding extreme * * * (but is usually a poor technique for other reasons). **50-24** ← To p. 318

unconditioned elicit	A neutral stimulus repeatedly paired with an unconditioned stimulus is soon able to elicit the response alone. _____ has occurred.
5-1	5-2
neutral stimulus	The unconditioned stimulus, food, will elicit salivation. Salivation is then called the _____ _____.
5-10	5-11
sweat	A rise in temperature is a(n) (1) _____ stimulus for increase in perspiration; similarly, a painful stimulus is a(n) (2) _____ stimulus for perspiration.
5-19	5-20
elicited	Many reflexes occur together in a(n) _____ state.
5-28	5-29
fear (anxiety)	The "lie detector" records some of the reflex responses which occur in fear (e.g., galvanic skin response, breathing pattern). In "detecting a lie," the instrument measures responses which became _____ through the pairing of lying and punishment.
5-37	5-38
is extinguished decreases, eases)	When the stutterer is no longer scolded, but encouraged to talk frequently, the reflexes involved in the state of anxiety are _____. (TT)
5-46	5-47
stimuli	The "tear-jerker" movie makes use of stimuli previously _____ to elicit crying and other emotional responses typical of states of sadness.
5-55	5-56

ositive

50-2

"Drowning one's sorrow" refers to the use of alcohol to escape from the (1) _____ properties of a(n) (2) _____ state.

50-3

---

vould
(will, does)

50-7

If caffeine and alcohol have opposite effects (i.e., are antagonists) and if alcohol decreases anxiety, one might interpret the "jitters" and wakefulness caused by coffee as due in part to _____ control exerted by aversive stimuli.

50-8

---

requently
more
requently,
often)

50-12

Alcohol decreases the aversive stimulation characteristic of anxiety. Drinking is therefore said to be (1) _____ -ly reinforced. Taking a drug which produces a state of well-being above the normal (*euphoria*) is (2) _____ -ly reinforced.

50-13

---

aversive
stimuli
(negative
einforcers)

50-17

Many habitual breakfast-coffee drinkers get a headache if they do not have coffee for breakfast on a given morning. These coffee drinkers have * * * (TT) when the morning coffee is skipped.

50-18

---

s not

50-22

Taking alcohol or morphine for the *first time* may be followed by a state of euphoria and by escape from ordinary aversive stimuli. From these facts alone, however, we * * * be sure that these drugs lead to addiction.

50-23

---

(1) withdrawal
    symptoms
(2) addict

50-27

End of Set

Conditioning 5-2	If a bell often rings a fraction of a second before something brushes the eye, the bell may become a(n) (1) ____ ____; in other words, the bell may (2) ____ a blink. 5-3
unconditioned response 5-11	When tone and food are repeatedly paired, ____ of a salivary reflex takes place. 5-12
unconditioned unconditioned 5-20	A special instrument (a galvanometer) is used to measure the electrical resistance of the skin. Perspiration lowers the resistance of the skin. This can be recorded by a(n) ____. 5-21
emotional e.g., state of fear, etc.) 5-29	A painful stimulus will (1) ____ the set of responses involved in "fear" and "anger." The painful stimulus is the (2) ____ ____ in this set of reflexes. 5-30
conditioned 5-38	Would the "lie detector" be successful with a person from a culture which never punishes lying? 5-39
extinguished 5-47	Any form of physical energy which is sufficient to cause a given bit of behavior without previous conditioning is called a(n) ____ ____. 5-48
conditioned 5-56	When a young child's fear of furry animals is eliminated by bringing him gradually more and more into contact with harmless furry animals, his fear is said to be ____. (TT) 5-57

negative 50-1	The "good flavor of coffee," unlike "getting a lift," is a stimulus property which is a(n) _____ reinforcer for drinking coffee. 50-2
have 50-6	From the use of black coffee to keep an intoxicated man awake, one would (correctly) predict that an injection of caffeine sulphate, a drug found in coffee, * * * reverse the process of "passing out" from too much alcohol. 50-7
1) aversive stimuli 2) is (may be) 50-11	That alcohol reduces the effect of conditioned aversive stimuli is shown when behavior which automatically generates aversive stimuli occurs * * * under alcohol. 50-12
withdrawal 50-16	Withdrawal symptoms furnish _____ _____ which exert powerful control over the behavior of drug-taking. 50-17
addiction 50-21	The "television habit" produces no true withdrawal symptoms. Therefore, it * * * an addiction in this sense. 50-22
are not 50-26	"I can take it or leave it alone" asserts that "leaving it alone" produces no overpowering (1) * * * and that the speaker is not a(n) (2) _____. 50-27

(1) conditioned stimulus (2) elicit 5-3	After conditioning, the bell alone will elicit a blink. The blink is a(n) ____ ____ which is similar to (but not quite identical with) the blink elicited by brushing the eye. 5-4
conditioning 5-12	During conditioning, the neutral stimulus (tone) acquires the power to (1) ____ salivation. Salivation elicited by the tone is called a(n) (2) ____ ____. 5-13
galvanometer 5-21	A sudden drop in the electrical skin resistance is called a *galvanic skin response* (GSR). When a painful stimulus produces this effect, it is an unconditioned ____ ____ response. 5-22
elicit unconditioned stimulus 5-30	The emotional states of "fear" and "anger" are marked by many reflexes (e.g., sweating, contraction of blood vessels, erection of hair or "goose flesh"). Many responses are elicited by the conditions which generate ____ states. 5-31
No 5-39	Hearing vulgar words may elicit a weak galvanic skin response, etc. This suggests that these words are conditioned ____ for some of the reflex responses involved in fear or anxiety. 5-40
unconditioned stimulus 5-48	The process by which a conditioned stimulus loses the ability to elicit a response is called ____. 5-49
extinguished 5-57	A young child is afraid of furry animals. Furry animals are brought closer during each meal. While enjoying food (an unconditioned stimulus), responses are conditioned which are ____ with fear. 5-58

▷	A man who drinks a cup of coffee "to get a lift" reduces the aversive properties of fatigue, of "being low," etc., and coffee drinking is reinforced by a(n) _____ reinforcer. 50-1
aversive stimuli (conditioned aversive stimuli) 50-5	Drinking strong, black coffee to keep from falling asleep after drinking too much alcohol suggests that the drugs, alcohol and caffeine, * * * opposing or antagonistic effects on behavior. 50-6
decrease (reduction) 50-10	Alcoholism may be due in part to the effect of this drug in decreasing the effects of (1) _____ _____. Alcoholism is a form of "neurosis" which (2) * * * the result of severe punishment or other avoidance contingencies. 50-11
reinforced 50-15	The aversive effects of withholding a drug after the drug has been repeatedly taken are called withdrawal symptoms. Further use of a drug is reinforcing in part by the avoidance of, or escape from, such _____ symptoms. 50-16
escape (relief) 50-20	A coffee drinker who gets a headache if he misses his morning coffee is suffering from a(n) _____ to caffeine. 50-21
withdrawal symptoms 50-25	The reinforcing effects of caffeine, alcohol, and morphine in producing euphoria * * * dependent on addiction. 50-26

In the conditioned eye-blink reflex just described, the ringing bell becomes the ____ ____.

5-5

For conditioning to occur, the tone must either coincide with the presentation of food or * * * it by a very short interval.

5-14

A painful stimulus elicits a GSR. This sequence of events (the stimulus and its response) is called the galvanic skin ____.

5-23

A child hurt by the dentist will be afraid when returning to the dentist's office at a later date. Through conditioning, the dentist's office has come to provide many ____ ____ for the reflex behavior in fear.

5-32

When a newspaper identifies the race of a person committing a particularly odious crime, the race label can become a(n) ____ ____ which will elicit the emotional responses aroused by other parts of the crime report.

5-41

After conditioning, the response elicited by a previously neutral stimulus is the ____ ____.

5-50

In an experiment, people learned to "like" modern music by hearing it while they ate. The music became the (1) ____ ____, and the food was the (2) ____ ____, for reflex responses characterizing "pleasure."

5-59

voidance

50-4

Alcohol is often said to reduce feelings of guilt. Technically speaking, it reduces the effect of _____ _____ generated by previously punished behavior.

50-5

---

unished

50-9

Laboratory animals, which normally refuse alcohol, drink alcohol under conditions in which reinforced behavior is also punished. They may then emit the punished behavior, suggesting a(n) _____ in the effectiveness of aversive stimuli.

50-10

---

habit

50-14

To say that a man has the "morphine habit" means more than that he frequently takes the drug. After repeated use, discontinuing morphine generates an extremely aversive condition. Further use of the drug will be strongly _____ by escape from this condition.

50-15

---

1) withdrawal
   symptoms
2) aversive
   stimuli

50-19

A man is said to be *addicted* to a drug if withholding the drug produces withdrawal symptoms. The addict's behavior of taking a drug is strongly reinforced by _____ from the withdrawal symptoms.

50-20

---

withdrawal
symptoms

50-24

A "chain smoker" avoids * * * by allowing no time for them to appear.

50-25

---

conditioned stimulus 5-5	If the bell is sounded many times when nothing brushes the eye, the conditioned eye-blink reflex will be ____. (TT) 5-6
precede 5-14	After a sufficient number of pairings of tone and food, the tone becomes a(n) (1) ____ ____ which will (2) ____ salivation. 5-15
reflex 5-23	Conditions which give rise to the so-called emotions of fear, anger, and anxiety produce a(n) ____ in the electrical resistance of the skin. 5-24
conditioned stimuli 5-32	If the dentist's behavior continues to provide unconditioned stimuli for fear reflexes, the child's conditioned fear of the dentist's office will not become ____. (TT) 5-33
conditioned stimulus 5-41	A favorable predisposition to a political candidate might be conditioned by serving a free lunch at a political rally. The food is a(n) ____ ____ used to condition many "favorable" reflex responses. 5-42
conditioned response 5-50	A stimulus which has acquired the ability to evoke a reflex response is the (1) ____ ____; the response it evokes is the (2) ____ ____. 5-51
conditioned stimulus unconditioned stimulus 5-59	**End of Set**

← To p. 313

conditioned unconditioned 49-3	We may punish a child for eating before others are served; yet eating is not usually punished. Thus, it (1) * * * always the *form* of behavior which makes it punishable but rather the (2) _____ (TT) under which it occurred. 49-4 ← To p. 313
not (cannot) 49-8	To say that we hurt someone with a careless remark unconsciously means that we do not notice a consequence of the behavior because of which it may be _____. 49-9 ← To p. 313
(results in) 49-13	We readily report that we have spanked a child "for his own good" because striking a child is *not* _____ under such conditions. 49-14 ← To p. 313
likely (more likely) 49-18	When we criticize a friend in anger, we may feel guilty when we are no longer angry because responses which hurt friends have been _____. 49-19 ← To p. 313
himself 49-23	In lying, a person recognizes the punishable reason for his behavior. Therefore, rationalization (1) * * * to be considered lying in this sense because the person (2) * * * "tell the whole truth" even to himself. 49-24 ← To p. 313
forgiveness 49-28	If you are *actually not* angry when a person has insulted you because you know he is maladjusted, then you * * * be rationalizing if you reported that reason for not returning his aggression. 49-29 ← To p. 313

xtinguished 5-6	(1) _____, the Russian physiologist, discovered the process called (2) _____. 5-7
1) conditioned stimulus 2) elicit 5-15	If the conditioned stimulus (tone) is presented a great many times *without* food, the tone eventually _____ to elicit salivation. 5-16
rop decrease) acceptable: hange) 5-24	A previously neutral stimulus repeatedly paired with a painful stimulus will acquire the power to elicit a GSR through _____. 5-25
xtinguished 5-33	Words like "bad" and "wrong" are frequently heard just before punishment. These words come to elicit responses characteristic of fear or anxiety. They become _____ stimuli. 5-34
nconditioned timulus 5-42	During the free lunch at a political rally, the candidate's name may become a(n) (1) _____ _____ which evokes favorable emotional responses similar to those evoked by the (2) _____ _____. 5-43

1) conditioned
    stimulus
2) conditioned
    response
 	
5-51
	We now have reason to believe that much of the apparently "spontaneous" flow of saliva when no food is in the mouth is caused by unnoticed _____ _____.
	
	5-52

conditioned 49-2	"Doing something else" avoids the (1) _____ aversive stimuli generated by a frequently punished response, as well as the possibly (2) _____ aversive stimuli of punishment. 49-3
punished 49-7	We may not realize that we are spanking a child because he made us angry rather than to correct his behavior. Thus, we * * * notice that our behavior is emitted for punishable reasons. 49-8
aversive 49-12	Striking the first blow is frequently punished; striking in self-defense is condoned. The same form of behavior * * * different consequences depending upon the circumstances. 49-13
1) punished (criticized) 2) reinforced (condoned) 49-17	A man who is late for work is * * * to say that he stayed in bed because he needed rest rather than because he was lazy. 49-18
rationalization 49-22	In rationalization, a person "believes" (tells himself) that his behavior was a function of variables with respect to which he is least likely to be punished. In rationalization, he deceives _____ as well as others. 49-23
...as ...has both) 49-27	Not striking a person who has just hurt you is reinforced as forgiveness or punished as cowardice, depending upon the circumstances. You might be rationalizing your behavior if you described it as _____. 49-28

← To p. 26

1) Pavlov 2) conditioning 5-7	Chemical irritants in the stomach elicit vomiting. Vomiting is, then, a(n) ____ ____ . 5-8 ← To p. 26
eases ails, loses ie power) 5-16	When the conditioned stimulus loses its power to elicit salivation because of repeated presentation without the unconditioned stimulus, the conditioned reflex is said to be ____ . 5-17 ← To p. 26
onditioning 5-25	A painful stimulus may also elicit changes in the breathing pattern: "catching the breath," and then deeper inhalation of air. This respiratory change and the GSR are, thus, two responses to the ____ unconditioned stimulus. 5-26 ← To p. 26
onditioned 5-34	Words like "bad" and "wrong" elicit (1) ____ ____ similar to the unconditioned responses elicited by painful stimuli. 5-35 ← To p. 26
onditioned timulus nconditioned timulus food) 5-43	A process through which we can eliminate conditioned responses is called ____ . 5-44 ← To p. 26
onditioned timuli 5-52	Words like "love" and "hate" are (1) ____ ____ which writers may use to elicit emotional (2) ____ ____ . 5-53 ← To p. 26

versive negatively einforcing) 49-1	Previously punished behavior generates ____ aver- sive stimuli. 49-2
versive 49-6	Society punishes the unjust. Unfairly adminis- tering punishment is itself sometimes ____ by others. 49-7
ontingent lependent) 49-11	It is easier for a man to notice and describe un- punished reasons for his own behavior because they are less ____ than punished reasons. 49-12
robable ikely) 49-16	Staying in bed late is often (1) ____ as laziness or indolence. It is often (2) ____ as wise self- therapy when one needs a rest. 49-17
tional(-izes) 49-21	You may admit, even to yourself, only the least punished reasons for a given response. This type of defective self-description is called ____. 49-22
nished 49-26	A man can rationalize his own conduct only if the behavior * * * punishable and non-punishable as- pects. 49-27

Read exhibit now and refer to it as needed.

Types of Response Mechanisms

1. Contractions of *striated* or striped muscles (so called because of their appearance under a microscope) move parts of the skeletal frame, as well as certain "flaps" of tissue such as the tongue, eyelid, and vocal cords.

2. Contractions of *smooth* muscles generally change the dimensions of various internal organs.

3. *Glands* secrete fluids into ducts or directly into the blood stream.

▷ Some behavior is criticized or otherwise punished by society, that is, it is frequently followed by _____ stimuli.

49-1

mitted
made)

49-5

If a man "does not notice" that he is engaging in behavior which is often punished, he avoids _____ stimuli generated by the behavior.

49-6

1) punishable
2) do not

49-10

When a response is a function of two variables, punishment may be _____ upon its relation to only one of them.

49-11

49-15

If a man can avoid reporting a punishable reason by reporting a non-punishable reason for his behavior, it is * * * that the non-punishable reason will be reported.

49-16

ess

49-20

Emphasizing the non-punishable aspects of one's own behavior is called rationalization. Thus, one _____-izes the behavior of striking a friend by saying, "I did it for his own good."

49-21

unished

49-25

Behavior which does not need to be, and in fact cannot be, rationalized is behavior which has never been _____ .

49-26

(1) rationalizing
(2) inadequate
(defective,
lack of,
incomplete)

49-30

End of Set

PART I Reflex Behavior

Set 6

Response Mechanisms

See exhibit on preceding page

Estimated time: 12 minutes

Turn to next page and begin

smooth
muscles

6-4

In vomiting, the _____ muscles of the stomach wall contract vigorously, thus forcibly ejecting the contents of the stomach.

6-5

---

glands
(gland)

6-9

Blushing and blanching result when _____ muscles change the diameters of small blood vessels near the skin.

6-10

---

(1) smooth
(2) glands

6-14

The pupil of the eye is the opening through the iris. Like other muscles controlling the diameters of organs, the iris contains _____ muscle.

6-15

---

smooth
muscles
(and) glands

6-19

Smooth muscles contract in which *three* of the following? (USE LETTERS) (a) vomiting, (b) running, (c) turning the head, (d) stomach cramps, (e) sweating, (f) reaching, (g) blushing, (h) eyes watering.

6-20

---

1) glands
2) smooth
  muscles
3) elicited

6-24

Responses of smooth muscles and glands are elicited by appropriate (1) _____. They are response mechanisms in the stimulus-response relations termed (2) _____. (TTs)

6-25

---

smooth
muscles
(and) glands

6-29

End of Set

Set 49

Rationalization

Estimated time: 11 minutes   **Turn to next page and begin** ▶

| is not
S^Ds (stimuli,
circumstances)

49-4 | Sometimes, as in a verbal slip, we may not notice that we have ____ a response which is often punished.

49-5 |

| punished

49-9 | In talking to others, we usually do not talk about our own (1) ____ behavior; similarly in thinking ("talking to ourselves"), we often (2) * * * think about our own punishable behavior.

49-10 |

| punished
(aversive)

49-14 | If a response is punished when controlled by Variable 1 and not punished when controlled by Variable 2, Variable ____ will more probably be recognized and reported.

49-15 |

| punished

49-19 | If we report that our friend has benefited from our criticism, it is ____ punishing to report having criticized him.

49-20 |

| (1) is not
(2) does not
(cannot)

49-24 | Claiming that bumping a rival on the dance floor was an "accident" is attributing the behavior to reasons for which bumping is not usually ____.

49-25 |

| would not

49-29 | When we admit only the least punishable reasons for our behavior, we are (1) ____. This is one of several forms of (2) * * * self-knowledge.

49-30 |

Contraction of _____ muscles moves parts of the skeletal frame.

6-1

---

mooth

6-5

Muscle fibers from the stomach appear _____ when viewed under a microscope.

6-6

---

mooth

6-10

Name the type of response mechanism (or organ) active in (1) walking, (2) stomach contraction, (3) salivation.

6-11

---

mooth

6-15

Tears which wash away irritants from the surface of the eye are provided by _____.

6-16

, d, g

6-20

Which type of response mechanism is usually involved in the organism's action upon the *external* environment?

6-21

) stimuli

) reflexes

6-25

Most of the behavior which acts upon the external environment is not elicited by stimuli in the form of simple reflexes. That is to say, eliciting stimuli are *not* the principal "causes" of the responses executed by _____ muscle.

6-26

D$_s$ (stimuli) 48-3	In a "description," verbal behavior is under the control of appropriate S^{D}s. Even in describing our own behavior, the behavior to be described must provide _____ for some verbal response. 48-4 ← To p. 308
einforce 48-8	The child who once cried when his stomach hurt later whines, "It hurts." Crying (1) * * * reinforced after a certain age, but a (similar) response, whining, (2) * * * reinforced (provided the child is not too old to whine). 48-9 ← To p. 308
D$_s$ (stimuli) 48-13	A man may fail to notice even rather advanced medical symptoms which presumably produce strong stimuli. Possibly these symptoms have never come to function as S^{D}s because the man has not been adequately _____ for reporting them. 48-14 ← To p. 308
ncompatible vith 48-18	I may not remember where I parked my car because appropriate self-observing behavior has not been (1) _____ or because I was preoccupied with some (2) _____ covert behavior at the time. 48-19 ← To p. 308
einforced 48-23	Repressed responses have (1) _____ consequences which provide conditions under which incompatible behavior is reinforced; but they have also probably had (2) _____ consequences which, alone, would make the response likely to occur. 48-24 ← To p. 308
ncompatible avoidance) 48-28	We interpret repression as the effect of incompatible behavior which avoids the (1) _____ consequences of the behavior the psychoanalyst would call (2) _____. 48-29 ← To p. 308

riated
triped,
keletal)

6-1

In the arm-flexion reflex, the response is executed by the contraction of ____ ____.

6-2

---

nooth
nstriped)

6-6

Smooth muscles change the (1) ____ of various (2) ____ organs.

6-7

) striated
muscles
) smooth
muscles
) glands

6-11

Reaching and throwing involve (1) ____ muscles. Nodding the head, making facial expressions, and talking involve (2) ____ muscles.

6-12

---

ands

6-16

A response may be the action of ____ ____, ____ ____, or ____.

6-17

---

riated
iscles

6-21

The types of response mechanisms principally active in maintaining the "internal economy" of the organism are ____ ____ and ____.

6-22

---

riated

6-26

In some cases, as in the flexion reflex, responses by striated muscles (1) * * * elicited by stimuli, but most responses of striated muscles (2) * * * under the control of eliciting stimuli.

6-27

id not was not ble to) **48-2**	We cannot describe someone's behavior if we did not notice it. That is, we can describe another's behavior only if that behavior provided ____ controlling some response. **48-3**
D_s (stimuli) **48-7**	As the child grows older, parents (and others) usually cease to reinforce crying and begin to ____ such verbal behavior as "It hurts." **48-8**
haped differentiated, onditioned) **48-12**	Some patients report very slight painful symptoms to their doctor. In their history of reinforcement, even weak painful stimuli have served as ____ for this verbal behavior. **48-13**
ncompatible /ith **48-17**	The "absent-minded" scholar cannot describe as much of his overt behavior as others because of covert verbal behavior which is * * * noticing or "thinking about" what he is doing. **48-18**
aversive (conditioned aversive) ·eduction (termination, alimination)**48-22**	We do not even think about severely punished behavior when we "repress" it. Doing, saying, or thinking something else is ____ by a reduction in conditioned aversive stimuli. **48-23**
epress (-ed) **48-27**	A laboratory analysis suggests that repressing is simply engaging in ____ behavior reinforced by the reduction of aversive stimuli generated by recalling an experience. **48-28**
ncompatible **48-32**	Inadequate self-knowledge may occur when the unreportable behavior generates conditions under which incompatible behavior is reinforced. This incompatible behavior is the main "force" or "agent" in ____. **48-33**

striated muscles (striped, skeletal) 6-2	Muscle fibers in the arms appear to be _____ when viewed under a microscope. 6-3
1) dimensions 2) internal 6-7	Not all responses involve muscles. Sweating is the action of _____. 6-8
1) striated 2) striated 6-12	Chewing food involves (1) _____ muscles. In swallowing, after food passes from the oral cavity, it is moved through the esophagus or gullet principally by (2) _____ muscles. 6-13
smooth muscles, striated muscles, or) glands (ANY ORDER) 6-17	Most of our interaction with the external environment involves gross or subtle movements of our skeletal frame. In other words, action upon the environment most directly involves _____ muscles. 6-18
smooth muscles and) glands 6-22	Name the response mechanism in the following: walking to the dinner table and chewing food (1) _____; moistening food with saliva (2) _____; passing food into stomach (3) _____; and providing the stomach with digestive juices (4) _____. 6-23
) are) are not 6-27	Action upon the environment involves (1) _____ muscles and usually does not fit the pattern of the simple (2) _____. 6-28

onditioned einforced, earned) 48-1	A person with an adequate verbal repertoire may not be able to describe a past event if he * * * verbalize it, at least covertly, at the time. 48-2
einforces conditions) 48-6	When crying in response to a painful stimulus has been reinforced, crying may become a verbal response emitted in the presence of other somewhat similar ____. 48-7
uccessive pproximations 48-11	When pain is reported in an unusually high pitch, a completely "natural" voice in reporting pain has apparently not yet been completely ____ by the verbal community. 48-12
ncompatible vith 48-16	A person doing one thing and "thinking about" something else may later be unable to describe what he was doing because covert verbal behavior is * * * noticing what he was doing. 48-17
einforced 48-21	Severely punished behavior generates stimuli which have become (1) * * * stimuli. Behavior which avoids (is incompatible with) the punished behavior is reinforced through the (2) ____ of these stimuli. 48-22
epression 48-26	We may not be able to recall an early childhood experience. Under some conditions a psychoanalyst would say we have ____ -ed it. 48-27
conditioned 48-31	Inadequate self-knowledge may result if we engage in behavior * * * with noticing some aspect of our other behavior. 48-32

striated
(striped)

6-3

Contraction of ____ ____ changes diameters of blood vessels.

← To p. 36 6-4

---

glands

6-8

Salivation is the action of the salivary ____.

← To p. 36 6-9

---

1) striated
2) smooth

6-13

Movements of the stomach and intestines in digestion involve (1) ____ muscles. Digestive juices are provided by (2) ____.

← To p. 36 6-14

---

triated

6-18

The internal economy of the body depends on secretion of digestive juices and on forcing substances through tubular organs by rhythmic changes in their diameters. The internal economy depends on the action of ____ ____ and ____.

6-19
← To p. 36

---

1) striated
   muscles
2) glands
3) smooth
   muscles
4) glands   6-23

Salivation and sweating are actions of (1) ____. Constriction of the pupil, vomiting, blushing, and blanching are actions of (2) ____ ____. Both types of response are (3) ____ by appropriate stimuli.

6-24
← To p. 36

) striated
) reflex

6-28

The principle of the simple reflex applies to responses by ____ ____ and ____ as well as some reflexes involved in posture, locomotion, and protective skeletal responses.

6-29
← To p. 36

We commonly lack "self-knowledge" in the sense that we cannot describe much of our past behavior. Many early childhood experiences cannot be recalled possibly because appropriate verbal behavior was not _____ (TT) at the time.

48-1

---

einforced

48-5

A very young child cries in response to a painful stimulus. Although this may be in part unlearned, a parent _____ this behavior if he provides needed attention.

48-6

---

einforced

48-10

When the verbal community reinforces first crying, next whining, and finally talking, behavior is being shaped through _____ _____ to a final form acceptable to the community.

48-11

---

annot
will not)

48-15

A driver carefully watching the road will later be unable to describe much of the roadside scenery. Watching the road is * * * looking at the scenery.

48-16

---

einforced
conditioned)

48-20

If talking about severely punishing situations generates strong aversive stimuli, we may be automatically _____ for talking about other things, as an example of avoidance behavior.

48-21

---

epressed

48-25

Self-knowledge is sometimes lacking because it is displaced by incompatible behavior which avoids the aversive stimuli generated by talking about punished responses. This kind of absence of self-knowledge has been called _____.

48-26

---

emitted

48-30

Inadequate self-knowledge may result because we have not been _____ to notice some aspect of our behavior.

48-31

en
, after)

7-4

Reinforcement and behavior occur in the temporal
order: (1) _____, (2) _____.

7-5

---

rived
food
ngry)

7-9

If an animal's response is not followed by reinforcement, similar responses will occur _____ frequently in the future.

7-10

---

ural
n-deliberate)

7-14

Food is not reinforcing unless the animal has first
been * * * food for some time.

7-15

---

force

7-19

In laboratory research, various devices are used
to reinforce responses. Heat can be used to _____
the responses of a cold animal.

7-20

---

ponse
havior)

7-24

The response of pressing a bar must be emitted at
least once in order to be _____.

7-25

---

s frequent
come
inguished)

7-29

No eliciting stimuli are observed for bar pressing,
flicking leaves in the park, etc. Therefore, responses of this type * * * classified as reflex behavior.

7-30

$s^D s$
(stimuli)

48-4

Discrimination results from a three-term contingency. Even though our behavior always generates potential stimuli, these are s^Ds only if a response has been _____ in their presence.

48-5

is not
is

48-9

When the *verbal community* (parents and others) considers a child too old to whine, whining is no longer _____, although saying, "my stomach hurts" in a normal voice may be.

48-10

nforced

48-14

If we have never learned to notice an aspect of our own behavior, it * * * be described by us.

48-15

conditioned
(reinforced,
shaped)
incompatible

48-19

If self-observation produces aversive stimuli, behavior incompatible with noticing one's own behavior is automatically _____.

48-20

aversive
(negative)
reinforcing
(positive)

48-24

When a person cannot recall some previously punished behavior, we say he has _____ it.

48-25

aversive
(negative,
punishing)
repressed

48-29

Repressed behavior will not undergo extinction if the behavior is seldom _____ and therefore does not go unreinforced.

48-30

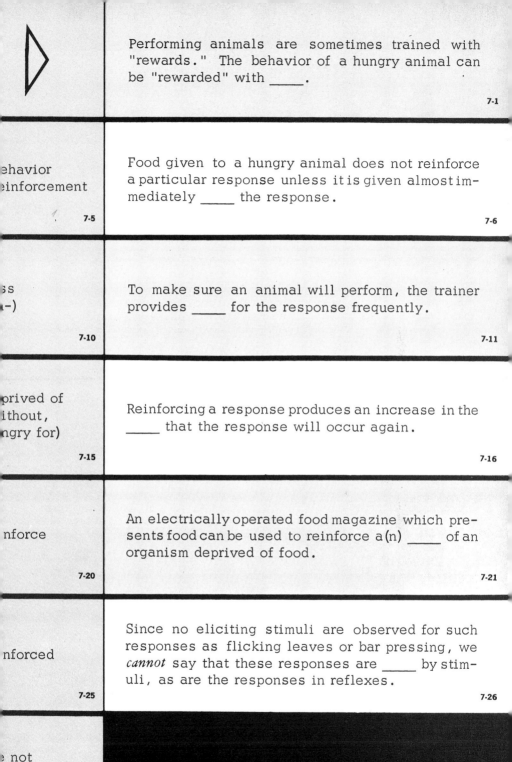

Performing animals are sometimes trained with "rewards." The behavior of a hungry animal can be "rewarded" with _____ .

7-1

behavior
reinforcement

7-5

Food given to a hungry animal does not reinforce a particular response unless it is given almost immediately _____ the response.

7-6

ss
(-)

7-10

To make sure an animal will perform, the trainer provides _____ for the response frequently.

7-11

prived of
ithout,
ngry for)

7-15

Reinforcing a response produces an increase in the _____ that the response will occur again.

7-16

nforce

7-20

An electrically operated food magazine which presents food can be used to reinforce a(n) _____ of an organism deprived of food.

7-21

nforced

7-25

Since no eliciting stimuli are observed for such responses as flicking leaves or bar pressing, we *cannot* say that these responses are _____ by stimuli, as are the responses in reflexes.

7-26

e not
nnot be,
ll not be)

7-30

End of Set

← To p. 303

) controlling
) controlled

47-3

In putting candy out of sight to keep from eating it, the (1) _____ to be controlled is eating candy, and the (2) _____ which controls is putting candy out of sight.

47-4
← To p. 303

) reinforces
) aversive
  (negative)

47-8

In self-control, the (1) _____ response is reinforced by the (2) _____ of conditioned aversive stimuli associated with the controlled response. (TTs)

47-9
← To p. 303

---

ive (and)
tive
forcing (and)
sive]

47-13

A delicious but indigestible food generates not only reinforcing stimuli but aversive stimuli which can result in the _____ of a controlling response.

47-14
← To p. 303

) voluntary
) involuntary

47-18

The weight-reducing pill which is simply a piece of candy to be taken before a meal controls ingestive behavior slightly by decreasing _____.

47-19
← To p. 303

) anxiety
) aversive

47-23

When a man sets a clock radio to awaken him, he is arranging for a(n) _____ (TT) to occur at a specified time to control his behavior.

47-24
← To p. 303

---

controll-)ing
einforced

47-28

A self-controlling response avoiding previously shamed behavior reduces the _____ _____ _____ generated by that behavior.

47-29
← To p. 303

) does (can)
) do not
  (need not)

47-33

End of Set

ood **7-1**	A technical term for "reward" is reinforcement. To "reward" an organism with food is to _____ it with food. **7-2**
after **7-6**	Unlike a stimulus in a reflex, a reinforcing stimulus * * * act to elicit the response it reinforces. **7-7**
einforcement(s) **7-11**	A hungry pigeon in the park flicks dead leaves about with quick movements of its beak. This behavior is _____ whenever it uncovers bits of food. **7-12**
robability likelihood, hances) **7-16**	We do not observe "probability" directly. We say that a response has become more probable if it is observed to occur more _____ under controlled conditions. **7-17**
esponse **7-21**	If the cold (or food-deprived) organism turns on an electrically operated heat lamp (or food magazine), the response of turning on will be _____. **7-22**
licited **7-26**	Responses such as bar pressing, flicking leaves, etc., are said to be *emitted* rather than *elicited* since there * * * (are or are no?) observed eliciting stimuli. **7-27**

Page 43

1) decrease
   (reduce,
   lower)
2) probability
 	
    47-2
	In analyzing cases in which one response controls another, we distinguish between the controlling response and the controlled response. Putting candy out of sight is the (1) ____ response; eating candy is the (2) ____ response.
	
	    47-3

forcing (and) rsive sitive (and) ative] HER ORDER) **47-7**	Candy in the mouth (1) ____ the behavior of reaching for candy and putting it in the mouth. This behavior has (2) ____ consequences associated with gaining weight. **47-8**

troll-)ed
 	
    47-12
	A delicious food may later cause severe indigestion. "Nature" has arranged both ____ and ____ consequences of eating such a food.
	
	    47-13

1) operant
2) respondent
   (reflex)
 	
    47-17
	The layman calls weeping "involuntary" and putting onion juice near one's eyes "voluntary." In these terms, the actress's technique shows (1) "____" control over (2) "____" behavior.
	
	    47-18

(controll-)ing
(controll-)ed
 	
    47-22
	An overly anxious man may "take to drink." In technical terms, he uses the drug, alcohol, to reduce the emotional state of (1) ____, which is frequently one effect of conditioned (2) ____ stimuli.
	
	    47-23

conditioned
 	
    47-27
	Behavior which "avoids sin" is (1) controll-____ behavior which is (2) ____ by the reduction of conditioned aversive stimuli.
	
	    47-28

einforces
 	
    47-32
	A man (1) * * * resist temptation by engaging in controlling behavior which is itself reinforced by external events. We * * * interpret this as the exercising of an inner power called "will."
	
	    47-33

einforce

Technically speaking, a thirsty organism can be _____ with water.

7-2

7-3

oes not
will not)

A reinforcement does not elicit a response; it simply makes it more _____ that an animal will respond in the same way again.

7-7

7-8

einforced

A pigeon is occasionally reinforced for flicking leaves about because of the common natural arrangement of leaves over _____.

7-12

7-13

equently
often)

When a response has been reinforced, it will be emitted _____ frequently in the future.

7-17

7-18

einforced

The response of turning on the electrically operated heat lamp or food magazine will be emitted more _____ in the future if the organism is cold or hungry.

7-22

7-23

re no

If pressing the bar does not operate the food magazine, the response * * * reinforced.

7-27

7-28

:ontrol :onditions 'variables, :ontingencies) 47-1	A mother may put candy out of sight to ____ the probability that her child will ask for it. She may do the same thing to reduce the (2) ____ that *she* will eat candy. 47-2
ontrols prevents, voids) 47-6	Self-control is often involved when the response to be controlled has both ____ and ____ consequences. 47-7
einforcement 47-11	The controll-____ response usually has both positive and negative consequences. 47-12
1) operant 2) reflex (respondent) 47-16	When the actress puts onion juice near her eyes, a(n) (1) ____ controls a(n) (2) ____. 47-17
motional 47-21	A man who is bothered by his own aggressive behavior toward others may take a "tranquilizer." Taking the drug is the (1) controll-____ response; aggressive behavior is the (2) controll-____ behavior. 47-22
aired 47-26	In shaming a man for unethical or immoral behavior, aversive stimuli are paired with the stimuli generated by that behavior and hence are ____ as aversive stimuli. 47-27
einforcement conditioning) 47-31	In ethical training, we are taught that certain behavior is "wrong." This behavior later generates conditioned aversive stimuli whose reduction ____ a variety of responses called "resisting temptation." 47-32

einforced
NOT:
ewarded)

7-3

The trainer reinforces the animal by giving it food
_____ it has performed correctly.

← To p. 41 7-4

---

probable
likely)

7-8

Food is probably not reinforcing if the animal is
not * * *.

← To p. 41 7-9

---

ood
seed, insects,
einforcers)

7-13

The reinforcement used by animal trainers is deliberately arranged, while the arrangement of leaves
and food in the park is * * *.

← To p. 41 7-14

---

nore

7-18

To get an animal to emit a response more frequently, we _____ the response.

← To p. 41 7-19

---

requently
often)

7-23

In a typical apparatus, the depression of a horizontal bar automatically operates a food magazine.
The apparatus selects "bar pressing" as the _____
to be reinforced.

← To p. 41 7-24

---

s not
will not be)

7-28

Reinforcement makes responses more frequent
while failure to receive reinforcement makes responses * * *.

← To p. 41 7-29

A man may (1) ____ the behavior of another man by arranging relevant conditions. Also, he may control his own behavior by arranging the same kinds of (2) ____.

47-1

---

controls
(weakens,
avoids)
removing
(taking away,
avoiding)   47-5

In exerting self-control by putting candy away to avoid eating it, one response ____ another response.

47-6

---

reinforces
(conditions)
(controll-)ing

47-10

The response to be controlled is often strong because it has received powerful ____.

47-11

(controll-)ing
elicits

47-15

Putting a handkerchief containing onion juice near one's eyes is (1) ____ behavior; weeping tears is (2) ____ behavior.

47-16

(controll-)ing
decrease
(decline,
disappear)
47-20

In "counting to ten" before acting in anger, we make use of the fact that a(n) ____ state often rapidly grows weak.

47-21

---

reinforcement

47-25

In shaming a man for unrestrained, unethical, or immoral behavior, stimuli generated by the behavior are being ____ with the aversive stimuli of shaming so that they will later generate anxiety or "feelings of guilt."

47-26

(controll-)ing
(controll-)ed

47-30

In so-called self-control, the controlling response is established through ____, just like any other response.

47-31

This is a hungry pigeon in a standard experimental space, an enclosed rectangular chamber or box. Stimuli eliciting reflex behavior may be neglected. The pigeon eventually pecks the small disk-shaped key. The food magazine operates automatically, making food available immediately after a peck *(response)* on the key. We observe that when the pigeon has pecked the key and received food, it soon pecks again (and receives food and pecks again, etc.), i.e., the *rate* or *frequency* of pecking is increased. Because the rate increases when the response is followed by food, food is said to reinforce the response. Food is called a *reinforcer,* and the event *reinforcement.* Because the response does not appear to be produced by an eliciting stimulus, it is said to be *emitted.* This type of behavior, which operates or acts upon the environment, is called *operant* behavior.[1]

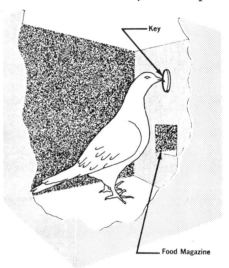

If after the operant (key pecking) has been *conditioned,* the pigeon no longer receives food when it pecks, the rate of emitting responses decreases until it reaches the low rate which prevailed before conditioning. This process is called *extinction.*

---

[1]When referring to behavior, generally, rather than to specific instances of it, we use the term *operant,* e.g., key pecking is an *operant;* but for specific instances, we use the term *response,* e.g., a peck on the key is a *response.* (Reflex behavior, which we have already studied, is called *respondent behavior.* It occurs only in response to eliciting stimuli.)

Set 47

Techniques of Self-Control

Estimated time: 15 minutes   **Turn to next page and begin** ▶

---

(1) response
   (behavior)
(2) response
   (behavior)
                              47-4

Putting candy out of sight to keep from eating it
(1) _____ the eating behavior by (2) _____ an S^D.

47-5

---

controlling
reduction
(termination,
avoidance)
                              47-9

In self-control, the reduction of conditioned aversive stimuli associated with the controlled response (1) _____ the (2) controll- _____ response.

47-10

---

einforcement
(conditioning)

                              47-14

An actress may make herself cry real tears by putting a handkerchief containing a bit of onion juice
near her eyes. The (1) controll- _____ response,
putting the handkerchief to the face, provides a
stimulus which (2) _____ tears.   47-15

---

deprivation

                              47-19

When we "count to ten" before acting in anger,
counting is a (1) controll- _____ response which
has its effect in allowing time for an emotional
state to (2) _____.

47-20

---

stimulus (S^D)

                              47-24

When a stout man's friends compliment him on his
success in taking off weight, they are supplying
additional _____ for the self-controlling responses
which have reduced the extent of his eating.

47-25

---

conditioned
aversive
stimuli
                              47-29

In self-control, the (1) controll- _____ response
affects variables in such a way as to change the
probability of the (2) controll- _____ response.

47-30

Set 8

The Standard Experimental Situation

Estimated time: 14 minutes

See exhibit on preceding page
Turn to next page and begin ▶

| 1) operant 2) responses 8-4 | When the first peck on the key is _____ (TT) by food, the probability of another peck on the key is increased. 8-5 |

| 1) stimulus 2) response 8-9 | It might be said that "the pigeon has acquired the habit of pecking the key," but the only thing observed is an increased _____ of responding after reinforcement. 8-10 |

| ot 8-14 | If a pigeon has not been in the box for a long time, its rate of responding upon returning to the box will be lower than previously in the box. This *forgetting* is due to the passage of _____ during which the response is not emitted. 8-15 |

| perates upon cts upon, nanges, fects, fluences) 8-19 | In the experiment described on the exhibit, the pecking response slightly moves the key. This is an instance of the fact that an operant * * * the environment. 8-20 |

| inforced 8-24 | A psychologist fed her infant son when he emitted a faint "cooing" sound. The rate of "cooing" when hungry was expected to (and did) _____ as a result of this reinforcement. 8-25 |

| 1) operant 2) reinforced (acceptable: conditioned) 8-29 | When you are thirsty and near a drinking fountain, it is (1) _____ that you will walk to the fountain because such behavior has been (2) _____ in the past, under a similar condition of deprivation. 8-30 |

) response
:) stimulus

46-3

The usual effects of reflexes explain the evolution of such mechanisms. The reflex of vomiting * * * survival value because organisms which possess it remove dangerous materials from their stomachs.

46-4
← To p. 298

ırvival

46-8

Dust in the eyes elicits lachrymal secretion. Tears further the survival of the organism by washing out dust. Any organism not possessing this ____ would probably suffer damage to its vision.

46-9
← To p. 298

ɔerant

46-13

The sneezing little boy who "only does it to annoy" exhibits (1) ____ behavior rather than (2) ____ behavior.

46-14
← To p. 298

) reflex
    (respondent)
) operant

46-18

When we keep from coughing by sucking a soothing or narcotic cough drop or sipping a little water, we control a reflex by removing or minimizing its ____.

46-19
← To p. 298

---

imulus

46-23

Vomiting in response to a feather in the throat is a(n) (1) ____; the behavior of tickling the throat with a feather is a(n) (2) ____.

46-24
← To p. 298

) involuntary
) voluntary

46-28

The term voluntary is a misleading description of operant behavior because operants * * * controlled through relevant variables as completely as respondents.

46-29
← To p. 298

When a pigeon is first placed in the experimental space, there is a low _____ that a peck on the key will soon be emitted.

8-1

---

nforced

8-5

When pecking the key is followed immediately with food, the _____ of the response is *observed* to increase.

8-6

.e
equency)

8-10

When a peck is followed by food, the event is described by saying, "The peck was followed by (1) reinforce-_____." The food is called a(n) (2) _____. (TT)

8-11

---

ie

8-15

Forgetting and extinction are technical terms for different processes. The response is *emitted* without reinforcement only in the process called (1) _____. The response is *not emitted* in the process called (2) _____.

8-16

---

erates upon
ts upon,
anges,
ects)

8-20

There are two classes of behavior, *operant* and *respondent*. (1) _____ behavior is influenced by the consequences of previous, similar responses whereas in (2) _____ behavior, a stimulus precedes the response.

8-21

---

rease
se)

8-25

The mother who feeds her baby when he "coos" increases the rate of "cooing." When the rate of "cooing" has increased because of the reinforcement, the operant has become _____. (TT)

8-26

---

probable
(likely)
reinforced
(acceptable:
conditioned)

8-30

If a water fountain consistently fails to operate, you cease to go to it when thirsty. Because of the lack of (1) _____ (TT), the operant has been (2) _____. (TT)

8-31

duces
liminates)

46-2

When a man pulls his hand away from a hot stove, the (1)____ terminates the (2)____ which elicited it.

46-3

---

eezing
oughing)

46-7

In struggling against an inadequate supply of air, "gasping for air" is respondent behavior which supplements defective respiration and increases the chances of____ of organisms possessing this reflex.

46-8

---

erant

46-12

In general, "operant reinforcement" of glandular responses has no direct effect. *Vocal* "crying for attention," however, is clearly a(n)____.

46-13

) avoid
) operant

46-17

To keep from "flinching" when firing a pistol, we can oppose the (1)____ response of flinching with an incompatible strong (2)____ response of holding the hand and arm steady.

46-18

---

not
annot be)

46-22

By tickling his throat with a feather or drinking an irritating solution of mustard and water, a man can regurgitate poisonous food. The operant behavior of tickling or drinking controls a respondent by producing the____ for it.

46-23

---

ntrol

46-27

Reflex behavior is commonly called *involuntary*; operant behavior is called *voluntary*. Thus, vomiting is said to be (1)____, while emptying one's plate into a garbage disposer is called (2)____.

46-28

---

probability 8-1	To say that there is, at first, a low probability of pecking the key, means that the pigeon will emit pecks at a low ____ or ____. (GIVE BOTH) 8
rate (frequency) (NOT: probability) 8-6	After the pigeon pecks the key and receives food, it begins to peck steadily. Presenting food is said to have ____ pecking, which has now become conditioned. 8
(1) (reinforce-) ment (2) reinforcer (reinforcing stimulus) 8-11	When food no longer follows pecking, the (1) ____ of emitting the response is observed to decline gradually. This process is called (2) ____. 8-1
(1) extinction (2) forgetting 8-16	Pecking the key is an example of behavior which operates upon the environment. Thus it is a(n) ____. 8-17
(1) Operant (2) respondent (reflex) 8-21	The diameters of visceral organs are changed by (1) ____ muscles. Parts of the skeletal frame are moved by (2) ____ muscles. 8-22
conditioned 8-26	The mother can reinforce an infant's vocal behavior only after at least one vocalization has been ____. 8-27
reinforcement extinguished 8-31	End of Set

stimulus 46-1	Heavy exercise overheats the body and produces sweating. The cooling effect of the evaporation of sweat from the skin _____ the stimulating condition which elicited the response of sweating. 46-2
survival value 46-6	Roughly speaking, the purpose of the reflex called _____ is to remove irritants from the *upper* respiratory passages. 46-7
is 46-11	If shedding tears increased in frequency when followed by displayed affection, we would call crying a conditioned _____ response. It is doubtful, however, that the case is ever that simple 46-12
(1) respondent (reflex) (2) operant 46-16	The yawning reflex often offends one's companions. We stifle a yawn by holding our jaw rigid in order to (1) _____ aversive social consequences. Holding the jaw rigid is a(n) (2) _____. 46-17
(1) terminated (eliminated, escaped) (2) avoids (prevents) 46-21	A man is told that food he has just eaten is dangerously spoiled; he does not regurgitate the food in a manner which resembles throwing food away. Vomiting * * * directly controlled by avoidance contingencies. 46-2
(1) avoids (2) reduces (terminates, escapes) 46-26	The operant "holding the breath" under water exerts control over reflex breathing. But the operant is itself under the _____ of avoidance contingencies. 46-2

rate (or) frequency (GIVE BOTH) 8-2	REFER TO THE FOOTNOTE ON THE EXHIBIT. A given peck on the key is a(n) (1) _____. The general behavior of "pecking a key" is a(n) (2) _____. 8-3
reinforced 8-7	In operant behavior, the temporal order of the response and the reinforcing stimulus is first the (1) _____ (TT) and then the (2) _____ _____. (TT) 8-8
(1) rate (frequency) (2) extinction 8-12	When the rate of pecking has returned to its initial low level as a result of withholding food, the operant is said to have been _____. 8-13
operant 8-17	Operant behavior has direct effects on the environment. One consequence which results in an increase in the subsequent rate of the operant response is called a(n) _____. (TT) 8-18
(1) smooth (2) striated (striped, skeletal) 8-22	Action upon the environment usually results from movement of the skeletal frame. Operants are usually contractions of _____ muscles. 8-23
emitted (made) 8-27	The psychologist fed the baby when he emitted "coos," but *not* when he cried. We should expect that crying when hungry would be (1) _____ because of the withholding of (2) _____. 8-28

> A reflex response may change the stimulus which elicits it. When coughing dislodges a bit of food in the throat, the response eliminates its own ____.
>
> 46-1

survival

46-5

The *purpose* of sneezing is the effect which gives the reflex ____ ____.

46-6

did not

46-10

The temporal relation between a child's weeping and a resulting display of parental affection * * * like the principal contingency in operant conditioning.

46-11

respondent
(reflex)

46-15

When a movie script calls for violent coughing, the director may ask a mediocre actor to inhale irritating fumes. He gets "realism" by demanding (1) ____ behavior rather than (2) ____ behavior.

46-16

response

46-20

A man is told that food he is starting to eat may be dangerously spoiled; he immediately throws it away. A conditioned aversive stimulus is thus (1) ____. This operant response (2) ____ actual poisoning.

46-21

(1) operant
(2) respondent
(reflex)

46-25

In holding one's breath under water, the operant which opposes reflex breathing (1) ____ the irritation of inhaled water and (2) ____ conditioned aversive stimuli established by previous inhalation of water.

46-26

(1) operant
(2) respondent
(reflex
response)

46-30

Breathing rapidly to hyperventilate before swimming under water is "voluntary" or (1) ____ breathing; the swimmer surfaces before "involuntary" or (2) ____ breathing becomes too powerful to be suppressed by an operant.

46-31

← To p. 47

1) response
2) operant

8-3

The experiment described on the exhibit is concerned with (1) _____ (TT) behavior. The apparatus reinforces specific (2) _____ (TT) when they are emitted.

← To p. 47 8-4

---

response
reinforcing
stimulus
reinforcer,
reinforcement)

8-8

A stimulus elicits a response in *respondent* (reflex) behavior. In respondent behavior, the temporal order is first the (1) _____, then the (2) _____.

← To p. 47 8-9

---

extinguished

8-13

A response is said to be extinguished when its rate has returned to its initial low level because responses have been emitted but _____ followed by reinforcement.

← To p. 47 8-14

---

reinforcement

8-18

The word *operant* is a noun or an adjective indicating something which is operative or has an influence. Operant behavior * * * the environment.

← To p. 47 8-19

---

riated
striped,
skeletal)

8-23

After a hungry infant begins crying, he is fed; soon he cries regularly when hungry. Feeding is said to have _____ crying which has now become conditioned.

← To p. 47 8-24

---

extinguished
decreased)
reinforcement
food)

8-28

Vocalizations are classed as (1) _____ behavior when they act upon the environment (social, in this case). In that case, their frequency depends on whether or not they are (2) _____.

← To p. 47 8-29

---

as (is of) 46-4	When overheating causes the small blood vessels in the skin to enlarge and suffuse the skin with blood ("flushing"), heat is more rapidly lost. The reflex has ____ value in lowering dangerous body temperatures.　　46-5
eflex 46-9	When a child's tears lead to a display of parental affection, the reflex response is followed by a consequence which probably * * * figure in its evolutionary development.　　46-10
1) operant 2) respondent 　(reflex) 46-14	When an actor imitates "gasping for air" in a scene in a disabled submarine, he engages in operant behavior, the topography of which closely approximates ____ behavior.　　46-15
stimulus 46-19	When we choke back a sob, we control a reflex with an incompatible response. The operant "choking back" suppresses a reflex ____.　　46-20
1) respondent 　(reflex) 2) operant 46-24	In holding one's breath under water, (1) ____ behavior is controlling (2) ____ behavior.　　46-25
are 46-29	Taking snuff to induce a sneeze might be called the "voluntary" control of "involuntary" behavior. The whole act represents a chain, the first member of which is a(n) (1)____response which produces a stimulus for a(n) (2) ____.　　46-30

Set 9

Positive and Negative Reinforcement

Estimated time: 14 minutes   **Turn to next page and begin** ▶

---

negative

9-4

Turning off a television commercial is reinforced by the *termination* of a(n) (1) _____ reinforcer; turning on a very funny program is reinforced by the *presentation* of a(n) (2) _____ reinforcer.

9-5

---

1) positive
   reinforcer
2) negative
   reinforcer

9-9

A man turns his face away from an ugly sight. Turning away is reinforced by the _____ of the ugly sight (a negative reinforcer).

9-10

---

einforced
acceptable:
onditioned)

9-14

"What does he see in her?" might mean "How does she _____ his courting behavior?" (TT)

9-15

---

ot reinforcing
xtinguishing)
ncompatible

9-19

A school teacher is likely, when possible, to dismiss a class when her students are rowdy because she has been _____ by elimination of the stimuli arising from a rowdy class.

9-20

---

ecreases
xtinguished
ot reinforced)

9-24

Absenteeism increases if employees are not sufficiently _____ with wages and suitable working conditions. (TT)

9-25

---

einforcer
einforcing
timulus)

9-29

End of Set

einforced conditioned) 45-3	As described in (A) and (B), it appears that the dog threw itself against the door primarily because of Mrs. Frazier's subsequent action in * * *. 45-4 ← To p. 293
termittent 45-8	If Mrs. Frazier acts in (B) to stop the dog's whining and banging *while* it is happening, her own behavior is an example of ____ behavior. 45-9 ← To p. 293
ontinuous 45-13	In (E), another new contingency has developed which can influence Mrs. Frazier's behavior. Spending so much time opening the door * * * an aversive condition for Mrs. Frazier. 45-14 ← To p. 293
ates requencies) 45-18	Mrs. Frazier controlled the dog's behavior in a satisfactory way principally through positive re-inforcement. She * * * resort to aversive control or punishment. 45-19 ← To p. 293
ositive (and) egative EITHER ORDER) 45-23	Removing the card while the dog was watching would ____ (TT) whatever the dog was doing. 45-24 ← To p. 293
voidance 45-28	The result as described in (H) was to prevent further damage to the door by eliminating certain behavior with an (1) S____. Only when the (2) S____ was present did Mrs. Frazier need to open the door at the first whine. 45-29 ← To p. 293

A hungry pigeon pecks a key and is immediately given food. The (1) _____ of the pecking response will increase since presenting food (2) * * * a reinforcement.

9-1

) negative
) positive

9-5

A stimulus is called a negative reinforcer if its _____-tion reinforces behavior.

9-6

rmination
nd, removal)

9-10

A food-deprived child will probably ask for food if the response "asking for food" has been (1) _____ in the past. This is an example of (2) _____ reinforcement.

9-11

inforce

9-15

The man who brings candy to his wife to end an argument may find later that his wife argues _____ (more or less?) frequently. An appeaser has worked as a reinforcer.

9-16

inforced
egatively
inforced)

9-20

The teacher who dismisses a class when it is rowdy probably causes the frequency of rowdy behavior to (1) _____, since dismissal from class is probably a(n) (2) _____ for rowdy children.

9-21

inforced

9-25

In looking for lost car keys, one may search the same littered table top several times before this behavior is _____ through consistent failure to find them.

9-26

ncreased

45-2

The dog may have mechanically opened some other door by throwing its forelegs against the door. If so, the response was ____ previously by a natural contingency.

45-3

1) in(-side)
2) out(-side)

45-7

In (B), "occasionally" means that Mrs. Frazier provided ____ reinforcement.

45-8

1) escape
2) avoidance

45-12

When, in (D), Mrs. Frazier starts opening the door after the dog's *first* faint whine, the dog's whining is on the schedule called ____ reinforcement.

45-13

was not
(is not)

45-17

The dog's "asking to be let in" soon occurred with two very different ____ depending on whether the card was or was not in place.

45-18

1) (S)$^\Delta$
2) (S)^D

45-22

Removing an S$^\Delta$ or *presenting* an S^D are two ways of describing the same change of stimulus. It is reinforcement although the distinction between ____ and ____ reinforcement cannot be made.

45-23

(S)$^\Delta$

45-27

In "turning back" in (J), the dog avoids an S$^\Delta$ which would have occurred if it had gone out on that occasion. We may interpret this "turning back" as ____ behavior.

45-28

negative

45-32

End of Set

) rate
  (frequency)
) is
  (constitutes,
  acts as)   **9-1**
	If, instead of presenting food after the pigeon pecks the key, a loud noise is turned *on*, the rate of pecking will *not* increase. Presenting a loud noise * * * a reinforcement. **9-2**

na(-tion) .ina(-tion)] **9-6**	Elimination of a television commercial may be a negative reinforcement. If so, the television commercial is a(n) ____ reinforce-____. **9-7**
:inforced :onditioned) ɔsitive **9-11**	Both positive and negative reinforcement ____ the rate of response. **9-12**
ɔre **9-16**	The man who brings his wife candy when she is especially agreeable may find that she argues * * *. He has reinforced responses which are incompatible with arguing. **9-17**
.crease inforcement **9-21**	A teacher who dismisses a class when it is quiet (1) ____ the probability of rowdy behavior. She is reinforcing responses which are (2) ____ with rowdiness. **9-22**
:tinguished **9-26**	If people continue to buy books, music, and works of art, we conclude that these objects ____ the behavior of purchasing them. **9-27**

espondents reflex esponses) 45-1	We can say that whining is an operant if we can show that its frequency _____ as the result of Mrs. Frazier's opening the door in (B). 45-2
einforced conditioned) 45-6	(B) describes reinforcement only if being outside is reinforcing when the dog is (1) _____-side, and being inside when the dog is (2) _____-side. 45-7
lowly 45-11	(D) suggests that Mrs. Frazier's own behavior is no longer (1) _____ behavior (which *terminates* whining and scratching) but (2) _____ behavior (which *prevents* door scratching). 45-12
iscrimination 45-16	The word "NO" on the card * * * more effective than, say, an equally conspicuous geometrical pattern. 45-17
D 45-21	Removing the card is a case of removing an (1) S_____ and presenting an (2) S_____. 45-22
ccidental 45-26	(I) may be interpreted as the avoidance of a long S_____ period which by that time often occurred when the dog was outside. 45-27
einforcing 45-31	In general, the dog reinforced Mrs. Frazier's own behavior by using _____ reinforcement since the dog stopped whining and scratching. 45-32

s not

9-2

When pecking a key *turns off* a very loud noise for a few moments, frequency of pecking in the presence of the noise may be observed to *increase*. In that case ending the loud noise * * * a reinforcement.

9-3

---

negative
(reinforce-)r

9-7

If a funny program is a positive reinforcer, presenting the program is a(n) ____ ____.

9-8

---

increase

9-12

When an infant emits the sounds "da-da," his father fondles him. We classify fondling as a reinforcer when we note that the infant (1) ____ this response more (2) ____.

9-13

---

ess
requently
less often,
ess)

9-17

Two responses are incompatible when they cannot be emitted at the same time. A wife who reinforces her husband when he is agreeable may find the rate of arguments decreasing because arguments are ____ with being agreeable.

9-18

---

decreases
incompatible

9-22

If we consistently get no answer when we dial a number, we stop dialing. This process is called (1) ____, and is due to lack of (2) ____.

9-23

---

reinforce
acceptable:
ondition)

9-27

To stop a dog from begging for food, one should ____ the operant by never again feeding it when it begs.

9-28

We cannot be sure that whining is an operant. It may be one of the many _____ which occur in an emotional state generated when a strong response cannot be executed.

45-1

---

would not

45-5

The expression "asking to be let out" suggests that the dog's behavior is similar to a human verbal response such as "open the door." Both responses are _____ by the action of a second organism.

45-6

---

variable (-)ratio

45-10

The schedule suggested in (B) should make the dog's behavior extinguish very _____ if reinforcement were discontinued.

45-11

---

(1) s^Δ
(2) s^D

45-15

When, in (F), Mrs. Frazier opened the door if the card wasn't in place but not if it was in place, she was establishing a(n) _____.

45-16

---

s^Δ

45-20

In (F), the door *without* the card became a(n) _____ for asking to be let in.

45-21

---

reinforce

45-25

The "silently" in (G) is important because it was advisable to remove the card without stimulating the dog in order to prevent _____ contingencies of reinforcement which might establish undesired superstitious behavior.

45-26

---

extinction
control
(discrimination)

45-30

Occasionally letting the dog in when the card was in place would spoil the result by _____ the response in the presence of s^Δ, thus breaking down the discrimination.

45-31

is	Reinforcement which consists of *presenting* stimuli (e.g., food) is called *positive* reinforcement. In contrast, reinforcement which consists of *terminating* stimuli (e.g., painful stimuli) is called _____ reinforcement.
9-3	← To p. 52 9-4
positive reinforcement	The rate of an operant can be increased by presenting a(n) (1) _____ _____ or by ending a(n) (2) _____ _____.
9-8	← To p. 52 9-9
(1) emits (2) frequently (often)	When the father fondles the infant after it has said "da-da," the infant may smile, repeat "da-da," etc. If he continues to fondle the infant frequently, we assume that the smile, etc., have _____ the father's behavior.
9-13	← To p. 52 9-14
incompatible	An undesired response can be eliminated by (1) * * * the response, or by reinforcing other responses which are (2) * * * with it.
9-18	← To p. 52 9-19
extinction reinforcement	If an airplane spotter never sees the kind of plane he is to spot, his frequency of scanning the sky (1) _____. In other words, his "looking" behavior is (2) * * *. (TT)
9-23	← To p. 52 9-24
extinguish	A stimulus which follows a response is called a(n) _____ if the rate at which similar responses are emitted is observed to increase.
9-28	← To p. 52 9-29

Set 45

A Problem in Behavioral Engineering

See exhibit on preceding page

Estimated time: 13 minutes

Turn to next page and begin ▶

---

opening
the door
(reinforcing it)

45-4

If the dog pushed the door open and slipped through without help, we * * * say that the dog was "asking to be let out. "

45-5

---

escape

45-9

If Mrs. Frazier acts in (B) only when there has been so much whining and banging that she "can't stand it any more, " the dog is probably being reinforced on a(n) _____ - _____ schedule.

45-10

---

is (may be,
was)

45-14

The card on the door became a(n) (1) _____ for the response of asking to be let in, and the door without a card became a(n) (2) _____ for the response.

45-15

---

did not

45-19

Because whining was never reinforced when the card was on the door, the card became a(n) _____ for the response of asking to be let in.

45-20

---

reinforce

45-24

It was important *not* to remove the card when the dog was whining or jumping against the door because that would _____ this behavior.

45-25

---

(1) $(S)^\Delta$
(2) $(S)^D$

45-29

A similar result could be achieved by completely extinguishing responses to the door, but the dog's "asking to be let in" was sometimes useful to Mrs. Frazier. Hence, (1) _____ was less suitable than establishing stimulus (2) _____.

45-30

Set 10

Basic Concepts Applied

Estimated time: 11 minutes **Turn to next page and begin** ▷

---

icreases

10-4

The receipt of candy as a result of "throwing a tantrum" is an example of _____ reinforcement.

10-5

---

compatible
ith

10-9

Two ways of effectively preventing unwanted conditioned behavior are: to (1) _____ it by withholding reinforcement and to condition some (2) _____ behavior.

10-10

---

te
equency)
cceptable:
obability)

10-14

Other things being equal, an operant which has been observed to occur at a high rate in the past has a high _____ of occurring at some future time.

10-15

) less
) extinction

10-19

Reaching for a glass of water and saying "Water, please" are (1) _____; any specific instance of such behavior, however, is called a(n) (2) _____.

10-20

---

erant

10-24

_____ usually control the internal economy of the organism.

10-25

---

itted

10-29

In forgetting, a response decreases in probability with the passage of time during which it * * * emitted.

10-30

Read exhibit now and refer to it as needed.

(A) Mrs. Frazier owned a dog which "asked to be let out or in" by whining softly and then standing on its hind legs and throwing its forepaws noisily against the door.

(B) Mrs. Frazier occasionally opened the door when the dog "asked to be let in or out."

(C) After the house was repainted and the door beautifully refinished, it became important for Mrs. Frazier to keep the dog from scratching the door.

(D) So Mrs. Frazier started responding to the dog's *first* faint whine, not waiting for the jump against the door.

(E) It was so easy to get in and out that the frequency of the behavior increased, and Mrs. Frazier began to spend a good share of the day letting the dog in and out.

(F) Mrs. Frazier solved the problem by hanging a card bearing the letters NO outside the door. The door was never opened when the card was in place; but when the card was *not* in place, the door was opened as soon as the dog whined.

(G) The card could be silently removed from the door through the mail slot.

(H) The dog quickly stopped "asking to be let in" when the card was in place. During this period, damage to the door was repaired. Henceforth, when it was convenient to let the dog in, Mrs. Frazier would remove the card. At other times the dog stayed outside without whining or throwing itself against the door.

(I) Because it was no longer easy to get back in, the dog now "asked to be let out" only infrequently.

(J) Sometimes, after asking to be let out, the dog would see Mrs. Frazier pick up the card to put on the door and would turn back and stay in the house.

▷

A child has a "temper tantrum," screaming for candy. The mother gives the child candy and the tantrum ceases. The *mother's* response of handing candy to the child is _____ by the termination of the tantrum.

10-1

---

ositive

10-5

When the mother placates the child with candy and the child ceases to scream, both mother and child are, perhaps unknowingly, _____ each other's behavior.

10-6

) extinguish
) incompatible

10-10

A man is said to have a tendency to listen to music or an interest in music if he _____ emits the behavior of listening to music.

10-11

---

obability
(kelihood)

10-15

A pigeon pecks a key and immediately receives food. After this, it is more _____ that the pigeon will again emit the response.

10-16

) operants
) response

10-20

After a response has been reinforced, the _____ is high that it will be repeated.

10-21

---

spondents
flexes,
ooth muscles,
l glands)

10-25

The pairing of two stimuli is necessary to condition (1) _____ behavior; reinforcement is necessary for conditioning (2) _____ behavior.

10-26

---

not

10-30

When, because a response is no longer followed by reinforcement, the response is emitted at a lowered rate, we say that _____ has taken place.

10-31

44-3

A man paid for tearing down walls is insulted by his employer. In working, he swings his sledge hammer with great vigor. The money he is paid affects this behavior as a(n) (1) _____, the insult as a(n) (2) _____ stimulus.

44-4
← To p. 287

44-8

As we write a paragraph, we create an elaborate chain of verbal stimuli which alter the probabilities of other words to follow. Sustained verbal behavior almost always involves _____ causes.

44-9
← To p. 287

44-13

Two responses which cannot be emitted simultaneously are _____ responses.

44-14
← To p. 287

44-18

A dog approaches a strange object. If the object is a positive reinforcer, (1) _____ the object is reinforced; if it is a negative reinforcer, withdrawing from the object is (2) _____.

44-19
← To p. 287

44-23

An organism may oscillate between approach and withdrawal. When a dog first approaches, then withdraws, and then approaches again, it is _____ between two responses.

44-24
← To p. 287

44-28

Many highly reinforced responses are also punished. A second response which terminates the conditioned aversive stimuli generated by a punished response may also be strong. These two responses are _____.

44-29
← To p. 287

44-33

End of Set

einforced 10-1	If termination of a temper tantrum reinforces a mother's response of giving candy to her child, the cessation of noise is an example of ____ reinforcement. 10-2
onditioning acceptable: einforcing) 10-6	To avoid conditioning temper tantrums, the mother should not ____ such behavior when it is emitted. 10-7
equently often) 10-11	We do not observe a "tendency" to listen to music or a "trait" such as a love for music. What we actually observe is that a man frequently ____ the behavior of listening to music. 10-12
robable ikely) 10-16	A pigeon pecks a key and immediately receives food. Technically speaking, the response is followed by ____ . 10-17
robability 10-21	There *is* an eliciting stimulus for ____ behavior. 10-22
) respondent (reflex)) operant 10-26	The magnitude of the response is related to the intensity of the preceding stimulus in ____ behavior. 10-27
xtinction 10-31	When, as a result of the *passage of time* with no opportunity to emit the response, a response is emitted at a lowered rate, we say that ____ has taken place. 10-32

an

44-2

A restaurant hires a pretty waitress and serves good food. Two different reinforcers, good food and a view of a pretty waitress, have a common _____ in increasing patronage.

44-3

D$_S$
stimuli)

44-7

A word which "expresses multiple meanings" is controlled by * * * stimuli.

44-8

D
stimulus,
ariable)

44-12

A single event may have (1) _____ effects on behavior and (2) _____ events may have a common effect.

44-13

---

ithdrawing

44-17

The separate probabilities of two conflicting responses may combine in *algebraic summation*. A timid man standing at the edge of a dance floor may show _____ _____ of the conflicting responses of approach and withdrawal.

44-18

---

ithdraw
turn back)

44-22

After the dog turns away from a strange object, the variables controlling approach may increase and the variables controlling withdrawal may decrease. The dog may again _____ this object.

44-23

---

1) algebraic
    summation
2) oscillation

44-27

In trying to decide about a purchase, we show _____ when we tentatively decide to buy, then not to buy, and then to buy, etc.

44-28

---

nxiety
emotion)

44-32

We might infer that an "anxiety neurosis" results when two (1) _____ responses are strong. Conditioned aversive stimuli are more or less continuously generated; hence the organism is nearly (2) _____ in a state of anxiety.

44-33

negative 10-2	With reference to the influence of the temper tantrum on the mother's behavior, the tantrum is a negative (1) reinforc-____; its cessation is a negative (2) reinforc-____. 10-3
reinforce 10-7	If temper tantrums have been previously conditioned, the mother can (1) ____ the response by consistently not (2) ____ it. 10-8
emits 10-12	We call a man a golf "enthusiast" if he frequently ____ the operant behavior of playing golf. 10-13
einforcement 10-17	When a pigeon is reinforced for pecking a key, the (1) ____ at which the response is (2) ____ increases. 10-18
espondent (reflex) 10-22	There *is no* eliciting stimulus for ____ behavior. 10-23
espondent (reflex) 10-27	Most (1) ____ behavior involves the activity of smooth muscles and glands. Most (2) ____ behavior involves the activity of striated muscles. 10-28
orgetting 10-32	**End of Set**

wo (both) 44-1	Two reinforcers * * * (can or cannot?) have a common effect in increasing the probability of a given operant. 44-2
he same (one, a single, a iven) 44-6	The verbal response "house" may be under the control of an actual house, a printed word, a spoken word, or words which frequently precede the word, as in completing "the White. . ." Many ____ exert control over the same response. 44-7
rompt 44-11	In puns, verbal slips, etc., the "multiple meaning" of a word is important. By "multiple meaning" we imply that more than one ____ (TT) is contributing to the probability of the response. 44-12
robability 44-16	If uncomplicated by other variables, a dog's history of negative reinforcement for withdrawing from strange objects determines its probability of ____ from another strange object. 44-17
lgebraic ummation 44-21	As a dog approaches a strange object, the variables controlling withdrawal may increase. When in algebraic summation, the tendency to withdraw exceeds the tendency to approach, the dog will ____. 44-22
ncreases 44-26	When a dog stands "not too close and not too far" from a strange object, its behavior shows (1) ____ ____. When it approaches, jumps back, approaches, etc., it shows (2) ____. 44-27
nxiety emotion) 44-31	When one or more of the variables controlling a response is aversive, prolonged conflict may result in a sustained state of ____. 44-32

einforc-)er einforc-)ement 10-3	When a temper tantrum results in the receipt of candy, the probability that the child will have a tantrum in the future _____. 10-4 ← To p. 57
1) extinguish 2) reinforcing 10-8	In addition to extinguishing temper tantrums, the mother may frequently reinforce "playing quietly." This would help to eliminate tantrums by conditioning behavior which is * * * them. 10-9 ← To p. 57
nits 10-13	Many so-called traits (aggressiveness, persistence, friendliness, etc.) are simply ways of indicating an individual's _____ of emitting certain types of behavior. 10-14 ← To p. 57
) rate (frequency)) emitted 10-18	If a previously reinforced response is no longer reinforced, it soon occurs (1) _____ frequently. This is called (2) _____. 10-19 ← To p. 57
perant 10-23	_____ (Operant or Respondent?) behavior usually acts upon the external environment. 10-24 ← To p. 57
) respondent) operant 10-28	In operant conditioning, a response can be reinforced only after it has been _____. 10-29 ← To p. 57

▷

Two "causes" may have a common effect. An operant reinforced with two reinforcers appropriate to two different deprivations will vary with ____ deprivations.

44-1

---

vo
multiple)

44-5

We may light a cigarette (a) on smelling cigarettes, (b) after seeing a friend light one, or (c) when watching a television advertisement for cigarettes. Three S^Ds can exert control over * * * response.

44-6

D_s (stimuli)

44-10

An actor may be unable to complete the recitation of a soliloquy until prompted. The soliloquy is a chain of verbal responses. The ____ (i.e., the added S^D) given to the actor is an additional source of stimulus control.

44-11

---

ncompatible
conflicting)

44-15

If uncomplicated by other variables, a dog's history of positive reinforcement for approaching strange objects determines its ____ of approaching another strange object.

44-16

---

pproach (and)
ithdrawal
EITHER ORDER)

44-20

When incompatible responses are *diametrically opposed*, there may be a(n) ____ ____ of their independent probabilities, as when a soldier moves slowly into combat.

44-21

---

scillation

44-25

There is oscillation in behavior when the act of beginning to execute a response ____ the strength of variables controlling a response diametrically opposed to it.

44-26

---

scillate

44-30

When behavior which is both reinforced and punished shows oscillation, conditioned aversive stimuli are repeatedly generated. These stimuli may in turn generate a state of ____.

44-31

Read exhibit now and refer to it as needed during the first half of this lesson.

(A) A pigeon is deprived of food for some time.

(B) The pigeon is placed in a standard experimental space where a feeding mechanism filled with grain is presented occasionally for a few seconds.

(C) The feeding mechanism or "food magazine" makes a characteristic noise, and the food is illuminated while available.

(D) Noise and light from the magazine initially have no power to reinforce behavior.

(E) On the other hand, food does reinforce any behavior it may follow. (Food is an *unconditioned* or *primary reinforcer*.)

(F) When the magazine has been operated many times, the pigeon immediately responds to the noise and light by approaching and eating.

(G) All food is removed from the feeding mechanism.

(H) The empty magazine now operates only when a key is pecked.

(I) Although the magazine is empty, the rate of pecking the key increases. The sound and light of the magazine have evidently become *conditioned reinforcers* (sometimes called *secondary reinforcers*).

(J) The sound and light became *conditioned reinforcers* when they were repeatedly paired with food.

(K) When pecking the key continues to operate the empty magazine, the rate declines.

(L) The sound and light of the magazine are no longer paired with food and, through extinction, lose the power to reinforce.

Set 44

Multiple Causes and Conflicting Responses

Estimated time: 12 minutes

Turn to next page and begin ▶

.) reinforcer
2) aversive
   (emotional)

44-4

A man paid for tearing down walls is insulted by his employer. His great vigor in swinging his sledge hammer may reflect the combined effect of ____ variables.

44-5

---

ultiple
many,
everal)

44-9

A quizmaster may give hints or prompts to a contestant. He is providing additional ____ to make the answer more probable.

44-10

---

ncompatible

44-14

In the condition we call "conflict," the variables active at the moment strengthen two or more ____ responses.

44-15

---

1) approaching
2) reinforced

44-19

A dog approaches a strange object slowly. (Strange objects in the past have provided both reinforcing and aversive stimuli.) The slow approach represents algebraic summation of the probabilities of ____ and ____.

44-20

---

scillating

44-24

Frequently "changing one's mind" about a purchase is an example of ____ between two responses.

44-25

---

ncompatible
conflicting)

44-29

When behavior is both strongly reinforced and severely punished, the organism may ____ between early phases of the two incompatible responses.

44-30

Set 11

Conditioned Reinforcers

See exhibit on preceding page

Estimated time: 26 minutes

Turn to next page and begin ▶

---

paired with (followed by)

11-8

After (G), operation of the food magazine will produce sound and light, but approaching the magazine will no longer be _____ by food.

11-9

---

paired

11-17

In the usual experiment, a peck operates a noisy magazine containing food. The peck is reinforced by both _____ and _____ reinforcement. (TTs)

11-18

---

conditioned reinforcer

11-26

The exhibit experiment demonstrates that an operant can be conditioned *without* using a(n) _____ reinforcer.

11-27

---

paired with (followed by, slightly precede)

11-35

When the chimpanzee drops tokens into the peanut vending machine, the tokens become (1) _____ reinforcers because they slightly precede the food, a(n) (2) * * *.

11-36

---

two (both)

11-44

If tokens have been paired with unconditioned reinforcers appropriate to many states of deprivation, there are _____ conditions of deprivation under which tokens reinforce behavior.

11-45

---

generalized reinforcers

11-53

A parent's *attention* can _____ (TT) the behavior of a child.

11-54

S^Ds (stimuli) 43-3	In (C), the taste of candy probably _____ (TT) the behavior of putting candy in the mouth. 43-4 ← To p. 282
(1) (B) (2) (C) (3) multiple (several, three) 43-8	In the laboratory, it (1) * * * possible to isolate simple functional relations; but in interpreting most events outside of the laboratory, we must be alert to the possibility of (2) _____ effects in complex situations. 43-9 ← To p. 282
(1) satiating (2) emotional 43-13	The event of presenting a single bit of candy had _____ effects on the child's behavior. 43-14 ← To p. 282
isolate (analyze, study) 43-18	An experimenter often holds all independent variables constant except the one he is investigating. In this way, he is * * * the effect this variable has upon the dependent variable. 43-19 ← To p. 282
reinforced (conditioned) 43-23	By reinforcing some specific behavior with small amounts of attention for a few moments, we can (1) _____ the behavior without producing satiation. In this way, we can (2) _____ the two effects of attention. 43-24 ← To p. 282
decrease 43-28	Oscillation, or alternation, of emotional effects in extinction after continuous reinforcement produces a record showing a(n) _____ in response rate as well. 43-29 ← To p. 282

(A) is necessary if ____ is to be used as a reinforcer.

11-1

---

einforced

11-9

After (G), the sound of the food magazine is no longer paired with the ____ reinforcer. (TT)

11-10

---

litioned (and)
onditioned
HER ORDER)

11-18

When the magazine operates after a peck, the pigeon approaches it and eats. Since approaching the magazine takes time, there is a short delay between the response and the ____ reinforcement. (TT)

11-19

---

unconditioned

11-27

When you are reinforced for services by a check, the check is analogous to the * * * in the present experiment.

11-28

---

conditioned
unconditioned
einforcer

11-36

We can demonstrate that a token has become a conditioned reinforcer by delivering a token immediately ____ some new response has been emitted.

11-37

---

nany

11-45

A reinforcer which is not dependent on any one specific deprivation is called a generalized reinforcer. A conditioned reinforcer becomes a generalized reinforcer when paired with * * * unconditioned reinforcers.

11-46

---

einforce
hence:
condition)

11-54

Feigning illness and being conspicuous (exhibitionism) often get attention. In other words, the attention of others ____ (TT) feigning illness and acting conspicuously.

11-55

elicits

43-2

In (C), visual stimuli from the candy are the _____ for eating the candy.

43-3

---

(1) decrease
(lower)
(2) S^Ds

43-7

The single piece of candy which elicited a reflex response in (1) _____ (USE LETTER) was an S^D for ingestive behavior in (2) _____ (USE LETTER) and an S^D for verbal behavior in (E). Thus, this single event had (3) _____ effects.

43-8

---

einforcer

43-12

The child may eat less in (H) partly because of the (1) _____ effect of eating the candy, (C), and partly because of the (2) _____ effect described in (G).

43-13

---

solated
analyzed,
separated,
distinguished)

43-17

By using simple organisms with controlled histories in simple environments, we hold many variables constant in order to _____ one effective variable at a time.

43-18

---

atiation

43-22

If a child who has stopped misbehaving after receiving much attention is *more* likely to misbehave on future occasions, then "attention" _____ (TT) misbehaving.

43-23

---

ncrease

43-27

As an emotional effect wears off, the organism returns to a higher rate of responding even though extinction is still proceeding. This means that more responses are now going unreinforced. The emotional effect may therefore return. There is another _____ in rate.

43-28

---

food 11-1	In (B), approaching the food magazine is _____ by food, provided the pigeon reaches the magazine in time to eat. 11-2
unconditioned (acceptable: primary) 11-10	In (H), the key is connected with the magazine for the first time. Thus the response to be conditioned can not have had a previous history of _____. 11-11
unconditioned 11-19	When a peck on the key operates a full magazine, a little time elapses between the response and the unconditioned reinforcement because of the time needed for the pigeon to * * *. 11-20
noise and/or light (conditioned reinforcer) 11-28	You will not continue to work for checks which "bounce" because the (1) _____ reinforcing power disappears in (2) _____. (TT) 11-29
after 11-37	Tokens are shown to be reinforcers if they _____ the subsequent rate of response similar to a response they have followed. 11-38
several (many) 11-46	If a chimpanzee exchanges tokens for food, water, a mate, and escape from pain, a token becomes a(n) _____ _____. 11-47
reinforces (ence: conditions) 11-55	"Paying attention" or "looking interested" when someone talks will usually increase the (1) _____ at which he talks since "attention" is a(n) (2) _____ _____ for most persons. 11-56

(B) describes the effect of candy as a stimulus which _____ a reflex response.

43-2

Even though (C) should slightly (1) _____ the deprivation level, the child now asks for candy at (E) although he did not at (A). This is due to the fact that the sight and taste of candy are (2) _____ for asking for more.

43-7

(G) describes an emotional effect produced by the withholding of a(n) _____, where reinforcement has previously been continuous.

43-12

We deliberately arrange experimental conditions to analyze (or isolate) the effects of a single variable. By changing the conditions specified in (D), the effect of stimulus control can be _____ from the effect of deprivation.

43-17

A child who misbehaves to get attention will stop when suddenly given almost constant attention. Here the most obvious effect of giving attention is an example of _____ rather than reinforcement.

43-22

The emotional effect of failure to receive reinforcement may wear off and the rate will _____ somewhat.

43-27

einforced
conditioned
by being
einforced)]

11-2

In (C), the noise and light of the magazine are being paired with _____ .

11-3

itioning
forcement)

11-11

In (I), when a first peck to the new key is emitted, it is followed by the sound of the magazine. Since the magazine is empty, its presentation * * * followed by an unconditioned reinforcer.

11-12

pproach the
agazine
jo to food)

11-20

When a peck operates the magazine, the noise of the magazine operation occurs immediately. The (1) _____ reinforcement is immediate, whereas the (2) _____ reinforcement is slightly delayed.

11-21

) conditioned
(secondary)
) extinction

11-29

A stimulus which acquires the property of a reinforcer is called a(n) _____ reinforcer.

11-30

crease

11-38

When a chimpanzee who has exchanged tokens for peanuts presses a telegraph key, a token is delivered. If the token is a conditioned reinforcer, the _____ of the response, pressing the key, will be observed to increase.

11-39

eneralized
inforcer
onditioned
eneralized
inforcer)

11-47

After the chimpanzee has exchanged tokens for food, water, a mate, etc., the tokens * * * effective if the chimpanzee is well-fed but deprived of water.

11-48

te
requency)
onditioned)
eneralized
inforcer

11-56

People frequently show *approval* just before they provide many different types of reinforcers. Smiles, the word "good," and other "signs of approval" become conditioned _____ _____ .

11-57

The single event described in (A) has several different _____.

43-1

---

re (were)

43-5

Ingestion of food produces satiation, an operation which (1) _____ the probability of "asking for food." At the same time, the discriminative stimuli generated by eating (2) _____ the probability of that response.

43-6

---

multiple
effects
(several, many,
three effects)

43-10

Although the verbal response "asking for more," (E), has been maintained by nearly continuous reinforcement, in (F), the parent _____ the positive reinforcer, candy.

43-11

---

would not

43-15

When stimuli from candy no longer serve as S^Ds, we should observe a decrease in the probability of asking for candy after eating a little candy. The decrease would be due to a(n) _____ in deprivation.

43-16

---

1) is not
2) is

43-20

A single aversive stimulus used in punishment elicits respondents, conditions other stimuli to elicit these respondents, and makes possible the conditioning of avoidance behavior. The single aversive stimulus has _____ effects.

43-21

---

decrease
(lower,
reduce)

43-25

The single operation of withholding positive reinforcement has two effects; both effects are a(n) _____ in rate.

43-26

---

food (reinforcement) 11-3	In (D), before being paired with food, the noise of the magazine * * * reinforce a response which it follows. 11-4
is not 11-12	In (I), because the rate of key pecking increases when followed by the sound of the empty food magazine, we conclude that this sound is a(n) ____ ____ 11-13
conditioned unconditioned 11-21	The conditioned reinforcer (noise of the magazine) occurs (1) ____ after a response to the key, but the unconditioned reinforcer is (2) ____ until the pigeon reaches the magazine. 11-22
conditioned (secondary) 11-30	A stimulus which has the property of a reinforcer without prior conditioning is called a(n) * * *. 11-31
rate (frequency) 11-39	The chimpanzee is being "paid" with tokens for pressing the key. Technically, we say its responses of pressing the key are ____. 11-40
are (will be, remain) 11-48	The effectiveness of a generalized reinforcer is relatively independent of the organism's condition of ____ at any given moment. 11-49
generalized reinforcers 11-57	You may show affection or approval to ____ (TT) a response you want another person to emit more frequently. 11-58

Page 67

Set 43

PART XII Scientific Analysis and the Interpretation of Complex Cases

Multiple Effects

See exhibit on preceding page

Estimated time: 15 minutes

Turn to next page and begin ▶

---

reinforces
(conditions)

43-4

Because of (D), the sight and taste of one piece of candy * * * S^Ds for asking for more candy.

43-5

---

(1) is
(2) multiple
(many,
various)

43-9

Events in everyday situations are often complex in that a single event may have multiple effects. In the episode described in the exhibit, the piece of candy had ____ ____.

43-10

---

multiple
(several)

43-14

If, once each day, we gave a single piece of candy (never followed by additional candy), the stimuli from the candy * * * serve as an S^D for asking for more.

43-15

---

analyzing
(isolating)

43-19

The relation between (A) and (E) is often called "whetting the appetite." It (1) * * * an example of a change in deprivation; it (2) * * * an illustration of the role of the candy in providing an S^D for further behavior.

43-20

---

(1) reinforce
(condition)
(2) isolate
(analyze,
separate)

43-24

When reinforcement is withheld after continuous reinforcement, response rate declines in extinction. Emotional behavior also occurs, and if this is incompatible with the response, it will ____ the rate further.

43-25

---

oscillation
(alternation,
fluctuation,
uneveness)

43-29

End of Set

:annot will not, vould fail to) 11-4	In (E), food **is termed** an unconditioned reinforcer (or primary reinforcer) because its reinforcing power * * * depend on previous conditioning. 11-5
:onditioned einforcer acceptable: :econdary einforcer) 11-13	Because the sound of the magazine *acquired* its power to reinforce, it is called a(n) ____ ____. 11-14
1) immediately (quickly) 2) delayed 11-22	In (I), the noise of the magazine will reinforce a response only if the pigeon is deprived of food. Both ____ and ____ reinforcers depend on food deprivation. 11-23
inconditioned einforcer 11-31	If a conditioned reinforcer is not occasionally paired with an unconditioned reinforcer, its effectiveness as a reinforcer is ____. 11-32
einforced acceptable: :onditioned) 11-40	If the chimpanzee can no longer use tokens in the vending machine, tokens will (1) ____ their power to reinforce through the process called (2) ____. 11-41
leprivation acceptable: :atiation, unger) 11-49	A conditioned reinforcer can become a(n) * * * by being paired with *several* unconditioned reinforcers appropriate to various kinds of deprivation. 11-50
einforce condition) 11-58	You may withhold affection or approval to ____ (TT) behavior you don't want another person to emit. 11-59

(A) A parent gives a child a small piece of candy, although the child has not recently asked for candy.

(B) The child salivates and

(C) eats the candy.

(D) In the child's history, getting and eating one piece of candy has usually been followed by getting another piece.

(E) The child asks for more candy; but

(F) although the parent usually gives more candy when asked, this time no more candy is given.

(G) The child cries, his face grows red, and finally he has a temper tantrum.

(H) Dinner is served a few minutes later, and the child eats less than usual.

does not 11-5	A synonym for "unconditioned reinforcer" is "____ reinforcer." 11-6
conditioned reinforcer (secondary reinforcer) 11-14	A synonym for "conditioned reinforcer" is "____ reinforcer." 11-15
conditioned (and) unconditioned (EITHER ORDER) 11-23	A conditioned reinforcer which has acquired its capacity to reinforce by being paired with food is effective only when the animal is * * *. 11-24
extinguished (decreased) 11-32	A chimpanzee drops tokens into a vending machine which delivers peanuts. The peanuts are ____-ed reinforcers which increase the frequency of depositing tokens into the machine. 11-33
1) lose 2) extinction 11-41	Food will reinforce a response only if the chimpanzee is deprived of food. Similarly, if the tokens have been paired only with food, they will be effective as reinforcers only if the chimpanzee is * * *. 11-42
generalized reinforcer (conditioned generalized reinforcer) 11-50	A generalized reinforcer is nearly ____ of the specific state of deprivation of the organism. 11-51
extinguish 11-59	Mr. X succeeds in coercing people into reinforcing him in many *different* ways. Signs of submissiveness in others then become ____ ____ which increase the frequency of new forms of coercion, independent of the particular deprivation. 11-60

| behavior | A meteorologist who attempts to bring about rain by "seeding" clouds with dry ice is attempting to ____ the weather. |
| 42-3 | 42-4 ← To p. 276 |

| (1) predicting
(2) controlling
(3) interpreting | A phenomenon is explained scientifically when we can state how it can be ____, ____, or ____. |
| 42-8 | 42-9 ← To p. 276 |

| dependent | A scientist manipulates (1) ____ variables to determine whether they affect the (2) ____ variable in which he is interested. |
| 42-13 | 42-14 ← To p. 276 |

| (1) independent
variable
(2) dependent
variable
(EITHER ORDER) | In a reflex, response magnitude is a(n) ____ of stimulus intensity. |
| 42-18 | 42-19 ← To p. 276 |

| (1) independent
(2) dependent
(3) functional
relation
(4) law | When a functional relation is known, we may be able to manipulate the (1) * * * to control the (2) * * *. |
| 42-23 | 42-24 ← To p. 276 |

| interpretation | By saying that nature is lawful, we mean that there are ____ relations between variables. |
| 42-28 | 42-29 ← To p. 276 |

| is | **End of Set** |
| 42-33 | |

primary 11-6	In (F), approaching the magazine when it operates has been ____ because it has been consistently followed by an unconditioned reinforcer (food). 11-7
secondary 11-15	In (L), when the sound of the magazine is never followed by food, its capacity to reinforce is ____. (TT) 11-16
deprived of food (hungry) 11-24	Establishing a conditioned reinforcer is similar to respondent conditioning in that both require that two stimuli be ____. 11-25
condition (-ed) 11-33	When the chimpanzee drops tokens into a vending machine, the visual and tactual stimuli provided by the token occur, in time, slightly ____ the food. 11-34
deprived of food (hungry) 11-42	The chimpanzee has "bought" only peanuts with tokens. If he has just eaten his fill of peanuts, the tokens * * * be capable of reinforcing. 11-43
independent 11-51	Money buys many things. Money is a(n) * * *. It must have acquired this property by being frequently paired with many *different* reinforcers in the behavior we call "buying." 11-52

oals (aims, urposes, ınctions) 42-2	A science of behavior has as its goal the prediction, control, and interpretation of the ____ of living organisms. 42-3
nterpret 42-7	The astronomer who gives the date of the next eclipse of the moon is (1) ____ an event; when he puts a satellite in orbit he is (2) ____ an event; when he explains the craters on the moon he is (3) ____ a thing or event. 42-8
1) dependent 2) independent 42-12	A variable which a science attempts to explain is called a(n) ____ variable. 42-13
ı function of 42-17	In a functional relation, there is an observed systematic relation between a(n) (1) * * * and a(n) (2) * * *. 42-18
.aw 42-22	We sometimes speak of cause-and-effect relations. A "cause" is a(n) (1) ____ variable, and an "effect" is a(n) (2) ____ variable. The relation is a(n) (3) ____ ____ and, when well established, it is formulated as a(n) (4) ____. 42-23
(1) predictions (2) control 42-27	When we show that an established relation between behavior and a given set of conditions may be exemplified in a given case, we engage in ____. 42-28
were not (was in-) 42-32	As a science succeeds in discovering functional relations, the assumption of lawfulness * * * confirmed. 42-33

← To p. 63

conditioned (acceptable: reinforced) 11-7	In (F), the sound of the magazine is repeatedly being * * * food in the mouth. 11-8 ← To p. 63
extinguished 11-16	In the usual experiment, the magazine always contains grain. The conditioned reinforcer (noise) is not extinguished because the conditioned and unconditioned reinforcers continue to be ____. 11-17 ← To p. 63
paired 11-25	Pavlov's dog salivated when a tone (conditioned stimulus) sounded. An operant could probably have been conditioned by letting the response produce the tone because the tone would be a(n) ____ ____ as well. 11-26 ← To p. 63
before (prior to) 11-34	When the chimpanzee regularly "buys" food with tokens, the tokens become conditioned reinforcers since the tokens repeatedly * * * food. 11-35 ← To p. 63
will not (should not) 11-43	If the chimpanzee has exchanged tokens for food when food-deprived and for water when water-deprived, then tokens will be able to reinforce behavior under ____ (HOW MANY?) kinds of deprivation(s). 11-44 ← To p. 63
generalized reinforcer conditioned generalized reinforcer) 11-52	A parent "pays attention" when he approaches a child, looks at him, touches him, etc. These activities generate stimuli affecting the child. The parent also provides food, water, loving care, etc. The stimuli arising from parental "attention" become (conditioned) ____ ____ for the child. 11-53 ← To p. 63

prediction 42-1	Prediction, control, and interpretation are the ____ of science. 42-2
predict 42-6	Pavlov became interested in conditioning when he noticed spontaneous secretion of saliva when no food was in the mouth. As a result of his experiments, he could ____ these spontaneous secretions as possibly resulting from conditioned stimuli. 42-7
dependent 42-11	In operant behavior, probability of response is the major (1) ____ variable; a condition of deprivation is one of the (2) ____ variables. 42-12
1) dependent 2) independent 42-16	When a functional relation exists between a dependent and an independent variable, the dependent variable is said to be a function of the independent variable. Rate of emission of an operant is * * * the level of deprivation. 42-17
law 42-21	An established functional relation is a scientific ____. 42-22
1) predict (determine, deduce) 2) dependent variable 42-26	When we state the probability of occurrence of a given response under a given set of conditions, we engage in (1) ____. When we arrange a set of conditions under which behavior has an assigned probability, we engage in (2) ____. 42-27
1) lawful 2) assuming 42-31	A science would not be successful in discovering functional relations if the assumption of lawfulness * * * valid. 42-32

Do not study exhibit in advance; use exhibit as needed in answering items.

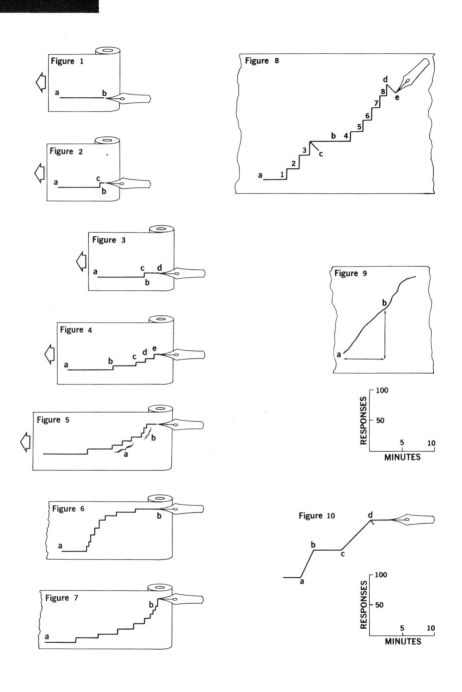

> ▷

Science has as its goal the prediction, control, and interpretation of natural events. A meteorologist makes a(n) _____ when he forecasts tomorrow's weather.

42-1

---

control

42-5

In a reflex, if we know the intensity of a stimulus, we can _____ the magnitude and latency of the response.

42-6

---

(1) stimulus
(2) dependent

42-10

In operant behavior, the frequency of a response is _____ upon reinforcement history, states of deprivation, and stimulus conditions.

42-11

---

functional
relation

42-15

When an independent variable is shown to affect a dependent variable, the (1) _____ variable is said to be a function of the (2) _____ variable.

42-16

---

independent

42-20

The statement of the functional relation between velocity of a freely falling body and time of fall is called "the _____ of gravity."

42-21

---

(1) predict
(2) control
(3) interpret

42-25

If we know the values assumed by an independent variable, we can (1) _____ the values of the (2) * * *.

42-26

---

(1) functional
     relations
(2) lawful
     (determined,
     ordered)
     42-30

In the beginning, a science merely assumes that its subject matter is (1) _____. Behavioral science begins by (2) _____ that behavior is lawful.

42-31

Set 12

The Cumulative Recorder

See exhibit on preceding page

Estimated time: 11 minutes

Turn to next page and begin ▶

) **a**

) **d**

12-4

In Figure 3, the time which elapsed between **a** and **b** is _____ than the time which elapsed between **c** and **d**.

12-5

---

shorter

shorter

12-9

In Figure 5, the higher the rate of responding, the (1) _____ the slope of the steplike line. We can determine the rate of responding from the (2) _____ of the steplike line.

12-10

12-14

Negative acceleration refers to a(n) (1) _____ in rate. Negative acceleration is shown in either Figure 6 or Figure 7. (WHICH?) Figure (2) _____.

12-15

---

and) 8

12-19

In Figure 10, a response was reinforced at _____.

12-20

---

ximately) 5

12-24

In Figure 10, the animal emitted about _____ responses between **a** and **b**.

12-25

---

vertical

horizontal

12-29

In a cumulative curve, the *slope* is a record of the animal's * * *.

12-30

Set 42

Goals and Techniques of Science

Estimated time: 12 minutes   **Turn to next page and begin** ▶

---

ontrol

42-4

A respondent is always under the ____ of a stimulus.

42-5

---

edicted,
ontrolled, (or)
terpreted

42-9

In a reflex, response magnitude is *dependent* upon the intensity of the (1) ____. The stimulus intensity is called the independent variable, and the response magnitude the (2) ____ variable.

42-10

) independent
) dependent

42-14

When changes in an independent variable provide systematic changes in a dependent variable, there is a functional relation between them. In reflexes, there is a(n) ____ ____ between stimulus intensity and response magnitude.

42-15

---

unction

42-19

A law of behavior is a statement of an established functional relation between responding and one or more of the ____ variables which control it.

42-20

) independent
variable
) dependent
variable

42-24

Knowing a set of conditions, we can (1) ____ behavior; manipulating a set of conditions, we can (2) ____ behavior; knowing an effect, we might be able to (3) ____ it in relation to its causes.

42-25

---

unctional

42-29

A science is only possible if there are (1) ____ ____ between variables, i.e., a science is possible only if its subject matter is (2) ____ as opposed to unlawful or capricious.

42-30

In Figure 1, a broad strip of paper is unwinding from a roll. The end of the paper is moving slowly toward the left. A pen held against the paper in a fixed position has drawn a line beginning at (1) _____ and ending at (2) _____.

12-1

---

onger
greater,
nore)

12-5

In recording the behavior of an organism, the pen moves upward and draws one short vertical line each time a response is made. In Figure 4, an experiment began when the pen was at **a.** The first response was made at _____.

12-6

---

1) steeper
(higher,
greater)
2) slope

12-10

In Figure 6, responding begins at a relatively high rate at **a.** The time between successive responses grows progressively _____.

12-11

---

1) decrease
2) 6

12-15

An increase in rate is called (1) _____ _____, and a decrease in rate is called (2) _____ _____.

12-16

12-20

If the paper moves slowly and if each vertical step is small, we cannot see the steplike record of a single response. The _____ of the curve at any point is still a valid indicator of rate of responding.

12-21

---

bout) 50

12-25

In Figure 10, the animal paused about (1) _____ minutes between positions (2) _____ and _____.

12-26

---

te of
sponding
esponse rate)

12-30

End of Set

not
annot)

t 31

41-2

When the hold-up victim turns over his wallet, he (1) _____ a threat and (2) _____ physical injury.

41-3
← To p. 272

---

tivation
ndrome

t 30

41-6

Punishment is effective in preventing a response when behavior which (1) _____ the punished behavior is established. But when this behavior has been extinguished, the (2) _____ response will again be emitted.

41-7
← To p. 272

---

wer

t 40

41-10

In avoidance behavior, the longer the response postpones the aversive stimulus, the _____ the rate.

41-11
← To p. 272

) A
) B
) C
) y
) z
t 35

41-14

Reinforcement consists of (1) _____ a positive reinforcer or (2) _____ a negative reinforcer. Punishment consists of (3) _____ a positive reinforcer or (4) _____ a negative reinforcer.

41-15
← To p. 272

) aversive
) reinforcing

t 36

41-18

It is poor technique to shape skillful behavior with (1) _____ reinforcers because the aversive stimuli, which must be presented in order to be terminated, elicit many respondents which (2) * * * the behavior to be shaped.

41-19
← To p. 272

---

ecrease
educe)

t 33

41-22

A person "can't remember" a very aversive childhood experience. This is called (1) _____. It can be interpreted as a case of engaging in other responses which (2) * * * thinking about the aversive experience.

41-23
← To p. 272

In Figure 2, the slow movement of the paper under the fixed pen has drawn the horizontal line (1) ____ - ____. At the end of **a - b**, the pen suddenly moved a short vertical distance to (2) ____.

12-2

In Figure 4, three responses were made fairly quickly (closely together) at ____, ____, and ____.

12-7

In Figure 6, the slope of the curve drawn by the pen near **a** indicates a(n) ____ initial rate of responding.

12-12

To record other events, the pen moves quickly "to the southeast" and back again. In Figure 8, the pen is shown in the process of drawing a line from (1) ____ to ____. The point of the pen will immediately return to (2) ____.

12-17

In Figure 10, the rate was highest between (1) ____ and ____, zero between (2) ____ and ____, and intermediate between (3) ____ and ____.

12-22

In the cumulative curves shown in the figures, time is shown by the (1) ____ distance traversed by the pen, and the number of responses by the (2) ____ distance.

12-27

The reflex activities comprising the activation syndrome occur together in emotions. We * * * define any one specific emotion (anger or fear) by listing the reflexes involved.

41-2

---

s

et 34   41-1

---

1) not be
2) is (will be)

et 40   41-5

Organisms in situations we call "emotional" frequently show the _____ _____.

41-6

---

xtinction (or)
daptation
EITHER ORDER)

et 36   41-9

With continuous punishment of a response maintained by positive reinforcement, the greater the severity of the punishment (after some minimum intensity is surpassed), the _____ the response rate.

41-10

---

1) quickens
2) dilate
3) begins
   (increases)

et 30   41-13

(1) _____ Control session
(2) _____ Stimulant injected
(3) _____ Tranquilizer injected
(4) _____ Buzzer onset
(5) _____ Shock

41-14

---

useful
(advantageous)
useless
(harmful, disadvantageous)

et 30   41-17

The exhilarating emotional reaction from riding a roller coaster or being in a speeding car is a reaction to stimuli which are often (1) _____ but in this instance are (2) _____ (TT).

41-18

---

s

et 31   41-21

The teacher who uses strong aversive control to get students to study may _____ the probability that they will study after graduation.

41-22

---

1) **a (–) b** 2) **c** 12-2	In Figure 3, the paper has moved on from the position shown in Figure 2. The fixed pen has drawn a second horizontal line ____ – ____. 12-3
, **d**, (and) **e** 12-7	In Figure 5, the three responses recorded at **a** were emitted ____ rapidly than the three at **b**. 12-8
igh (rapid) 12-12	In Figure 7, the rate increases fairly steadily from a low value near (1) ____ to a high value near (2) ____. 12-13
1) **d** (to) **e** 2) **d** 12-17	In Figure 8, the short mark ("hatch" or "pip") at ____ was made by a movement of the pen like the one shown at **e**. 12-18
1) **a** (and) **b** 2) **b** (and) **c** 3) **c** (and) **d** 12-22	When the steps are small, we cannot count responses. But in Figure 9, the scale *at the right* tells us that approximately ____ responses were made between **a** and **b**. 12-23
) horizontal) vertical 12-27	The rate of responding is indicated by the ____ of the cumulative record. 12-28

In the experiment demonstrating shock avoidance, the low initial rate suggests that anxiety * * * necessary for adequate avoidance.

41-1

---

xtinction

Set 38   41-4

The rate of a response maintained by positive re-inforcement may (1) * * * decreased by a *mild* con-tinuous punishment, but it (2) * * * decreased by a strong continuous punishment while punishment remains in effect.

41-5

;Δ

Set 33   41-8

If a timid person forces himself to attend many group meetings, his timidity may undergo the process of ____ or ____ .

41-9

---

1) eliminate
2) decreases
3) anxiety

Set 38   41-12

In the activation syndrome, inhalation (1) ____ , bronchioles (2) ____ , and adrenalin secretion (3) ____ .

41-13

---

1) avoidance
2) escape

Set 32   41-16

The activation syndrome would usually be biolog-ically (1) ____ to a cave man, and it would usually be biologically (2) ____ to a public speaker.

41-17

---

slowly
(seldom)
rapidly
(frequently)
anxiety

Set 35   41-20

A given emotion * * * defined by the events which serve as reinforcers or by the increased probability of a group of responses.

41-21

---

c (–) d

In Figure 3, the pen has been in the four lettered positions **a**, **b**, **c**, and **d**. It occupied position (1) ____ first, and (2) ____ last.

12-3
12-4
← To p. 73

---

less

The more rapid the responding, the (1) ____ the pauses between two responses and the (2) ____ the horizontal lines drawn by the pen.

12-8
12-9
← To p. 73

---

(1) a
(2) b

An increase in rate is called *positive acceleration*. Positive acceleration is shown in either Figure 6 or Figure 7. (WHICH?) Figure ____ .

12-13
12-14
← To p. 73

---

c

The "southeast" mark or hatch is most often used to indicate that a response has been reinforced. In Figure 8, the responses numbered ____ and ____ were reinforced.

12-18
12-19
← To p. 73

---

roximately)

If paper speed is very slow, we may not be able to accurately measure the time between any two responses; but in Figure 9, the scale tells us that responses at **a** and **b** were approximately ____ minutes apart.

12-23
12-24
← To p. 73

---

slope

Rate of responding means responses/time (responses ÷ time). The slope of a cumulative record is (1) ____ distance/(2) ____ distance.

12-28
12-29
← To p. 73

---

(1) escapes
(2) avoids

Set 33   **41-3**

In the experiment showing the ineffectiveness of punishment in removing a response from the repertoire, punishment was in effect for the first 10 minutes of ＿＿＿ of a food-reinforced response.

41-4

---

avoids (is incompatible with) punished

Set 39   **41-7**

A pigeon reinforced with food for pecking a key during an S^D but not during an S^Δ will peck a second key which delays the appearance of ＿＿＿.

41-8

---

lower

Set 34   **41-11**

Punishment does not (1) ＿＿＿ a response. Rate of responding temporarily (2) ＿＿＿, in part, because punishment and the resulting conditioned aversive stimuli generate (3) ＿＿＿.

41-12

---

presenting
terminating (removing)
terminating (removing)
presenting   **41-15**
Set 37

Operant behavior which postpones an *un*conditioned aversive stimulus is called (1) ＿＿＿ behavior. Behavior which terminates an *un*conditioned aversive stimulus is called (2) ＿＿＿ behavior.

41-16

---

negative
are
incompatible with (interfere with)   **41-19**
Set 32

In the presence of a conditioned aversive stimulus, a food-reinforced response is emitted more (1) ＿＿＿, and a response with an avoidance history more (2) ＿＿＿. These and similar changes define (3) ＿＿＿.

41-20

---

repression
avoid
(are incompatible with)   **41-23**
Set 39

End of Set

EXPERIMENT 1.

Preliminary treatment. A food-deprived pigeon is placed for the first time in a standard experimental box, and the feeding mechanism is operated *by the experimenter* from time to time. When the mechanism operates, there is a loud click. When first placed in the box, and for the first several clicks of the mechanism, the pigeon may jump, flap its wings, and rush about. After a while, this "emotional" behavior ceases. We say that *adaptation* has taken place. The pigeon eventually learns to turn toward and approach the feeding mechanism, or food magazine, whenever it hears the click.

Conditioned key pecking. A plastic disk is now attached behind a circular opening in the wall of the box above the feeding mechanism. The disk acts as an electric key. When the pigeon pecks the key, a circuit is closed causing the feeding mechanism to operate. (The experimenter no longer operates the mechanism.) Cumulative records of all responses to the key are made. Two examples are shown in Figures 1A and 1B. All responses were reinforced, but the usual sideward movements of the pen to indicate reinforcement are omitted.

Figure 1A   Pigeon A

Figure 1B   Pigeon B

EXPERIMENT 2.

An inexperienced pigeon is placed in the box. No preliminary magazine training is given, that is, no attempt is made to adapt the pigeon to the box and the click, or to establish the click as a conditioned reinforcer. The key is connected to the feeding mechanism from the start. The cumulative record is shown in Figure 2.

Figure 2   Pigeon C

"THE LEARNING CURVE"

Early investigators observed organisms in puzzle boxes, mazes, and similar situations. They measured successive delays in responding and plotted these in a "learning curve," believing that they were plotting the course of a basic learning process. Experiment 2 (Pigeon C) is comparable.

Plotted on the right are the delays between successive reinforced responses on the key.

Figure 3

SUCCESSIVE RESPONSES

← To p. 265

is not
(is no longer)

40-5

In Figure 1, the record for the control or "no punishment" procedure has many slight variations in
slopes which indicate some moment-to-moment
variation in (1) _____ of _____. Such variations (2)
* * * common in variable-interval reinforcement.

40-6
← To p. 265

---

punished

40-12

Figure 1. Except for the first 4 minutes, the slope
of the record for the tenth 1-hour session of continuous (1) _____ is about (2) * * * the slope for
the last of the "no punishment" sessions.

40-13
← To p. 265

---

higher

40-19

Experiment 2. On the first day of the stronger
punishment, the rate of responding is nearly _____.

40-20
← To p. 265

---

lower

40-26

When even more intense shocks were used, more
time was required to stabilize the rate. The more
intense the punishment the _____ the rise in rate to
a stable level.

40-27
← To p. 265

---

increased

40-33

Figure 3. Every response was again punished
beginning at the (1) _____ arrow. The response
rate immediately (2) _____.

40-34
← To p. 265

---

(1) increases
    (rises)
(2) higher

40-40

End of Set

Set 13

PART III   Operant Conditioning: Precise Contingencies

Factors Affecting Speed of Conditioning

See exhibit on preceding page

Estimated time: 24 minutes

Turn to next page and begin ▶

1) adaptation
2) conditioned
   reinforcer

13-8

After preliminary treatment, a key is connected to the feeding mechanism (magazine). For the first time in the history of the pigeon, a peck on the key will * * *.

13-9

horter (less)

13-17

The rate of responding in Figure 1A (Pigeon A) between **b** and **c** is roughly the same as between _____ and _____.

13-18

13-26

Experiment 2. Since the preliminary treatment was omitted for Pigeon C, there * * * opportunity for adaptation of unconditioned responses to the un-familiar experimental box.

13-27

horter

13-35

As the pigeon adapts to the click, the time elapsing between the click of the mechanism and contact with food decreases. This hastens the process of _____ the click as a reinforcer.

13-36

arning
rve

13-44

When the times between successive responses in Experiment 2 are plotted in a "learning curve" such as Figure 3, the falling curve means that these times are growing progressively _____.

13-45

spondent
flex)

13-53

(1) _____ behavior maintains the internal economy of the organism. (2) _____ behavior affects the environment.

13-54

ill not :annot) 40-4	The variable-interval schedule, in (A), furnishes a base line on which the effects of added punishment can be observed. The experimenter maintains this base line long enough before introducing shock to be certain that the rate * * * changing. 40-5
.) punished !) the same as (equal to) 40-11	Experiment 1. The tenth session of punishment was preceded by nine 1-hour sessions during which each response was _____. 40-12
l) variable- interval 2) stable (uniform, constant)₄₀₋₁₈	In Experiment 2, the same procedure was followed as in Experiment 1 except that the shock intensity was _____ in Experiment 2. 40-19
ecrease 40-25	Experiment 2. When a sufficiently intense shock follows every response, rate of responding remains _____ than in the absence of a punishing contingency. 40-26
l) discontinued 2) arrow 40-32	Figure 3. Within a very few seconds after punishment was discontinued, the rate of responding _____ drastically. 40-33
ower 40-39	Immediately after continuous punishment is discontinued, response rate (1) _____ and is, for a while, (2) _____ than that normally generated by the reinforcement schedule. 40-40

Experiment 1. During the preliminary treatment, "emotional" behavior is elicited by the strange box, the click of the magazine, etc. This "emotional" behavior * * * compatible with pecking the key or eating.

13-1

---

inforced
ate feeding
anism,
t in food)

13-9

The wiring of the apparatus is such that the click of the food mechanism as a(n) ____ ____ follows *immediately* upon the pigeon's response to the key.

13-10

(and) **d**

13-18

Figure 1A shows that the reinforcement of the response at **b** produced an immediate, substantial increase in rate. This is shown by the change in the ____ of the curve at **b**.

13-19

---

as no

13-27

In Experiment 2, the first response produced a click of the magazine. Unconditioned emotional responses to the click have not undergone ____.

13-28

·nditioning

13-36

One might say that Pigeon C learns much more slowly than A and B. The apparent slow learning of C is due to the time needed for (1) ____ of unconditioned responses and for establishing a(n) (2) ____ reinforcer.

13-37

.orter

13-45

Experiment 2 (Figure 2). Pigeon C's record does not reveal the speed of acquiring a key-pecking response because other processes are also involved. The pigeon must first ____ to the box and the click.

13-46

) Respondent
  (Reflex)
) Operant

13-54

(1) ____ behavior usually consists of the activity of striated muscle. (2) ____ behavior usually consists of the activity of smooth muscle and gland.

13-55

By inserting the electrodes beneath the skin, in
(C), a shock of constant intensity can be delivered
because variations in skin resistance * * * influence the voltage reaching the pain receptors.

40-4

Figure 1. Although every response is (1) ____
during the punishment procedure, by the end of
the first day the rate of responding is nearly (2)
* * * the rate during the "no punishment" procedure.

40-11

In (H), responses continued to be reinforced on a(n)
(1) * * * schedule without punishment until the
experimenter was certain that the rate was (2) ____
at the value which prevailed before the introduction
of shock.

40-18

Experiment 2 indicates that if punishment is sufficiently intense it will ____ the rate of a response
maintained on a variable-interval schedule of reinforcement.

40-25

Experiment 3. As described in (K), punishment was
(1) ____ at the point marked by the first (2) ____
in Figure 3.

40-32

With continuous punishment of a response maintained by positive reinforcement, the greater the
severity of the punishment (after some minimum
intensity is surpassed), the ____ the response rate.

40-39

is not (is in-) 13-1	Experiment 1. We cannot relate the first reactions to the click and the box to any known history of conditioning. In that sense, this "emotional" behavior is ____ . 13-2
conditioned reinforcer 13-10	Experiment 1. Every peck on the key is *instantly* reinforced by the (1) ____ , but there is a short delay before reinforcement with (2) ____ because the bird must first bend down to the feeding mechanism. 13-11
slope 13-19	Pigeon A (Figure 1A) reached its maximal rate of responding after only ____ reinforcement(s). Conditioning was immediate. 13-20
adaptation 13-28	In Experiment 2, the click occurs at the very instant the response is emitted, but it is not yet a(n) ____ ____ , and little or no reinforcement occurs. 13-29
(1) adaptation (2) conditioned (secondary) 13-37	Pigeon A demonstrates that conditioning can occur very ____ when adaptation is already complete and when each response is immediately reinforced. 13-38
adapt 13-46	The click must also become a(n) ____ ____ before the key-pecking response can be conditioned effectively. 13-47
(1) Operant (2) Respondent (Reflex) 13-55	To condition an operant, a reinforcing stimulus is arranged to follow the ____ . 13-56

all

40-2

Aversive stimuli elicit the many respondents of the (1) ____ ____. One of these, sweating, (2) ____ the electrical resistance of the skin.

40-3

---

(1) lower
(2) were not

40-9

Figure 1. During the first day of punishment, the slope of the record gradually * * * as the session progresses.

40-10

---

increased
(rose)

40-16

In (G), the increased response rate was (1) ____ than while punishment was in effect and also (2) ____ than it had been in the session preceding the introduction of punishment.

40-17

---

were not

40-23

Figure 2. When every response is punished by a moderate intensity of shock, the rate of responding after daily 1-hour sessions is substantially ____ than it was without punishment.

40-24

---

positive
acceleration

40-30

Figure 3. During the second 15 minutes of the session, rate of responding has become relatively ____.

40-31

---

higher

40-37

The rate of a response maintained by positive re-inforcement may (1) * * * decreased by a *mild* continuous punishment, but it (2) * * * decreased by a strong continuous punishment while punishment remains in effect.

40-38

---

unconditioned (unlearned) 13-2	Experiment 1. As adaptation proceeds, the "emotional" behavior ceases. The elimination of this behavior is similar to the _____ of conditioned behavior. 13-3
click (conditioned reinforcer) food (unconditioned reinforcer) 13-11	The click is effective as a reinforcer for pecking the key because it follows the response (1) _____, whereas there is a short (2) _____ before the appearance of the unconditioned reinforcer. 13-12
one 13-20	Experiment 1. In everyday terminology, we would say that Pigeon A shows a(n) _____ speed of learning to peck the key. 13-21
conditioned reinforcer 13-29	In Figure 2, the pause **a - b** is (1) _____ than in Figure 1A mainly because unconditioned behavior to the experimental box had to undergo (2) _____. 13-30
fast (quickly, rapidly) 13-38	Pigeon C's record does not show a difference in speed of conditioning so much as (a) the lack of (1) _____ to the box and click, and (b) the lack of a conditioned reinforcer (2) _____ following early responses. 13-39
conditioned reinforcer (secondary reinforcer) 13-47	Does the "learning curve" of the early investigators actually reveal the learning process for the key-pecking response as an isolated bit of behavior? 13-48
response (behavior, operant) 13-56	To condition a respondent, a neutral stimulus is paired with the _____ _____ repeatedly. 13-57

stable (uniform, constant) 40-1	As indicated in (B), the 1-minute variable-interval schedule was in effect at * * * times during Experiments 1, 2, and 3. 40-2
reinforced 40-8	Figure 1. During the first half-hour of the first day of punishment, response rate is considerably (1)____ than it was on the previous day when responses (2) * * * being punished. 40-9
was not (is not) 40-15	NOW READ EXPERIMENT 2. In (G), when punishment was discontinued, the response rate____for a while. 40-16
thirty-second 40-22	Figure 2. For Days 22, 27, and 32 there were many irregularities in response rates but the over-all rates * * * very different. 40-23
(1) reinforced (2) punished 40-29	Figure 3. During the first 15 minutes of the session, the response rate showed a gradual change found in most of the sessions with this combination of variable-interval food reinforcement and continuous punishment (e.g., Figures 1 and 2). Specifically the rate showed a(n) ____ ____. 40-30
punished 40-36	Figure 3. The response rate between the arrows is much higher than this schedule normally generates. When continuous punishment is discontinued, the response rate is, for a while, ____ than it would have been had there been no punishment. 40-37

tinction

13-3

Adaptation differs from extinction, however, in that no previous ____ of the behavior has taken place, so far as we know.

13-4

immediately
elay
nterval)

13-12

In Figure 1A at **a**, the key was connected and the recorder started. Pigeon A emitted the first peck at point ____.

13-13

gh
apid, great)

13-21

In Figure 1B (Pigeon B), the first response occurred at ____.

13-22

) longer
) adaptation

13-30

The relatively long pauses between **b** and **c** and between **c** and **d** in Figure 2 are partly explained by the need for ____ to both the box and the click.

13-31

daptation
uickly
closely,
nmediately)

13-39

After looking at Pigeon C's record, we may suspect that Pigeon B also may not have undergone complete (1) ____ to the click as a novel stimulus, or that the click was not fully established as a(n) (2) * * *.

13-40

b

13-48

A "learning curve" for Pigeon A in Experiment 1 would drop to a low constant level after only ____ response(s).

13-49

conditioned
imulus

13-57

A conditioned reinforcer acquires its power by being ____ with an unconditioned reinforcer.

13-58

(A) describes the schedule used throughout all three experiments. When uncomplicated by other variables, this schedule generates a(n) _____ and moderate rate of responding.

40-1

---

very (each)

40-7

Experiment 1. While punishment is in effect, every response is followed by shock. Responses are also still _____ on a variable-interval schedule.

40-8

:celeration

40-14

Experiment 1. By the tenth day of punishment, after many thousands of responses have been mildly punished, the over-all rate of responding * * * appreciably lowered.

40-15

---

gher

40-21

Experiment 2. The highest over-all rate during punishment shown in Figure 2 occurred on the _____ day of punishment.

40-22

---

ronger
nore intense)

40-28

NOW READ EXPERIMENT 3. Pecking the key was (1) _____ on a variable-interval schedule. Except for the 10-minute period described in (K), every response was (2) _____.

40-29

)

40-35

Figure 3. The rate of responding during the 10 minutes without punishment was substantially higher than during the parts of this session in which responses were _____.

40-36

---

itioning
ning)
eptable:
orcement)

13-4

Experiment 1. The preliminary procedure is important because it provides an opportunity for *un*conditioned emotional behavior to undergo _____.

13-5

13-13

Throughout Experiment 1, the click of the magazine, a conditioned reinforcer, is followed by _____, an unconditioned reinforcer.

13-14

13-22

The record for Pigeon B differs from that for Pigeon A mainly in the fact that a(n) _____ time elapsed between the first, second, and third responses.

13-23

---

daptation

13-31

Figure 2 shows a fairly smooth _____ acceleration. (positive or negative?)

13-32

) adaptation
) (conditioned)
reinforcer

13-40

On the day following the experiment in Figure 2, Pigeon C was again placed in the box. It responded immediately. All emotional responses to the box which might be incompatible with the behavior had evidently undergone full _____.

13-41

---

ie

13-49

The "learning curve" for Pigeon C could be interpreted as showing the gradual strengthening of a key-pecking "habit." But Experiment 1 shows that the acquisition of key pecking does not always occur _____-ly.

13-50

---

aired

13-58

A stimulus paired with food acquires the power to _____ an operant response.

13-59

Set 40

---

1) rate (of)
   responding
2) are

40-6

Experiment 1. In (E), a brief, mild shock follows
_____ response.

40-7

---

1) punishment
2) the same as

40-13

Figure 1. During the first 4 minutes of the tenth
day, the response rate shows positive _____.

40-14

---

ero

40-20

Experiment 2. By the fifth day of the stronger
punishment, the over-all response rate is _____
than on the first day.

40-21

---

lower

40-27

When a shock stronger than that in Experiment 2
was used, the stable rate eventually reached was
lower than that of the thirty-second day in Experiment 2. The _____ the punishment, the lower the
stable rate of responding.

40-28

---

1) second
2) decreased
   (dropped,
   declined)

40-34

Figure 3. As described in (K), between the points
marked by the arrows _____ response was punished.

40-35

---

adaptation 13-5	Experiment 1. During the preliminary treatment, the pigeon is eventually conditioned to approach the feeding mechanism just after hearing the click. Two stimuli, _____ and food, therefore tend to occur close together. 13-6
ood 13-14	Since food follows the click throughout the experiment, the reinforcing property of the click does not undergo _____. (TT) 13-15
onger greater) 13-23	Figure 1B. Pigeon B reaches a constant rate of responding after _____ responses have been reinforced. 13-24
ositive 13-32	The positive acceleration in Figure 2 simply means that, in general, the intervals between successive responses become progressively _____. 13-33
daptation 13-41	The pigeon is also likely to respond immediately on the second day because it has been _____ many times for pecking the key. 13-42
radual(-ly) slow(-ly)] 13-50	In Experiment 1, it is important to establish the click as a reinforcer, *not* because a conditioned reinforcer is more effective than an unconditioned reinforcer, but because the click follows the response more _____. 13-51
inforce 13-59	A stimulus paired with food acquires the power to _____ a respondent. 13-60

Do not read Experiment 3 until instructed
to do so.

EXPERIMENT 3.

(J) A pigeon was reinforced with food on a 1-minute variable-interval schedule. A moderately intense shock followed each response, as in Experiment 2.

(K) Halfway through a session, punishment was abruptly discontinued for 10 minutes and then reinstated. The cumulative record is shown in Figure 3.

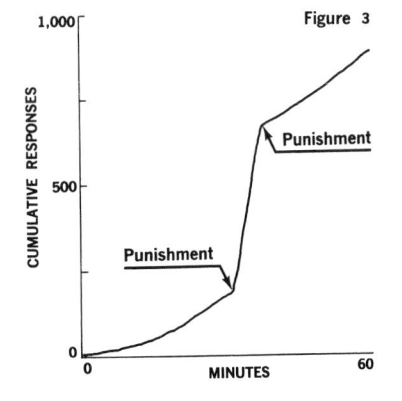

Figure 3

lick 13-6	Experiment 1. In the preliminary procedure, the click becomes a conditioned reinforcer because the click and food are being ____. 13-7
xtinction 13-15	In Figure 1A, the time elapsing before the pigeon made the first response can be determined by the length of the part of the curve between ____ and ____. 13-16
ıree 13-24	Figure 1B. Some evidence that the reinforcement of the response at **b** was effective is obtained from a comparison of distance **a - b** with distance ____ - ____. 13-25
ıorter 13-33	In Experiment 2, the "startle reflex" elicited by the click of the feeding mechanism takes a few seconds to subside. There is, therefore, a slight ____ before the occurrence of the unconditioned reinforcer. 13-34
∈inforced 13-42	The early procedure for obtaining learning curves, exemplified by Figure 3 in the exhibit, is most like that for the pigeon labeled ____. 13-43
ıickly apidly, losely) 13-51	A "learning curve" * * * (does or does not?) describe the acquisition of an isolated response because it reflects, in part, a change in a conditioned reinforcer which only eventually provides immediate reinforcement. 13-52
.icit 13-60	A rat in an experimental apparatus is presented with food by a feeding mechanism which makes a noise. The noise acquires the power to (1) ____ salivation and to (2) ____ pressing a lever. 13-61

Do not read Experiment 2 until instructed
to do so.

EXPERIMENT 2.

(G) At the end of Experiment 1 punishment was discontinued. For the first
few sessions, the rate of responding was actually *higher* than before
punishment was introduced.

(H) After several sessions without punishment, the rate of responding
dropped to the original level and again became stable. The cumulative
record from the last day of this period without punishment is shown
in Figure 2 labeled "No Punishment."

(I) Each response was then followed by a shock as in Experiment 1, but
a moderately strong shock was used, 50 volts instead of the milder 30
volts. Cumulative records from many days under this procedure are
shown in Figure 2 (Days: one through thirty-two).

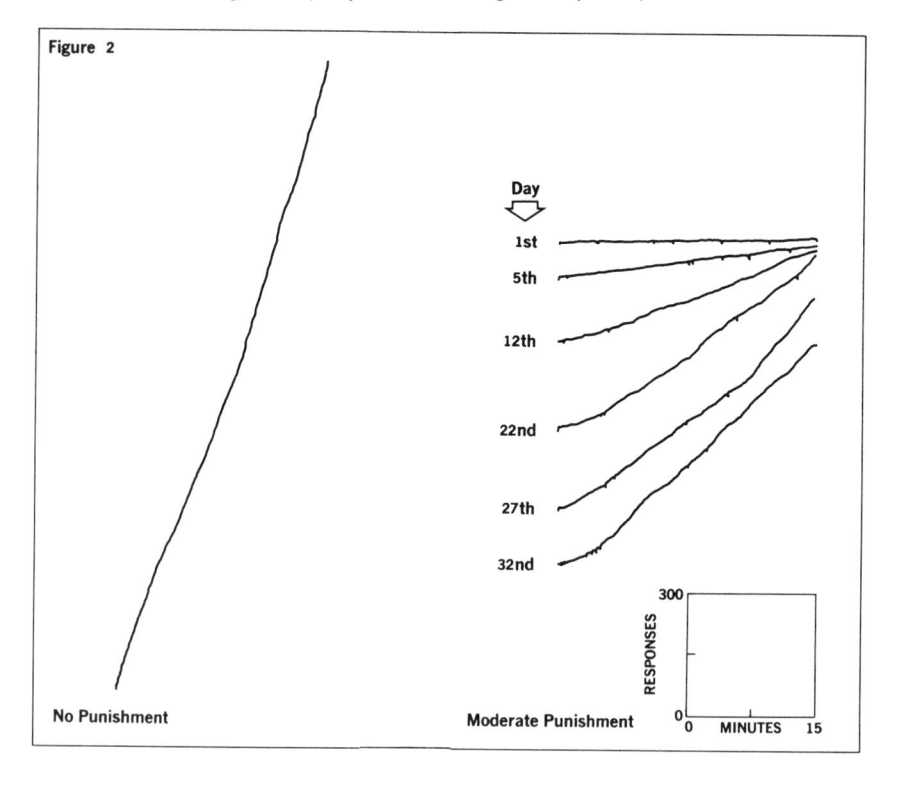

Figure 2

paired 13-7	Experiment 1. The preliminary treatment has two effects important for later conditioning of key pecking. It allows time for (1) _____ of the "unconditioned" behavior, and it establishes the click as a(n) (2) _____ _____. 13-8 ← To p. 79
a (and) b 13-16	The time elapsing between the first and second responses in the record for Pigeon A, Figure 1A, is very much _____ than the time elapsing before the first response. 13-17 ← To p. 79
b (−) c 13-25	Speed of conditioning is sometimes thought to indicate "intelligence." The pigeon is surely less intelligent than a man, yet a man cannot acquire a comparable response more rapidly than the pigeon labeled _____ on the exhibit. 13-26 ← To p. 79
delay (interval of time) 13-34	As "startle" responses to the click disappear, the times between the peck and the unconditioned reinforcer grow _____. 13-35 ← To p. 79
C 13-43	In the procedures of earlier investigators, the basic learning process was thought to be shown graphically in a(n) _____ _____. 13-44 ← To p. 79
does not 13-52	Pecking a key is an example of operant behavior, and, as such, is to be distinguished from _____ behavior. 13-53 ← To p. 79
(1) elicit (2) reinforce 13-61	**End of Set**

EXPERIMENT 1.

(A) A food-deprived pigeon was placed in a standard experimental chamber each day for a 1-hour session. Key pecking was reinforced with food on a variable-interval schedule (average interval of 1 minute) until rate of responding was stable from one day to the next.

(B) This schedule of food reinforcement remained in effect throughout all the experiments which follow.

(C) Small electrodes were inserted beneath the pigeon's skin. Through these electrodes a brief shock (lasting 100 milliseconds) could be delivered.

(D) The last day of the variable-interval schedule uncomplicated by punishment can be seen in Figure 1 where it is labeled "No Punishment."

(E) On the next day, *every* response was followed by a brief mild shock (30 volts). The cumulative record from this session is labeled "Punishment (1st hour)" in Figure 1.

(F) Every response continued to be punished through many daily sessions, and the variable-interval schedule of food reinforcement remained in effect. The cumulative record from the tenth session of continuous punishment is shown in Figure 1.

Mild Punishment

No Punishment

Punishment 1st hour

Punishment 10th hour

Figure 1

300 RESPONSES

0   MINUTES   15

Read exhibit now and refer to it as needed.

The experimenter places several pigeons in separate experimental boxes. A food magazine delivers a small amount of food to each pigeon every 15 seconds regardless of what the pigeon is doing. When the experimenter returns later, he finds one bird sitting very still, another hopping from one foot to the other, another bowing, another turning around and around, another raising and lowering its head, etc. Each bird continues to repeat its own "ritual" between deliveries of food.

Whether a shock is delivered following a response
or independently of any response, it is effective in
temporarily (1) ____ the rate of food-reinforced
behavior. In either case, shock produces a(n) (2)
____ state.

39-4
← To p. 257

A pinched child may not giggle for a while. Even
though the pinch had not followed his giggle
closely, the effect would have been * * *.

39-9
← To p. 257

---

conditioned
aversive
termination
(reduction,
elimination)
39-13

Situations in which responses have been punished
generate conditioned aversive stimuli. Behavior
which terminates these stimuli is ____.

39-14
← To p. 257

Punishment eventually leads to the reinforcement
of "doing something else." Because "doing something else" prevents the occurrence of unconditioned aversive stimuli, it is an example of ____
behavior.

39-19
← To p. 257

When incompatible behavior is extinguished, the
punished response emerges in full strength. The
punished response has not been emitted while in
competition with the incompatible behavior, and
hence extinction of this behavior * * * occurred.

39-24
← To p. 257

A person described as "awkward," "timorous," or
"inhibited" is often actively "not behaving," thereby avoiding the execution of behavior which has
been ____ in the past.

39-29
← To p. 257

Set 14

Accidental Contingencies and Superstitious Behavior

See exhibit on preceding page

Estimated time: 17 minutes

Turn to next page and begin ▶

---

dent(-ally)
ntention(-ally)]

14-7

In the "accidental contingency experiment," the feeding mechanism operates every 15 seconds *regardless* of what the pigeon is doing. This differs from the usual experiment because _____ is not contingent upon any specific response.

14-8

---

einforcement

14-15

A response reinforced often enough to be emitted at a high rate continues to be reinforced even though there is no deliberate connection between the _____ and the operation of the food magazine.

14-16

---

uperstitions

14-23

A student may scratch his head while trying to solve a problem. If he finds a solution at that moment, the response of scratching his head will be _____.

14-24

---

inforced

14-31

The accidental nature of the reinforcing contingency explains the variety of _____ conditioned in experiments on "accidental contingencies."

14-32

---

inforcement

14-39

You may rub a rabbit's foot because you have been told it will bring good luck. Being told it will bring good luck makes it more likely that you will _____ (TT) the response for the first time.

14-40

---

ten
equently)

14-47

We have already seen that, under ideal conditions, a pigeon may reach a high stable rate after only _____ reinforcement of a very simple response.

14-48

nconditioned
versive
timulus
ctivation
yndrome   39-2

A shock is delivered to a rat which has received food for lever pressing. Even if the shock is not contingent on the response, the rate immediately (1) _____ because the resulting emotional condition is (2) * * * lever pressing.

39-3

---

versive
timulus

          39-7

The parent who pinches the child for giggling is (1) _____ by the termination of the giggling. The (2) _____ is increased that the parent will use punishment in similar situations in the future.

39-8

---

einforced

          39-12

As the early components of a frequently punished chain of responses are emitted, they generate (1) _____ _____ stimuli. Any behavior of "doing something else instead" will be reinforced by the (2) _____ of these stimuli.

39-13

---

voidance
ncompatible)

          39-17

By actively holding still, you may _____ making a movement which resembles one which has been punished.

39-18

---

einforcement
conditioning)

          39-22

When punishment is discontinued, the avoidance behavior resulting from earlier punishment undergoes (1) _____. The previously punished behavior may then (2) * * *.

39-23

---

epression
ncompatible
vith

          39-27

A person may "talk about other things" (or just not talk) and thereby (1) _____ talking about aversive situations. We need not refer to this as a process of (2) _____ which forces response out of "consciousness."

39-28

In the usual experiment on operant conditioning, a specific _____ is followed by reinforcement because of a mechanical or electrical device deliberately arranged by the experimenter.

14-1

---

einforcement
magazine
operating)

14-8

By operating the feeding mechanism automatically every 15 seconds regardless of what the pigeon was doing, the experimenter showed the effects of _____ reinforcing contingencies.

14-9

---

esponse
behavior)

14-16

A man playing a slot machine may pull the handle a particular way. If the machine then pays off, it is more _____ that he will pull the handle the same way on the next play.

14-17

---

einforced
ence:
onditioned)

14-24

If a student solves a problem while scratching his head, he is (1) _____ likely to scratch when he has another problem, and the behavior has a good chance of being (2) _____ again by the solving of the new problem.

14-25

---

sponses
ituals,
uperstitions)

14-32

A man who has occasionally thrown a seven while calling "Come, seven!" may call the same words for some time during a losing streak, but if he never again gets a seven, the response will eventually be _____.

14-33

---

nit

14-40

If you receive good news shortly after rubbing a rabbit's foot, the superstitious behavior is accidentally _____.

14-41

---

e

14-48

A response accidentally reinforced is unlikely to be accidentally reinforced again if the first reinforcement resulted in a(n) _____ rate of responding.

14-49

1) eliminate
   (get rid of
   weaken)
2) decreases
   (declines)
3) anxiety

A shock delivered to the feet of a rat is a(n) (1) ____ ____ ____ which will elicit the respondents characteristic of the (2) ____ ____.

39-2

---

not

39-6

The child who is pinched for giggling during a ceremony stops giggling immediately. Pinching is a(n) ____ ____; the responses to it are incompatible with giggling.

39-7

---

1) punished
2) conditioned
   aversive
   stimuli

39-11

A response which terminates an aversive stimulus is ____.

39-12

---

ncompatible

39-16

Any behavior which "displaces" a frequently punished response prevents the appearance of the unconditioned aversive stimulus. The response which replaces the usually punished response is an example of ____ behavior.

39-17

---

unished

39-21

Punishment *in*directly lowers the rate of the punished response by providing conditions for the ____ of incompatible avoidance behavior.

39-22

---

ncompatible
ith
displacing)

39-26

A person "can't remember" a very aversive childhood experience. The clinician calls this (1) ____. It is probably, in part, the effect of other responses which are (2) * * * "thinking about" the aversive experience.

39-27

---

1) reinforced
2) may not be
   (is not)

39-31

End of Set

...esponse 14-1	When the experimenter deliberately arranges re-inforcing contingencies, it * * * accidental that reinforcement follows a particular response. 14-2
...ccidental 14-9	When the magazine operates independently of the pigeon's behavior, it is only by accident that any particular _____ is reinforced. 14-10
...robable ...ikely) 14-17	A bowler may snap his fingers just as the ball hits the pins. Although this behavior has no effect on the ball, a "strike" will _____ snapping the fingers. 14-18
...) more ...) reinforced 14-25	Head scratching, pencil chewing, table tapping, etc., do not actually solve problems; thus, they are generally (1) _____ forms of behavior resulting from (2) _____ contingencies of reinforcement. 14-26
...xtinguished 14-33	When *termination* of a stimulus increases the rate of a contingent response, it is a case of _____ re-inforcement. 14-34
...einforced 14-41	If rubbing the rabbit's foot had not been emitted, it could not have been reinforced. Once the verbally suggested superstitious behavior has been (1) _____, it is possible for (2) _____ reinforcement to follow. 14-42
...w 14-49	A particularly slow learner may require many re-inforcements before developing a high rate of responding. He is _____ likely to develop super-stitious behavior than a faster learner. 14-50

Mild unsustained punishment does not permanently (1) _____ an operant. Rate of responding temporarily (2) _____ because punishment, and the resulting conditioned aversive stimuli, generate (3) _____ .

39-1

) contingent
(dependent)
) aversive
stimulus
(negative
reinforcer)₃₉₋₅

For an aversive stimulus to lower the rate of a positively reinforced response, it * * * necessary for the stimulus to be response-contingent.

39-6

---

s not

39-10

When a response is followed immediately by an aversive stimulus, the response is said to have been (1) _____ . Stimuli which accompany punishment become (2) _____ _____ _____ .

39-11

---

onditioned
versive

39-15

By getting out of a situation in which punishment is common, a man can prevent the occurrence of the punished behavior and the resulting aversive stimuli. This is a case of avoidance. The behavior is _____ with the punished behavior.

39-16

---

xtinction

39-20

While displaced by an avoidance response, a punished response is not extinguished. When incompatible behavior is extinguished, the _____ response will be emitted again.

39-21

---

ncompatible
avoidance)

39-25

When a response prevents the occurrence of punished behavior, the clinician may say that the punished behavior is "repressed." Repression may be interpreted as avoidance behavior which is * * * the punished behavior.

39-26

) reinforced
) decrease
(decline)

39-30

Since the behavior of punishing others is (1) _____ by its quick effects, it is frequently repeated even though the effect (2) * * * permanent.

39-31

The environment provides many natural contingencies of reinforcement. An animal stalks its prey silently because a silent response is often reinforced. This * * * an example of a natural contingency.

14-3

, not

14-2

Whether accidentally or deliberately arranged, the operation of the food magazine _____ (TT) whatever a bird happens to be doing. Therefore, the rate of emitting this response increases.

14-11

sponse
ehavior,
)erant)

14-10

A bowler may make movements as though he controlled the ball after it has left his hand. These movements are frequently reinforced by a(n) _____ (accidental or natural?) reinforcement even though they do not actually affect the ball.

14-19

inforce

14-18

A desperate man playing roulette may shout his number as the wheel turns. If he then wins, he will * * * shout the next time he plays.

14-27

iperstitious
ccidental

14-26

A man has a cold. A friend recommends a "cure" which is in fact worthless. The man tries it and feels fine the next day. This *termination* of the "miseries of a cold" is an example of _____ reinforcement.

14-35

gative

14-34

Accidental *respondent* conditioning is also possible. In a city under bombardment, the odor of a bomb shelter may be _____ with unconditioned stimuli for the pattern of respondents in "fear."

14-43

) emitted
) accidental

14-42

An "intelligent" person may be defined as one who learns quickly even under less than ideal conditions. Thus, he is especially prone to developing

_____ .

14-51

ss

14-50

) decreasing
(reducing,
lowering)
) emotional

39-4

The rate of positively reinforced behavior is lowered by an aversive stimulus whether response-
contingent or not. In punishment, an aversive
stimulus is (1)_____ upon a response, but the emotional effect is the same as with a non-contingent
(2) _____ _____.

39-5

---

ie same
lecreased
iggling)

39-9

To lower the rate of giggling temporarily, it * * *
necessary for a pinch to follow a giggle closely
(to be response-contingent).

39-10

---

einforced

39-14

A situation in which some response has been punished frequently or severely provides _____ _____
stimuli.

39-15

---

voidance

39-19

If punishment is repeatedly avoided by executing
incompatible behavior, the conditioned negative
reinforcer undergoes _____ and the incompatible
behavior is no longer reinforced.

39-20

---

as not
did not,
ould not have)

39-24

A person may be unable to talk about a very aversive experience. The experience is sometimes said
to be "forced into the unconscious" in a process
called "repression." We may interpret repression
as the displacement of punished behavior by _____
behavior.

39-25

---

unished

39-29

When we ridicule a man for doing something we
find undesirable, our behavior is (1) _____ by an
immediate (2) _____ in the frequency of the undesirable behavior.

39-30

s

14-3

Under both natural and arranged contingencies, reinforcement occurs just _____ a given response.

14-4

---

einforces

14-11

If a bird happens to raise its head just before the magazine operates, then * * * is reinforced.

14-12

---

ccidental

14-19

A poker player leaves the table briefly. Upon his return he gets a very good hand. A good hand is shown to be a(n) (1) _____ if his frequency of leaving the table (2) _____ .

14-20

---

robably

14-27

Since in the experiment the relation between receipt of food and ritualistic behavior is accidental, we say the behavior is _____ .

14-28

---

egative

14-35

A man tries a cold "cure" which has *no* medicinal value; if he then feels better, relief from the "miseries of a cold" is an example of a(n) _____ (accidental or natural?) contingency involving a negative reinforcement.

14-36

---

aired

14-43

When the odors, colors, etc., of a particular bomb shelter are paired with unconditioned stimuli resulting from an air raid, it is an example of a(n) _____ pairing.

14-44

unished

38-3

Experiment 1. A second group described in (E) (1)
* * * punished. Their extinction curve provides a
control in determining the effects of (2) ____.

38-4
← To p. 252

igher
steeper)

38-8

Experiment 1. Punishment results in a(n) (1) ____
rate while the punishing contingency is in effect,
and the rate continues to be (2) ____ for a while
after punishment ceases.

38-9
← To p. 252

s not
cannot be)

38-13

Experiment 1. Slapping the forepaws is an aversive stimulus which elicits many respondents of
the (1) ____ ____. If these respondents (2) * * *
compatible with lever pressing, the lowered rate
during punishment is, in part at least, explained.

38-14
← To p. 252

unished

38-18

Experiment 2. During (H), various stimuli in the
experimental situation were (1) ____ with an aversive stimulus, a slap on the forepaws. The stimuli became (2) ____ ____ stimuli as in Experiment
1.

38-19
← To p. 252

isappeared
been
xtinguished,
ecreased)

38-23

Experiment 2. During the 2 hours described in (I),
lever pressing could not be extinguished because
the lever was * * *.

38-24
← To p. 252

1) decreases
2) increases
3) anxiety

38-28

If the experimental box had had a door, a punished
rat would have been reinforced for leaving through
the door since this response would have ____ the
conditioned aversive stimuli generated by the box.

38-29
← To p. 252

fter **14-4**	Giving food to a food-deprived organism is always temporally related to *some* behavior (perhaps just the behavior of standing still) and must, therefore, function to ____ that behavior. **14-5**
ead raising :hat, that ehavior) **14-12**	In the "accidental contingency experiment," if head raising has been accidentally reinforced once, it is much more (1) * * * that the pigeon will be raising its head just before the next (2) ____, 15 seconds later. **14-13**
I) reinforcer 2) increases **14-20**	A player throwing dice when a great deal of money is at stake exclaims "Come on, baby!" and wins. The verbal behavior has no effect on the (1) ____, but the outcome of the throw may have an effect on the player's (2) ____. **14-21**
uperstitious **14-28**	If a previously reinforced response is never again reinforced, it is eventually ____. **14-29**
ccidental **14-36**	A loud disturbing noise from an electrical appliance ended just as a man barely touched a dial. If touching the dial actually had no effect, this was an example of a(n) (1) ____ contingency involving a(n) (2) ____ reinforcement. **14-37**
ccidental **14-44**	If the odor of a bomb shelter later elicits the respondent pattern of "fear," it is an example of a(n) (1) ____ reflex which is superstitious because the stimulus pairing was (2) ____-al. **14-45**

extinction 38-2	Experiment 1. During the first 10 minutes of extinction as described in (C), one group of four rats was _____ (TT) for each lever-pressing response. 38-3
punished (slapped) 38-7	Experiment 1. During the second hour, the record for the punished group showed a somewhat _____ slope than the record for the unpunished group. 38-8
(1) lower (2) number 38-12	Other things being equal, behavior * * * permanently eliminated by punishment if the punishment is discontinued in the immediate future. 38-13
(1) punished (2) extinction 38-17	For the first 10 minutes of extinction in Experiment 2 (described in H), the procedure was the same as for the _____ group in Experiment 1. 38-18
aversive 38-22	Experiment 2. During the 2 hours described in (I), the state of anxiety should have _____. 38-23
(1) extinction (2) punishment 38-27	In anxiety, behavior reinforced with food (1) _____ and avoidance behavior (2) _____. Thus, the temporary decreases in Experiments 1 and 2 seem to be examples of the type of change which we call (3) _____. 38-28

einforce hence: ondition) **14-5**	Presenting food to a food-deprived organism _____ the operant behavior which it follows, even though no one "intends" it to have such an effect. **14-6**
robable (likely) peration (of the ood magazine) reinforcement) **14-13**	If a response which has been accidentally rein-forced does not happen to occur just before a sec-ond presentation of the magazine, it will be _____. (TT) **14-14**
1) dice (outcome) 2) behavior (responses) **14-21**	*Superstitious* behavior means behavior in which there is no causal relation between response and reinforcement. In the experiment on accidental contingencies, the pigeon's behavior is _____ since it does not cause the operation of the magazine. **14-22**
extinguished **14-29**	If the intervals at which food is given are too long, any superstitious behavior resulting from one ac-cidental reinforcement may suffer _____. **14-30**
1) accidental (2) negative **14-37**	Verbally transmitted superstitions which are com-mon in a culture involve many factors. When acted upon for the first time, an accidental _____ may occur. **14-38**
conditioned accident(-al) **14-45**	A reinforcement may follow a response (a) because of a *natural* causal relation, (b) because someone so arranged it, or (c) by accident. The result * * * the same in all of these cases. **14-46**

reinforcement positive 38-1	Experiment 1. In (B), food reinforcement was discontinued; the resulting change in behavior is called ____. 38-2
lower 38-6	Experiment 1. During the first hour of extinction, the over-all slope of the record for the ____ group was lower than that for the other group. 38-7
an equal (the same) 38-11	Experiment 1. Conclusion: In the case of a brief period of mild punishment, the rate of responding is (1) ____ during and just after punishment, but the (2) ____ of responses emitted in complete extinction may not be changed. 38-12
extinction 38-16	READ EXPERIMENT 2 NOW AND REFER TO IT AS NEEDED. From (G) and (H) we know that the new rats were (1) ____ (TT) for each response during the first 10 minutes of (2) ____ (TT) of the response. 38-17
unconditioned aversive 38-21	Experiment 2. During (H), the various stimuli provided by the box acquired aversive properties. In the 2 hours without the lever, the unconditioned aversive stimulus was absent and the stimuli from the box could lose their ____ properties. 38-22
extinguished decrease (depression) 38-26	Experiment 2. The data described in (L) demonstrate that although an operant can be eliminated by (1) ____, it is not eliminated by a brief period of mild (2) ____. 38-27

← To p. 89

einforces hence: onditions) **14-6**	In the experiment on accidental reinforcing contingencies described in the exhibit, the feeding mechanism operated every 15 seconds regardless of what the pigeon was doing. A response was only _____ -ally reinforced. **14-7** ← To p. 89
xtinguished **14-14**	Since substantial conditioning is produced by a single reinforcement, it is highly probable that a response accidentally reinforced will occur again and receive additional _____. **14-15** ← To p. 89
uperstitious **14-22**	Pulling a slot-machine handle in a fancy way, talking to dice, etc., are examples of _____ because they depend on accidental reinforcement. **14-23** ← To p. 89
xtinction **14-30**	If the experiment on accidental contingencies is repeated with many different pigeons, each pigeon develops its own "ritual." Each pigeon does whatever it was accidentally _____ for doing. **14-31** ← To p. 89
einforcement (reinforcing) ontingency] **14-38**	A response which is never emitted cannot be followed by _____ and, hence, cannot be conditioned. **14-39** ← To p. 89
s (will be, nay be) **14-46**	If a single reinforcement has only a small effect, it is unlikely that a response followed by one accidental reinforcement will occur sufficiently _____ to be accidentally reinforced again. **14-47** ← To p. 89

▷

Experiment 1. In (A), lever pressing was maintained on a fixed-interval schedule of (1) _____. *Presentation* of food following a response is defined as (2) _____ reinforcement.

38-1

---

(1) reinforced
(2) punished

38-5

Experiment 1. While responses were being punished, the response rate was _____ for the punished rats than for the unpunished rats.

38-6

---

higher

38-10

Experiment 1. By the end of the second extinction day, the two groups had made approximately * * * total number of responses.

38-11

---

(1) conditioned
(2) anxiety
(emotion)

38-15

Experiment 1. When punishment is discontinued, we expect the rate to remain low until the stimuli provided by the situation cease to be conditioned aversive stimuli through _____.

38-16

---

could not
(would not)

38-20

Experiment 2. During 2 hours, in the absence of the lever, the forepaws were not slapped. This means that the conditioned aversive stimuli in the box were not being paired with the _____ _____ stimulus, the slap.

38-21

---

1) had
2) had no
(did not
have an)

38-25

Experiment 2. Conditioned aversive stimuli from the lever (and from the behavior of pressing it), which could not be (1) _____ under condition (I), probably caused the slight (2) _____ in rate described in (K).

38-26

Example: How to train a dog to touch a doorknob with its nose.

You will need a reinforcer which can be presented very quickly when the behavior is emitted. A *conditioned* reinforcer is most convenient, for example, an *auditory* stimulus such as the sound of a dime-store noisemaker or "cricket." Condition the dog by sounding the cricket just before tossing a small piece of food into a dish. Repeat until the dog goes to the dish as soon as the cricket sounds.

You could condition the desired response by waiting until the dog's nose touched the knob and then reinforcing, but you might have to wait a long time. To avoid this, *shape* (or *differentiate*) the behavior. At first, reinforce any response remotely related to the final form. For example, the dog may be sitting still, and it will never touch the knob doing that. Therefore, reinforce *any slight movement* by sounding the toy cricket as soon as the dog moves, tossing a small scrap of food into the dish. (The advantage of an *auditory* conditioned reinforcer is that it reaches the dog instantly no matter where the dog is looking.) When the dog is moving about, reinforce movements in the general direction of the door and withhold reinforcements for movements in any other direction (*differential reinforcement*). Gradually shape the behavior of moving closer to the door and then closer to the knob. Then reinforce bringing the head closer to the knob. Finally deliver a reinforcement only when the dog is touching the knob with its nose. This gradual shifting of the criterion of differential reinforcement is known as *successive approximation*. The entire process should take only a few minutes.

Although the goal is to get the dog's nose to touch the doorknob, a large pattern of behavior is strengthened by reinforcement. The dog must approach the door, assume a particular posture, and so on. The various *elements* of the total response must all be conditioned in the shaping process.

If we now want to condition a different response, a first response may be a help or a hindrance, depending on whether the two responses share *common elements.*

Set 38

Part XI Punishment

Effects of Punishment During Extinction of Reinforced Behavior

See exhibit on preceding page

Estimated time: 16 minutes

Turn to next page and begin ▶

---

1) was not
2) punishment

38-4

Experiment 1. While the data shown in the figure were being collected, responses were not (1) _____. For the first 10 minutes each response by one group was (2) _____. (TT)

38-5

---

1) lower (decreased)
2) lower (low)

38-9

Experiment 1. During the second day of extinction, the group which had been punished showed a slightly _____ over-all rate as indicated by the slopes.

38-10

---

(1) activation syndrome
(2) are not (are in-)

38-14

Experiment 1. During punishment, the stimuli provided by the experimental box, the rat's behavior, the lever, etc., are paired with an aversive stimulus. Thus, they become (1) _____ aversive stimuli and produce a state of (2) _____.

38-15

---

(1) paired
(2) conditioned aversive

38-19

Experiment 2. When the lever was removed at (I), further responses could not be emitted, and therefore extinction * * * be completed.

38-20

---

absent (not present, removed)

38-24

Experiment 2. Only the lever was absent during the 2-hour period. The conditioned aversive stimuli from other parts of the box (1) * * * an opportunity to be extinguished while those from the lever (2) * * * opportunity to be extinguished.

38-25

---

terminated (removed, escaped from)

38-29

Leaving the box would have lowered the rate of lever pressing because it would have been incompatible with lever pressing. Merely turning away from the bar is also reinforced as avoidance behavior and is also * * * lever pressing.

38-30

Set 15

PART IV   Shaping

Principles of Shaping New Behavior

See exhibit on preceding page

Estimated time: 20 minutes

Turn to next page and begin ▶

---

does not
(will not)

15-7

In training a high jumper, the coach reinforces *successive approximations* to good form by ____ the crossbar a little, after a few successful jumps.

15-8

---

differential

15-15

There are two aspects in shaping skillful behavior: (a) reinforcing only certain responses, which is called (1) ____ ____; and (b) gradually raising the requirement for reinforcement, which is called (2) ____ ____.

15-16

---

successive
approximation

15-23

A brief technical way of saying, "We reinforce movements toward the door and do not reinforce movements away from the door" is: "We ____ ____ movements toward the door."

15-24

---

temporal

15-31

Touching the knob of a door is similar to touching some other part—say, the hinge; the two behaviors have common ____. (TT)

15-32

.me
delay,
interval,
ait)

15-39

Bowling and many similar skills are shaped rather slowly because of the lack of an effective reinforcer which ____-ly follows the behavior.

15-40

---

haping

15-47

On the rifle range, we begin at close range and move to longer and longer ranges as we become more skilled. Moving to longer ranges applies the principle of * * *.

15-48

EXPERIMENT 1.

(A) Eight rats were reinforced with food on a fixed-interval schedule for pressing a lever.

(B) After three daily sessions of 1 hour each, food reinforcement was discontinued. Responses made without reinforcement were recorded for two sessions of 2 hours each.

(C) For four rats, the apparatus was so arranged that each lever-pressing response during the first 10 minutes of extinction resulted in a slap on the forepaws by a return kick of the lever.

(D) After 10 minutes, the rats were no longer slapped.

(E) The other four rats were not slapped at all.

(F) The averaged cumulative records for the two groups of rats for the two extinction sessions are presented in Figure 1.

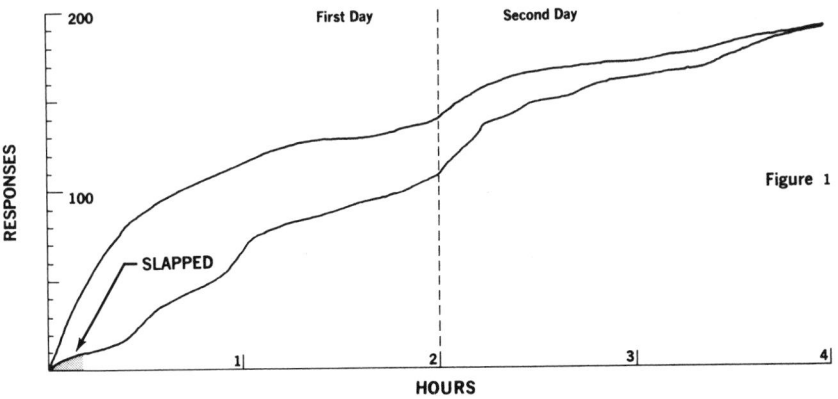

EXPERIMENT 2.

(Wait until instructed to read Experiment 2.)

(G) A group of new rats were treated like the punished group in Experiment 1 until the extinction session.

(H) For the first 10 minutes in extinction, every response was followed by a slap.

(I) After this short period of punishment, each rat was left in the box for 2 hours, but the lever was removed.

(J) Two hours later, the lever was replaced and extinction continued with no further slapping of the forepaws.

(K) Except for a very slight initial depression in rate,

(L) the extinction curve was like that for the unpunished rats in Experiment 1.

> The high-jump star in a track meet is reinforced for clearing the crossbar. The height of the crossbar determines which form or energy of response will be successful and hence _____ .
>
> 15-1

---

raising

15-8

> Gradually shifting the criterion as to what form of response will be reinforced alters behavior through *successive approximation*. By requiring a slightly higher jump each time, behavior is gradually shaped through _____ _____ .
>
> 15-9

---

differential
reinforcement
successive
approximation

15-16

> In differential reinforcement, one form of behavior is (1) * * * and other, possibly rather similar, forms are (2) * * * .
>
> 15-17

---

differentially
reinforce

15-24

> It is more than simple conditioning when we differentially reinforce successive approximations to a final form of behavior. When we follow the procedure, we are said to be _____ behavior.
>
> 15-25

---

elements

15-32

> Response differentiation * * * a synonym for shaping.
>
> 15-33

---

immediate(-ly)
quick(-ly)]

15-40

> Eventually the *stimuli* resulting from successful movements of the bowler's body (i.e., the "feel" of bowling) become conditioned as a (n) _____ through being paired with falling pins.
>
> 15-41

← To p. 246

(1) presented (2) withdrawn 37-3	Reinforcement, whether it be presenting a positive reinforcer or removing a negative reinforcer, _____ the rate of a response it follows. 37-4
(1) B (2) positive 37-8	One procedure, which we call punishment, is to _____ a positive reinforcer immediately after a response. 37-9
(1) positive (2) negative 37-13	Removing an aversive stimulus is a(n) (1) _____ -ment. Presenting an aversive stimulus is a(n) (2) _____ -ment. 37-14
D A reinforcement 37-18	A response might be followed by a change from S^D to S^Δ. Terminating S^D might be classed as (1) _____ (USE LETTER) and presenting S^Δ might be classed as (2) _____. (USE LETTER) Both cases are (3) _____. 37-19
emotional 37-23	If an emotional state elicited by punishment is incompatible with the operant behavior punished, the frequency of the incompatible operant will _____ so long as the emotional state continues. 37-24
conditioned aversive stimuli (conditioned negative reinforcers) 37-28	When a buzzer sounds for 3-minute periods and is consistently followed by shock, behavior with an avoidance history (1) _____ and food reinforced behavior (2) _____ in frequency. 37-29

reinforced 15-1	In practicing the high jump, a form of jump which clears the crossbar is reinforced while a slightly different form which does not clear the bar is * * *. 15-2
successive approximations 15-9	When the crossbar is relatively low, many different ____ of responses are reinforced. 15-10
reinforced (conditioned) not reinforced (extinguished) 15-17	READ THE EXHIBIT ON PAGE 97 NOW AND REFER TO IT AS NEEDED. In the experiment described in the exhibit, we differentially reinforce the dog for moving about by withholding (1) ____ until the dog (2) ____. 15-18
shaping (differentiating) 15-25	The very first step in the procedure described in the exhibit is to establish an auditory stimulus as a(n) (1) ____ reinforcer by repeatedly pairing it with a(n) (2) * * *. (TT) 15-26
s 15-33	The procedure with which we train the dog to touch the doorknob is called (1) ____-ing or response (2) ____. 15-34
einforcer 15-41	When "feedback" from the bowler's body has become a conditioned reinforcer, it ____-ly reinforces bowling behavior. 15-42

D 37-2	Reinforcement may be either positive as when a positive reinforcer is (1) ____ , or negative as when a negative reinforcer is (2) ____ . (CAUTION, REFER TO EXHIBIT) 37-3
present 37-7	Making a child go without dinner for drawing on the wallpaper is an example of ____ (USE LETTER) since food is a(n) ____ reinforcer. 37-8
reinforcement (reinforcing) 37-12	Punishment is the withdrawal of a(n) (1) ____ reinforcer or the presentation of a(n) (2) ____ reinforcer following a response. 37-13
is not 37-17	A response may be followed by a change from S^Δ to S^D. Terminating S^Δ might be classed as (1) ____ (USE LETTER) and presentation of S^D might be classed as (2) ____ . (USE LETTER) Both cases are (3) ____ . 37-18
punishment (B) 37-22	An aversive stimulus such as shock elicits a(n) ____ state. 37-23
activation syndrome 37-27	Stimuli accompanying or just preceding a punished response become ____ ____ ____ by being paired with the punisher. 37-28
(1) punished (2) accident(-al) 37-32	**End of Set**

not reinforced
(extinguished)

15-2

The term *differential* reinforcement indicates that only responses surpassing some specific criterion are reinforced. In high jumping, the height of the crossbar sets the criterion for the _____ reinforcement of jumps.

15-3

---

forms (types)

15-10

In raising the bar after a few successful jumps, the coach is raising the criterion for differential _____.

15-11

---

reinforcement
(food)
moves
(responds)

15-18

The behavior of a dog in sitting and looking at a person who often feeds it is (probably unintentionally) _____ by the novice trainer.

15-19

---

conditioned
unconditioned
reinforcer

15-26

The auditory conditioned reinforcer is useful because (as explained in the exhibit) a reinforcement is most effective if it occurs * * * after a response.

15-27

---

shap(-ing)
differentiation

15-34

Any operant response which occurs immediately (1) * * * reinforcement increases in (2) _____.

15-35

---

immediate(-ly)
quick(-ly)]

15-42

Learning to bowl is speeded up if an instructor immediately says "good" when the form is good, but not when it is not. In reinforcing only relatively good form, he is * * * (TT) good form.

15-43

A rat presses a lever and escapes shock. This is an example of ____ in the table. (USE LETTER)

37-2

One procedure, which we call punishment, is to ____ a negative reinforcer immediately after a purpose.

37-7

In defining punishment as B and C in the table, we do not refer to any effect on behavior. Punishment refers to procedures which are the reverse of those which have proved to be ____. (TT)

37-12

We discover the effects of punishment only by carrying out an experiment. Unlike reinforcement, punishment * * * defined in terms of any particular effect on behavior.

37-17

A child is refused permission to go out because he has misbehaved. If "outside" is a positive reinforcer, this is an example of ____.

37-22

Regardless of the effectiveness of punishment, an aversive stimulus used as a punisher will elicit the respondents (sweating, increased heart rate, etc.) comprising the ____ ____ which occurs in many emotional states.

37-27

A passenger on the "Andrea Doria" pressed a light switch just as the ship collided with the "Stockholm." The response was (1) ____. This was a(n) (2) ____-al contingency.

37-32

differential 15-3	Differential reinforcement is the reinforcement of one form or magnitude of a response when other rather similar forms or magnitudes * * * reinforced. 15-4
reinforcement 15-11	In gradually ____ his standards, the coach is differentially reinforcing successive approximations to the desired behavior. 15-12
reinforced (conditioned) 15-19	When reinforcement for sitting still is withheld, the dog soon ____ sitting still. 15-20
immediately (instantly, quickly) 15-27	Food tossed into a dish will not immediately stimulate the dog if it is not looking, but a(n) ____ stimulus, such as the sound of a "cricket," affects the dog immediately. 15-28
1) before (prior to) 2) rate (frequency) 15-35	After the behavior of "touching the doorknob" has been shaped, we can quickly condition "touching the hinge." We profit from the previously reinforced elements which the two behaviors * * *. 15-36
differentially reinforcing 15-43	If the bowling instructor says "good" at the very instant the learner completes a movement, reinforcement is ____ and thus most effective. 15-44

▷	A pigeon pecks a key and a food magazine operates. This is an example of _____ in the table. (USE LETTER) **37-1**

---

ncreases **37-5**	Spanking a child for drawing on the wallpaper is an example of (1) _____ (USE LETTER) because spanking constitutes the (2) _____ of a (3) _____ reinforcer. **37-6**

---

1) response 2) withdrawal 3) presentation **37-10**	A reinforcement is defined as an event which_____ the rate of a response which it follows. **37-11**

---

punishing (punishment) reinforcing (reinforcement) **37-15**	Punishment is defined as a procedure which is the _____ of reinforcement. **37-16**

---

reinforcement punishment **37-20**	A child is not permitted to go outside to play until he cleans his room. "Inside" is an (1) S_____ for playing and "outside" an (2) S_____. Cleaning the room will, therefore, be (3) _____ by presentation of S^D and withdrawal of S^Δ. **37-21**

---

einforced **37-25**	When pressing a lever turns *on* a shock, pressing the lever is being _____. **37-26**

---

1) decreases 2) increases **37-30**	A child reaches out and touches a flame. The child's behavior was _____ by a natural contingency. **37-31**

are not

15-4

We speak of differential reinforcement when we want to indicate that some responses are (1) * * * (TT), and some rather similar responses are (2) * * *. (TT)

15-5

---

raising

15-12

In gradually shifting the criteria of differential reinforcement, the coach is shaping the desired behavior through successive ____.

15-13

---

stops (quits)

15-20

Moving and sitting still are incompatible. When we reinforce moving, the dog stops sitting still, not only because one response (sitting still) is extinguished but because a different response (moving) which is * * * sitting still is reinforced.

15-21

---

auditory

15-28

An auditory conditioned reinforcer (the "cricket") is especially convenient in shaping behavior because the sound reaches the dog-* * * delay.

15-29

---

have in common (share)

15-36

After shaping "touching the doorknob," we shall be handicapped in shaping "lying in the corner" since we shall first have to ____ the incompatible behavior of "touching the doorknob."

15-37

---

immediate

15-44

The instructor should not wait for perfect form before saying "good." He should use both the principles of differential reinforcement and successive approximation to ____ good form.

15-45

---

increases 37-4	Reinforcement may be positive as in A or negative as in D. In either case it ____ the future rate of the response. 37-5
withdraw (remove) 37-9	In punishment, a(n) (1) ____ is followed by (2) ____ of a positive reinforcer or (3) ____ of a negative reinforcer. 37-10
reinforce(-ment) punish(-ment) 37-14	Removing a positive reinforcer after a response is (1) ____. Presenting a positive reinforcer after a response is (2) ____. 37-15
(1) B (2) C (3) punishment 37-19	When contingent upon a response, a change from S^Δ to S^D is (1) ____, and a change from S^D to S^Δ is (2) ____. 37-20
decrease (decline, fall) 37-24	When pressing the lever turns *off* a shock, pressing the lever is ____ (TT) by termination of the shock. 37-25
(1) increases (2) decreases 37-29	The conditioned aversive stimuli generated by regularly punished behavior will result in a state of anxiety in which positively reinforced behavior (1) ____ and avoidance behavior (2) ____ in frequency. 37-30

We must speak loudly to be heard at a noisy party. At a noisy party, loud speech is _____ (TT) reinforced.

15-6

---

approximations

15-13

Complex skills must be shaped very gradually. As the criterion for differential reinforcement is shifted, _____ _____ to the final behavior are made.

15-14

---

ncompatible
vith

15-21

When we reinforce movements toward the door *but not movements* in other directions, we are _____ _____ movements toward the door.

15-22

---

vithout (with
virtually no)

15-29

Using a "cricket" to reinforce the dog's responses is superior to merely tossing pieces of food into a dish because the temporal relation between _____ (TT) and _____ (TT) can be better controlled.

15-30

---

extinguish

15-37

In learning to bowl, a specific pattern of movements must be shaped. The falling pins _____ the behavior.

15-38

---

hape
differentiate)

15-45

When the instructor slowly raises his standards for saying "good," he is making _____ _____ to the desired form.

15-46

Read exhibit now and refer to it as needed.

The table refers to different possible *contingencies* between a response and events which *immediately follow* a response. You may find it convenient to reproduce this table on scratch paper, using abbreviations, for reference in answering items.

	PRESENTATION	WITHDRAWAL
POSITIVE REINFORCER	A. Positive Reinforcement	B. Punishment
NEGATIVE REINFORCER	C. Punishment	D. Negative Reinforcement

ifferentially

15-6

In learning the high jump, you begin with the crossbar fairly low and gradually raise it. If a jump barely clears the bar when it is low, this same jump * * * clear it when it is higher.

15-7
← To p. 98

---

uccessive
pproximations

15-14

The high jumper is reinforced if he clears the crossbar, but not if he does not. The height of the crossbar automatically selects the criterion for _____ reinforcement.

15-15
← To p. 98

---

ifferentially
einforcing

15-22

In shaping any given behavior, we gradually change the criterion of what to reinforce. The desired behavior is approached by * * *.

15-23
← To p. 98

---

sponse (and)
inforcement
ITHER ORDER)

15-30

For best results in shaping behavior, the conditioned reinforcer should be presented in a close _____ relation to the response.

15-31
← To p. 98

---

inforce
ifferentially
inforce)

15-38

In bowling, there is a relatively long _____ between the release of the ball and the fall of the pins.

15-39
← To p. 98

---

uccessive
pproximations

15-46

When the bowling instructor differentially reinforces closer and closer approximation to good form, we call the process _____ behavior.

15-47
← To p. 98

---

inforcer

36-2

When we say that a man is "suffering from" anxiety, we imply that a(n) _____ state is aversive.

36-3
← To p. 241

) extinction
) adaptation

36-6

In recommending that a man should change his job to get relief from worrying about his work, we propose to change an emotional condition by removing the * * *.

36-7
← To p. 241

---

inforcing

36-10

By slowing down, the speeding driver * * * the conditioned aversive stimuli which his speeding has elicited.

36-11
← To p. 241

---

egative

36-14

A man can sometimes get rid of the aversive effects of hating someone by getting away from him. The emotion is reduced or eliminated by removing its _____.

36-15
← To p. 241

---

ncompatible

36-18

An emotional reaction may quickly grow weaker as time passes. "Counting to ten" before acting in anger _____ the magnitude of the reaction by making it more remote from the inciting event.

36-19
← To p. 241

---

ncrease

36-22

When an employee is severely criticized for an error made during a period of anxiety, the probability of errors may _____ as a result of the increase in anxiety.

36-23
← To p. 241

Set 16

---

differentially

16-4

When parents differentially reinforce a young child only for the sounds of their language, these sounds (1) * * * in frequency while "foreign" sounds (2) * * *.

16-5

---

(1) elements
(2) reinforced

16-9

When we push a heavy object, it moves only if our push exceeds a given force. The contingencies determining which force of pushing will be ____ ____ are determined by the physical properties of the situation.

16-10

---

(1) is
(2) is

16-14

If the shot-put coach never *reinforces* unless the world's record is broken, he (1) * * * using successive approximation; he (2) * * * have a criterion which, if reached, would direct him to provide differential reinforcement.

16-15

---

shaping
(response
differentiation)

16-19

Most of the elements of newly shaped behavior have already been followed by ____ in earlier approximations.

16-20

---

immediately
(quickly)

16-24

A baseball pitcher acquires skill slowly, in part, because there is some ____ between his throwing movements and the reinforcement of seeing the ball cross the plate, seeing the batter swing and miss, or hearing the umpire call "Strike!"

16-25

---

differentially
reinforced

16-29

End of Set

motional 36-1	In saying that someone "enjoys a good cry," we imply that an emotional state or some stimulus accompanying it is a(n) ____. (TT) 36-2
1) positive 2) negative EITHER ORDER) 36-5	If a timid person forces himself to attend many group meetings, his timidity may undergo the process of (1) ____ (if the emotion was conditioned) or (2) ____ (if it was unconditioned). 36-6
litioned sive stimuli rsive stimuli, ative forcers) 36-9	Strong conditioned anxiety generated by speeding may make a driver drive slowly. The anxiety is aversive rather than ____. 36-10
einforcing 36-13	When getting rid of a strong emotion is reinforcing, it is an example of ____ reinforcement. 36-14
ncompatible 36-17	Doing good to someone who "despitefully uses" you is ____ with the emotional behavior usually strengthened by "despiteful use." 36-18
versive emotional) 36-21	The employee who makes an error because of anxiety may be criticized by his boss. This will probably ____ his anxiety. 36-22

Learning to fire a *pistol* is relatively easy after good performance in firing a *rifle* has been shaped. Certain ____ ____ (e.g., squeezing the trigger, not flinching) may help in learning to fire a second firearm.

16-1

---

increase
are
extinguished
(decrease)

16-5

Learning to say "ball" makes it easier for the child to learn to say "fall" because the two responses have * * *. Part of the response "fall" has already been reinforced when the child said "ball."

16-6

---

differentially
reinforced

16-10

When calling to someone at a distance, only loud calls are reinforced. Shouting is ____ reinforced.

16-11

---

1) is not
2) does

16-15

A child may get his mother's attention only by raising his voice. Unintentionally, the mother is ____ ____ loud talking.

16-16

---

reinforcement

16-20

When slightly exceptional cases are differentially reinforced just as they are emitted, a new unit of behavior is ____ through successive approximation.

16-21

---

delay
(time)

16-25

A good pitch can be *instantly* reinforced if the pattern of stimulation from the muscles (the "feel" of good form) has become a(n) ____ reinforcer.

16-26

A "tear-jerker" is a book, play, or movie designed to reinforce the reader or viewer by generating mild _____ effects.

36-1

---

versive

36-4

Some types or degrees of emotional states are (1) _____ reinforcers and others are (2) _____ reinforcers.

36-5

---

einforcing

36-8

When we warn someone of the dangers of fast driving, show him pictures of crashes, corpses, etc., we pair stimuli generated by speeding with aversive stimuli. The stimuli from speeding become * * *.

36-9

---

ncreases
conditions)

36-12

A reduction in strong states of "rage," "anger," etc., is _____ (TT) to most people.

36-13

---

xtinction

36-16

A man's hatred may be reduced if he can engage in emotional behavior which is _____ with hatred.

36-17

---

ncompatible
vith

36-20

Skilled behavior learned while one is calm may be disrupted in anxiety. "Putting the pressure on" an opposing baseball pitcher is using a(n) _____ stimulus in an effort to disrupt behavior.

36-21

---

einforced
(conditioned)
xtinction

36-24

The parent who attempts to extinguish a child's display of bad temper must be sure to ignore it *consistently*, otherwise he will maintain the behavior on _____ reinforcement.

36-25

:ommon :lements 16-1	An infant's operant behavior is composed of un-differentiated wiggles, squirms, waving of arms and legs, etc. Out of this activity, skilled move-ments of the child are very gradually ____ through differential reinforcement. 16-2
:ommon ·lements 16-6	In learning a second language, new vocal patterns will already have been shaped through ____ rein-forcement when the first language was learned. 16-7
ifferentially 16-11	The soft-loud range of normal speech is ____ by the use of differential reinforcement by members of the verbal community. 16-12
ifferentially einforcing 16-16	When the mother becomes accustomed to the child's moderately loud voice, she may answer only still louder calls. The intensity of the child's voice gradually ____ through unintentional differential reinforcement. 16-17
haped lifferentiated) 16-21	A person skilled in one sport will probably be quick to acquire skill in a new sport if the two require "similar" movements, timing, etc. By "similar," we mean that the required responses have * * *. 16-22
onditioned econdary) 16-26	The pitching coach who knows good form speeds learning by supplying ____ (TEMPORAL ANSWER) differential reinforcement, as by saying "Good!" 16-27

emotional
(anxiety)

36-3

In going to a psychiatrist to get relief from worry, a man is escaping from an emotional condition which has the properties of a(n) ____ stimulus.

36-4

---

stimulus
(aversive
stimulus,
cause)

36-7

The exhilaration of riding a roller coaster or being in a speeding car is an example of an emotional condition which is ____ .

36-8

---

escapes
(decreases,
terminates)

36-11

Society usually condemns strong emotional reactions such as "jealousy," "fear," "anger," "rage," "hatred," etc. Society's condemnation ____ the aversive properties.

36-12

---

stimulus
(cause)

36-15

If a person loses a conditioned hatred for someone as the result of frequently being near him under conditions which do not arouse hatred, the emotional condition disappears through ____ .

36-16

---

decreases
(lowers)

36-19

"Love thine enemies" directs one to engage in emotional behavior * * * hatred.

36-20

---

increase

36-23

We may advise a parent to ignore a child's display of bad temper if we believe that the behavior has been (1) ____ (TT) by the parent's reactions and can therefore be eliminated through (2) ____ . (TT)

36-24

shaped
(differentiated)

16-2

In the nursery, crude vocal responses are reinforced. As the child grows, listeners reinforce
increasingly accurate vocalizations. Requiring
better speech at age three than at age two illustrates _____ _____ in shaping.

16-3

---

differential

16-7

When an American learns Chinese, skill in drawing
characters must be shaped; but when he learns
French, the required writing skills (1) * * * been
shaped. French and English writing have many
(2) _____ _____ .

16-8

---

shaped
(differentiated)
(acceptable:
conditioned)

16-12

If in teaching the shot-put, a coach is satisfied
with *every* throw, no matter how bad, he (1) * * *
using successive approximation, and he (2) * * *
using differential reinforcement.

16-13

---

increases

16-17

We generate "new" forms of behavior by differentially reinforcing forms which gradually approxi-
mate the final form. We call this procedure _____
the behavior.

16-18

---

common
elements

16-22

When we acquire skill in driving one car, the skill
"transfers" to driving other cars. This is to be
expected because the behaviors of driving the two
cars * * * really very different.

16-23

---

immediate

16-27

Annoyance at hearing loud speech and failure to
hear faint whispers, set the upper and lower limits
of the intensity of verbal responses which the lis-
tener will _____ _____ .

16-28

← To p. 236

conditioned aversive (aversive) 35-3	Experiment 1. In (F), part of a pattern of behavior characterizing (1)＿＿＿is described. This pattern is now produced by a (2) ＿＿＿ ＿＿＿ stimulus. 35-4 ← To p. 236
(1) decrease (2) increase 35-8	Experiment 1. A stimulant (amphetamine, pronounced am-fet'-a-meen) ＿＿＿ the rate when the buzzer is *not* sounding. 35-9 ← To p. 236
lowers (decreases) 35-13	Experiment 1. Under the tranquilizer, the buzzer (a conditioned aversive stimulus) has * * * influence on the rate. 35-14 ← To p. 236
after 35-18	Experiment 2. In earlier sessions, pressing the lever had (1) ＿＿＿ a shock. Therefore, lever pressing in this experiment is (2) ＿＿＿ behavior. 35-19 ← To p. 236
(1) high (2) low 35-23	Figure 2. While the buzzer is sounding, as between points 2 and 3, the rate of the food-reinforced response is (1) ＿＿＿ while the rate of the response having an avoidance history is (2) ＿＿＿ than before the buzzer onset. 35-24 ← To p. 236
(1) high (2) decreases 35-28	Figure 2. Just before the onset of the buzzer (e.g., point 2) the rate of both responses is nearly ＿＿＿ for a short while. Note the repetition of all the complex details of the record as the cycle repeats. 35-29 ← To p. 236

← To p. 106

successive approximation **16-3**	The babblings of a very young child presumably contain all the basic sounds of all languages. But the parents _____ (TT) reinforce only the sounds of their own language. **16-4** ← To p. 106
have (have already) common elements **16-8**	Reinforcing one operant may often increase the strength of another. Common (1)_____ are strengthened when either operant is (2) _____. ← To p. 106 **16-9**
(1) is not (2) is not **16-13**	If a shot-put coach says "good" each time a man makes a throw better than his last, he (1) * * * using successive approximation, and he (2) * * * using differential reinforcement. **16-14** ← To p. 106
shaping **16-18**	It is true that to be reinforced a response must first be emitted; nevertheless, by the procedure called _____, it is possible to create complicated units of behavior which would never otherwise appear. **16-19** ← To p. 106
are not **16-23**	To be most effective, reinforcement must follow a response _____. (TEMPORAL ANSWER) **16-24** ← To p. 106
differentially reinforce **16-28**	When we walk on the deck of a ship at sea, a slightly different form of walking ("sea-legs") is shaped by the special contingencies determining which forms of walk will be _____ _____ on a slowly tilting surface. **16-29** ← To p. 106

adaptation 35-2	Experiment 1. The contingency described in (E) establishes the buzzer as a(n) * * * stimulus which will produce anxiety. 35-3
decreases (drops) zero 35-7	Experiment 1. When the buzzer has sounded for a short time, the rat behaves in the manner described in (F). Thus, while there is a(n) (1) ____ in rate of food-reinforced behavior, there is a(n) (2) ____ in crouching, etc. 35-8
greater 35-12	Experiment 1. While the buzzer is absent, the tranquilizer (reserpine) ____ the over-all rate, as compared with the control session. 35-13
fixed-ratio high pauses (breaks) 35-17	Experiment 2. Reinforcements are not marked in Figure 2. However, since the schedule is a fixed ratio of 12, the steplike character of the record between points 1 and 2 suggests that the very short horizontal sections occur just ____ reinforcement. 35-18
was absent (was not present, was off) was present (was on) 35-22	Experiment 2, Figure 2. When the conditioned aversive stimulus is absent, the rate of the food-reinforced response is (1) ____, and the rate of the response with an avoidance history is rather (2) ____. 35-23
decreases increases 35-27	Figure 2. Some additional "fine grain" effects can be seen. During most of the buzzer interval, the rate of avoidance behavior is (1) ____, but just before the shocks at points 1 and 3, the slope of the avoidance record (2) ____. 35-28

(1) negative (2) positive Set 9 17-5	Name the response systems involved in the following: walking to the table, putting food in the mouth and chewing it, (1) * * * muscle; moistening food with saliva, (2) * * *; passing food into stomach, (3) * * *; and providing stomach with digestive juices, (4) * * *. 17-6
temporal Set 3 17-11	After a chimpanzee has exchanged tokens for food, water, a mate, etc., the tokens * * * effective as reinforcers if the chimpanzee is well-fed but deprived of water. 17-12
shaping Set 15 17-17	Persistent head scratching, pencil chewing, table tapping, etc., while studying are frequently conditioned (1) _____ operants resulting from (2) _____ contingencies of reinforcement. 17-18
adapted quickly (immediately) Set 13 17-23	In shaping any given behavior, we gradually change the criterion for reinforced responses. The desired behavior is approached by * * *. 17-24
(1) respondent (reflex) (2) operant Set 10 17-29	Reaching for a glass of water or saying "Water, please" are examples of (1) _____ behavior; any specific instance of such behavior, however, is called a(n) (2) _____. 17-30
(1) dimensions (2) internal Set 6 17-35	A conditioned reinforcer can become a(n) * * * by being paired with several unconditioned reinforcers appropriate to various deprivations. 17-36

(1) variable-interval (2) uniform (steady, constant, stable) 35-1	Experiment 1. (C) describes the emotional effect of an unfamiliar stimulus. In (D), exposure to the buzzer has been sufficient for complete ____. 35-2
is no 35-6	Experiment 1. In the non-drugged control session, *after* the first half minute or so of the buzzer, the rate (1) ____ nearly to (2) ____ and remains there until the period ends with a shock. 35-7
(1) increases (2) decreases 35-11	Experiment 1. The anxiety shown by the suppression of the response rate during the conditioned aversive stimulus is ____ in the stimulant sessions than in the normal (control) sessions. 35-12
(1) decreases (2) increases 35-16	READ EXPERIMENT 2 NOW. Experiment 2. Chain pulling was on a(n) (1) * * * schedule of food reinforcement. This schedule produces a(n) (2) ____ and steady rate of responding with (3) ____ after reinforcement. 35-17
conditioned aversive shock (unconditioned aversive stimulus) 35-21	Experiment 2, Figure 2. Between points 1 and 2 (and the other comparable portions of the session), the conditioned aversive stimulus (1) * * *, and between points 2 and 3 it (2) * * *. 35-22
anxiety 35-26	In anxiety, the rate of food-reinforced behavior (1) ____ and the rate of avoidance behavior (2) ____. 35-27

On a cumulative record, the slope of the line indicates (1) * * *, and the hatch marks or pips usually indicate (2) * * *.

17-1

---

triated
striped)
lands
mooth muscle
lands
et 6   17-6

Many so-called traits ascribed to individuals (aggressiveness, persistence, friendliness, etc.) are simply alternate ways of indicating an individual's _____ of emitting certain types of behavior.

17-7

---

re (remain,
ill be)

et 11   17-12

Conditioned operants are eliminated in two contrasting ways: the response is emitted without reinforcement in the process called (1) _____, but is not emitted in the process called (2) _____.

17-13

---

uperstitious
ccidental

et 14   17-18

Two ways of effectively preventing unwanted conditioned behavior are: (a) to (1) _____ it by withholding reinforcement, or (b) to condition some (2) _____ behavior.

17-19

---

uccessive
pproximation

et 15   17-24

To condition a reflex, a neutral stimulus is (1) _____ with a(n) (2) _____ _____.

17-25

---

1) operant
2) response

et 10   17-30

Lying generates stimuli which have acquired the power to elicit the conditioned responses which occur in _____.

17-31

---

eneralized
einforcer

et 11   17-36

The reinforcers used by animal trainers are (1) _____ arranged, but a pigeon foraging for food among leaves in a park is working under (2) _____ contingencies.

17-37

Experiment 1. In (A), the base line against which anxiety is to be observed is provided by a(n) (1) * * * schedule of reinforcement by water. This schedule yields a fairly moderate and (2)____ rate of responding.

35-1

During the "normal" or control (saline) session (comparing the no-buzzer period with the first half minute of each buzzer period) there * * * change in response rate when the buzzer begins.

35-6

Experiment 1. The stimulant (1) ____ the rate of bar pressing while the conditioned aversive stimulus is absent, and it (2) ____ the rate of bar pressing in the presence of the conditioned aversive stimulus.

35-11

Experiment 1. By definition, a drug which decreases anxiety is one which (1) ____ the effect of a conditioned aversive stimulus. A drug which increases anxiety (2) ____ the effect of a conditioned aversive stimulus.

35-16

Figure 2. At point 2, the buzzer began sounding. The buzzer had become a(n) (1) ____ ____ stimulus because of many earlier pairings with (2)____, as at point 3.

35-21

Figure 2 illustrates two changes occurring simultaneously in a single organism. These changes characterize a state of ____.

35-26

rate (of responding) reinforcements Set 12 17-1	(1) _____ behavior is strongly influenced by the consequences of previous similar responses, whereas (2) _____ behavior depends upon a preceding stimulus. 17-2
rate (frequency, probability) Set 10 17-7	In differential reinforcement, one form or magnitude of behavior is (1) * * * and other, possibly rather similar forms or magnitudes, are (2) * * *. 17-8
(1) extinction (2) forgetting Set 10 17-13	In conditioning a reflex, as the number of pairings of the conditioned and unconditioned stimuli increases, the latency of the conditioned reflex (1) _____ and the magnitude of the conditioned response (2) _____, until both reach a limit. 17-14
(1) extinguish (2) incompatible Set 10 17-19	A stimulus which elicits a response without previous conditioning is called a(n) (1) _____ _____; a stimulus which elicits a response only after conditioning is called a(n) (2) _____ _____. 17-20
paired unconditioned stimulus Set 3 17-25	In the usual experiment, when a peck operates the food magazine the (1) _____ reinforcement is immediate, whereas the (2) _____ reinforcement is slightly delayed. 17-26
fear (anxiety) Set 5 17-31	A particularly slow learner may require many reinforcements before developing a high rate of responding. He is _____ likely to develop superstitious behavior than a faster learner. 17-32
deliberately natural (non-deliberate) Set 7 17-37	When behavior decreases in frequency and when, so far as we know, no previous conditioning of the behavior has taken place, we call the process not extinction but _____. 17-38

Set 35

---

(1) anxiety
(2) conditioned
aversive

35-4

Figure 1. The short segments between the straight and broken arrows were recorded while the (1) _____ was operating. These portions of the records were displaced (2) _____ -ward slightly to isolate them from the rest of the record.

35-5

---

increases

35-9

Experiment 1. When the buzzer *is* sounding, the stimulant produces a(n) _____ in rate compared with the rate during the buzzer in the normal (or saline-control session).

35-10

---

little (no)

35-14

Experiment 1. The buzzer, as a(n) (1) * * * produces a state of anxiety shown by the fact that it (2) _____ the rate of bar pressing maintained by positive reinforcement.

35-15

---

(1) delayed
(postponed,
avoided)
(2) avoidance

35-19

Experiment 2. During this session (and several previous sessions like it), the only shocks were those at the (1) _____ of the buzzer periods. These were unavoidable shocks in the sense that they (2) * * * contingent upon an absence of avoidance behavior.

35-20

---

(1) low
(almost zero)
(2) higher

35-24

A conditioned aversive stimulus changes the probability of many responses. We call the change produced by a conditioned aversive stimulus a state of _____.

35-25

---

zero

35-29

Experiment 2. Conclusion: Presenting a(n) (1) _____ _____ stimulus results in a state of (2) _____, shown in part by a(n) (3) _____ in food-reinforced behavior and a(n) (4) _____ in behavior which has an avoidance history.

35-30

(1) Operant (2) respondent (reflex)	
et 10 17-2	

In a conditioned reflex, when a conditioned stimulus is repeatedly presented alone, the magnitude of the conditioned response (1) _____ and the latency of the conditioned reflex (2) _____, until (3) _____ is complete.

17-3

---

reinforced
(conditioned)
not reinforced
(extinguished)

et 15   17-8

The experimenter deliberately arranges reinforcement for key pecking, but superstitious behavior is conditioned by _____ reinforcement.

17-9

---

1) decreases
2) increases

et 4   17-14

A psychologist fed a baby when he emitted "coos," but *not* when he cried. We would expect that crying when hungry would be (1) _____ (TT) because of the withholding of (2) _____. (TT)

17-15

---

unconditioned
stimulus
conditioned
stimulus

et 3   17-20

If an airplane spotter never sees the kind of plane he is to spot, his frequency of scanning the sky (1) _____. In other words, his "looking" behavior is (2) * * *. (TT)

17-21

---

conditioned
(secondary)
unconditioned
(primary)

et 13   17-26

In a reflex, the more intense the stimulus, the greater the (1) _____ of the response and the shorter the (2) _____ of the reflex.

17-27

---

ess

et 14   17-32

Operant behavior has direct consequences on the environment. A consequence which results in an increase in the subsequent rate of the operant response is called a(n) _____. (TT)

17-33

---

daptation

et 13   17-38

Learning to say "ball" makes it easier for the child to learn to say "fall" because the two responses have * * *.

17-39

Read Experiment 1 now. Wait until instructed to read Experiment 2.

EXPERIMENT 1.

(A) A water-deprived rat is reinforced with water on a variable-interval schedule until responding stabilizes at a moderate rate – a base line on which anxiety is to be observed.

(B) Every 10 minutes a buzzer sounds for 3 minutes.

(C) When the buzzer is first sounded, the rate of lever pressing is decreased.

(D) Soon, the buzzer has no effect on rate.

(E) The rat is now shocked at the end of each 3-minute buzzer period.

(F) Soon, when the buzzer sounds, the animal begins to crouch and remains fairly immobile. Erection of hair, defecation, etc., occur.

(G) Sample records taken at this stage are given in Figure 1 marked "SALINE." The straight arrow indicates the onset of the buzzer. The broken arrow indicates the brief shock, followed immediately by termination of the buzzer.

(H) To isolate the performance in the presence of the buzzer, the record is displaced downward between the arrows.

(I) Saline solution injected into the rat has no effect. The performance is typical of uninjected rats.

(J) Reserpine is a tranquilizer.

(K) Amphetamine is a stimulant.

Figure 1

FOOD CHAIN (FR-12)

AVOIDANCE LEVER

Figure 2

30 MINUTES

EXPERIMENT 2.

(Wait until instructed to read Experiment 2.)

A food-deprived monkey receives food after every twelfth pull of a chain. At the same time, a lever is present which in the past has been used in an avoidance procedure (a response to it delayed shock 20 seconds). In the session represented by the record in Figure 2, the avoidance contingency was *not* in effect but extinction is not yet complete. Periods of quiet and buzzer-terminated-by-shock were alternated every 6 minutes. Between points 1 and 2 on Figure 2 the buzzer and shock remained off; then at point 2, the buzzer was sounded, continuing to point 3; at 3, a brief shock was presented and the buzzer was terminated.

1) decreases
   (declines)
2) increases
   (lengthens)
3) extinction

et 4   17-3

When a pigeon is reinforced for pecking a key, the reinforcing stimulus occurs (1) _____ a peck, and the (2)_____at which this response is (3) _____ (TT) increases.

17-4

ccidental

et 14   17-9

In a reflex, the (1) _____ of a stimulus is the intensity which is barely sufficient to (2) _____ a(n) (3) _____.

17-10

xtinguished
einforcement

et 10   17-15

Certain groups of responses, such as those elicited by a sudden loud noise, are characteristic of a state of _____.

17-16

ecreases
xtinguished
(not reinforced)

et 9   17-21

You will not continue to work if your pay checks "bounce" because the (1) _____ generalized reinforcing effect of such a check disappears in (2) _____.

17-22

) magnitude
) latency

t 1   17-27

When a response is elicited by a stimulus without previous conditioning, the sequence is called a(n) _____ _____.

17-28

inforcer

t 8   17-33

If in teaching the shot-put, a coach is "satisfied" with every throw, no matter how bad, he (1) * * * using successive approximation and he (2) * * * using differential reinforcement.

17-34

s not

Figure 1. The "hatch marks" or "pips" on the record indicate ____.

34-3

34-4
← To p. 230

---

ever pressing
ar pressing)

Experiment 1. Pressing the lever does not generate the various conditioned aversive stimuli generated by other responses in the box. These other responses generate ____ which are paired with shock.

34-8

34-9
← To p. 230

,000
TO THE
EAREST
HOUSAND)

Experiment 1. The animal must receive an occasional shock or the conditioned aversive stimuli generated by other behavior will lose their aversive properties through ____.

34-13

34-14
← To p. 230

---

minutes

Figure 2. Each point shows, for a particular session, the (1) ____ of responses on the key which (2) * * *.

34-18

34-19
← To p. 230

---

maller
ower)

Figure 2. During the early sessions, an S$^\Delta$ was presented whenever (1) * * * had elapsed after the last (2) ____.

34-23

34-24
← To p. 230

---

horter
esser)

Experiment 2 demonstrates that a(n) (1) ____ may be an aversive stimulus capable of maintaining (2) ____ behavior.

34-28

34-29
← To p. 230

← To p. 111

1) after 2) rate (frequency) 3) emitted et 8 17-4	Turning off a television commercial is reinforced by termination of a(n) (1) _____ reinforcer; turning on a very funny program is reinforced by the presentation of a(n) (2) _____ reinforcer. 17-5 ← To p. 111
1) threshold 2) elicit 3) response et 1 17-10	An important aspect of respondent conditioning is the _____ relation between presentations of the initially neutral stimulus and of the unconditioned stimulus. 17-11 ← To p. 111
motion fear, nxiety) et 5 17-16	When we differentially reinforce successive approximations to a final form of behavior, we are _____ behavior. 17-17 ← To p. 111
1) conditioned 2) extinction et 11 17-22	A simple operant can be conditioned very rapidly if the organism is (1) _____ to the situation and if a reinforcer follows the response (2) _____. 17-23 ← To p. 111
nconditioned eflex et 3 17-28	The pairing of two stimuli is necessary for conditioning (1) _____ behavior; reinforcement is necessary for conditioning (2) _____ behavior. 17-29 ← To p. 111
) is not) is not t 16 17-34	Smooth muscles change the (1) _____ of various (2) _____ organs. 17-35 ← To p. 111

1) postpones
   (delays,
   avoids)
2) avoidance

34-2

Experiment 1. The rat has already responded under this procedure in many sessions. Thus, initial conditioning * * * shown in Figure 1.

34-3

---

onditioned
versive

34-7

Experiment 1. The only behavior in the box which is never accompanied by shock is * * *.

34-8

---

our

34-12

Experiment 1. Each full excursion of the pen across the paper represents about 1,000 responses. Once the animal begins responding, it presses the lever _____ times (TO THE NEAREST THOUSAND) before receiving another shock.

34-13

---

voidance

34-17

Experiment 2. During Sessions 1-19 (excluding 2 and 12), if no response was made on the key which postponed S^Δ for as long as * * *, then a 1-minute S^Δ (or "time-out") occurred.

34-18

---

ere not

34-22

Figure 2. The numbers of responses emitted during Sessions 2 and 12 were very much _____ than during the other sessions.

34-23

---

gher
reater)

34-27

Each response delayed the shock in Experiment 1 by only 8 seconds. The response rate was higher in Experiment 1 than in Experiment 2 partly because each response delayed the aversive stimulus for a(n) _____ period of time.

34-28

When every response is reinforced, we speak of *continuous reinforcement*. Often, however, an operant is reinforced only occasionally, that is, reinforcement is *intermittent*. In one type of intermittent reinforcement, a response is reinforced only after a certain number of responses have been emitted (*ratio reinforcement*). In another type, a response is reinforced only after a certain time has passed (*interval reinforcement*). A given schedule is programmed by apparatus composed of timers, counters, relays, etc.

Food-deprived pigeons were reinforced with food for pecking a key in a standard experimental box. Typical portions of actual cumulative records are given to show the rate, and changes in rate, at which each pigeon pecked the key under various schedules of reinforcement.

Experiment 1.

A **fixed-interval schedule.** The experimental equipment includes a timer which starts just after reinforcement. After 10 minutes has elapsed, the key and magazine are connected and the next response is reinforced. Responses during the 10-minute interval are not reinforced.

Figure 1

(1) 8
(2) response

34-1

Experiment 1. Pressing the lever (1) _____ shock for 8 seconds. Since the rat is not shocked if it presses the lever frequently enough, this is an example of (2) _____ behavior.

34-2

---

(1) aversive
stimulus
(negative
reinforcer)
(2) anxiety

34-6

Experiment 1. Many responses emitted by the animal (except pressing the lever) have been followed by shock. Such behavior generates stimuli which are paired with shock and become _____ _____ stimuli.

34-7

---

(1) is
(2) deprivation

34-11

Experiment 1. After a few minutes, the rat begins to respond at a fairly high rate. No more shocks are received until the pen has traveled across the paper nearly _____ times.

34-12

---

(1) food
(2) S^Δ

34-16

Experiment 2. Responses on one of the keys were effective only in avoiding S^Δ, therefore, responding on this key was an example of _____ behavior.

34-17

.wo

34-21

Experiment 2. During Sessions 2 and 12, S^Δs * * * presented. Responding on the key which previously postponed S^Δ had no effect.

34-22

---

ncreases

34-26

The shorter the period of postponement of an aversive stimulus, the _____ the response rate.

34-27

---

naintained

18-5

When reinforcement ceases altogether, the operant
* * *.

18-6

---

atio
variable-ratio)

18-11

A worker on "piecework" is paid $1 for every lot
of 20 articles he produces. When finishing a lot
is thus reinforced, the reinforcement is on a(n)
_____ schedule.

18-12

.0 minutes
einforcement

18-17

Experiment 1. Another response is reinforced after
a fixed (1) _____ has elapsed since the last reinforcement. The schedule is called a(n) _____ - _____
schedule of reinforcement.

18-18

---

lopes

18-23

A rough estimate of the response rate represented
in a cumulative record can be obtained by comparing
the (1) _____ of the record with the slopes shown
in the (2) _____.

18-24

L) reinforced
2) after

18-29

Experiment 1. After B, the next reinforced response
is represented at (1) _____, and the indicated rate
just (2) _____ this point is about 2.5 responses per
second.

18-30

---

einforced

18-35

Experiment 1. Responding "immediately after reinforcement" is extinguished through lack of _____
during this part of the interval. (Extinction under
one condition and not under another is called *discrimination* and is to be studied later.)

18-36

▷

Experiment 1. The rat gets shocked only when more than (1) _____ seconds elapse after the last (2) _____ by the rat or the last shock.

34-1

---

(1) low
(2) shocks

34-5

Experiment 1. Shock is an unconditioned (1) _____ _____. A stimulus frequently preceding shock generates the emotional predisposition called (2) _____.

34-6

---

irst (early)

34-10

Experiment 1. The low initial rate suggests that anxiety (1) * * * necessary for adequate avoidance behavior. This is similar to providing a condition of (2) _____ before using a positive reinforcer.

34-11

---

1) avoidance
2) avoids
(postpones, delays)

34-15

READ EXPERIMENT 2 NOW AND REFER TO IT AS NEEDED. Experiment 2. There were two keys in this apparatus. Responses on one key were rein- forced with (1) _____ on a variable-interval schedule *except* when the (2) _____ (TT) was present.

34-16

---

1) reinforced
2) avoidance

34-20

Figure 2. During Sessions 1-19 (excluding 2 and 12) about _____ hundred responses per session were made on the S^Δ-avoidance key.

34-21

---

hortened
decreased)

34-25

Figure 2. Decreasing the interval by which a re- sponse delays an S^Δ (from 2 minutes to 45 seconds) considerably _____ the number of responses per session.

34-26

---

ate
frequency)

34-30

In avoidance behavior, one variable shown to be of considerable importance is the * * * during which the response postpones the aversive stimulus.

34-31

The "acquisition," or conditioning, of behavior refers to an increase in frequency of occurrence of a response resulting from _____.

18-1

---

extinguished
creases in
, ceases)

18-6

When an operant is only occasionally followed by reinforcement, the schedule of reinforcement is said to be _____.

18-7

---

atio
fixed-ratio)

18-12

In a ratio schedule, the number of responses required per reinforcement may be constant (fixed-ratio schedule) or variable (variable-ratio schedule). Gambling is analogous to a(n) (1) * * * schedule and "piecework" to a(n) (2) * * * schedule.

18-13

---

1) interval
   (period)
2) fixed-
   interval

18-18

Experiment 1. The schedule is called a(n) (1) _____ - _____ schedule because only after 10 minutes have elapsed will another (2) _____ occur (and then, only if the organism (3) _____).

18-19

---

1) slope
2) scale

18-24

Experiment 1. Responses are reinforced at points B and E. The slope of the record from D to E is between the two slopes _____ and _____ shown on the scale.

18-25

---

1) E
2) before

18-30

Experiment 1. On a fixed-interval schedule of reinforcement, response rate is (1) _____-est just after reinforcement and (2) _____-est just before the next reinforcement.

18-31

---

einforcement

18-36

Experiment 1. The pattern of responding, typical of the fixed-interval schedule, develops in part because of the _____ of responses occurring soon after reinforcement.

18-37

Set 34

PART IX Avoidance and Escape Behavior

Avoidance Experiments

Estimated time: 17 minutes

See exhibit on preceding page
Turn to next page and begin ▶

shocks
(aversive
stimuli)

34-4

Experiment 1. In the first few minutes of the session, shown at **a** in Figure 1, the rate was (1) _____ and the animal received many (2) _____.

34-5

---

stimuli

34-9

Figure 1. In spite of a long history of avoiding shock, the rat receives many shocks during the _____ part of the session, as shown at **a**. These generate emotion.

34-10

---

extinction

34-14

Experiment 1 demonstrates (1) _____ behavior. This behavior (2) _____ the unconditioned aversive stimulus.

34-15

---

(1) number
(2) postponed S△
     (avoided S△)

34-19

Experiment 2. Responses in the presence of S△ were never (1) _____. Thus, postponing the loss of an opportunity to be reinforced on one key maintained (2) _____ behavior on the other key.

34-20

---

(1) 2 minutes
(2) response

34-24

Experiment 2. At the forty-fourth session, the interval between the last response and the presentation of an S△ was _____ to 45 seconds.

34-25

---

1) S△
2) avoidance

34-29

The length of time for which a response postpones an aversive stimulus is an important determinant of the _____ of an avoidance response.

34-30

reinforcement 18-1	A previously acquired operant which is consistently not reinforced will be _____. 18-2
intermittent 18-7	There are many different ways in which intermittent reinforcement may be scheduled. Under some schedules an operant may be extinguished; under others it will be _____ in strength. 18-8
(1) variable- ratio (2) fixed-ratio 18-13	When you telephone a friend at his home and there is no answer, time must elapse before he will have returned home to answer a second call. You are reinforced by getting an answer only if you call at the right _____. 18-14
fixed-interval reinforcement responds 18-19	On a cumulative recorder, the (1) _____ moves one small step with each response. Rate of responding is indicated by the (2) _____ of the line. 18-20
(and) 3 18-25	Experiment 1. The response rate represented by the record between D and E is approximately 2.5 _____ per _____. 18-26
1) low(-est) 2) high(-est) 18-31	Experiment 1. After C there is a(n) (1) _____ in the slope, but between C and D the rate is still (2) _____ than between D and E. 18-32
-reinforcement inction) 18-37	*Unlike* the "superstition" experiment, in a fixed-interval schedule of reinforcement a specific response (e.g., pecking) must occur after the interval elapses. Reinforcement is contingent upon a(n) _____ in fixed-interval schedules. 18-38

EXPERIMENT 1.

A rat is placed in a standard experimental box, the floor of which is an electric grid through which the rat can be shocked. A brief shock occurs every 8 seconds unless the rat presses a lever; such a response postpones the shock for a full 8 seconds. The rat is shocked whenever it fails to emit a response within 8 seconds after the previous response or shock. The animal has been under the same contingencies for many sessions. (White space has been cut out of the record and the separate segments brought together to facilitate reproduction.) Occasional shocks are indicated by the short downward movements of the pen (not to be confused with the fragments of the reset lines).

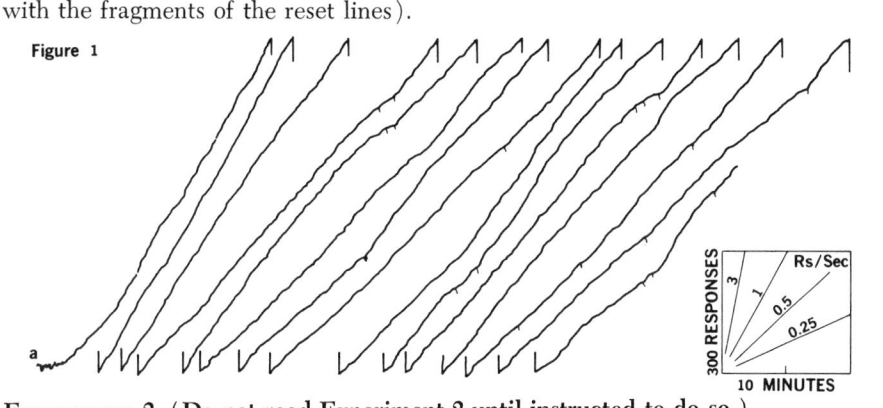

Figure 1

EXPERIMENT 2. (Do not read Experiment 2 until instructed to do so.)

In a standard apparatus a food-deprived pigeon pecked a key which delivered food on a variable-interval schedule when an S^D (lighted key) was present. In S^Δ responses produced no food. A second key was also present. Whenever the pigeon failed to respond on this key for a certain interval of time (2 minutes in first part of Figure 2 and 45 seconds in second part), S^Δ appeared for 1 minute on the food-reinforcement key. This procedure had been in effect for several days before data in Figure 2 were collected. In Figure 2 a point has been plotted for each session showing the total number of responses on the key which postponed S^Δ. On days 2 and 12 (open circles) no S^Δs were presented whether or not the pigeon responded.

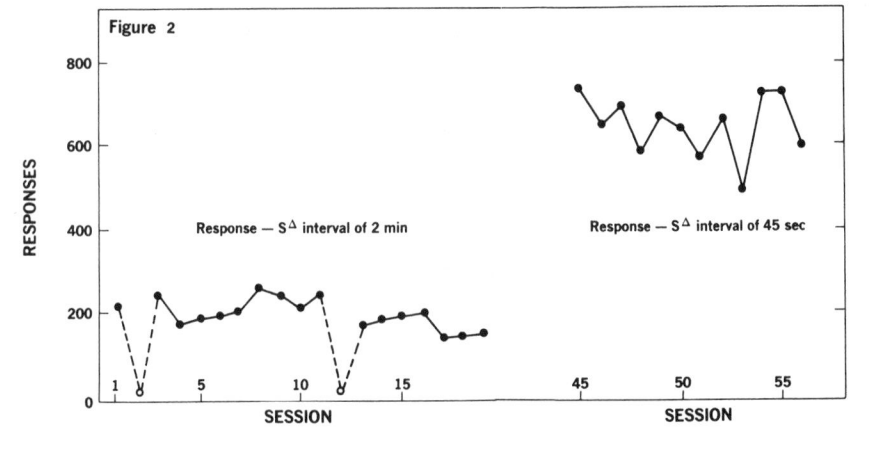

Figure 2

xtinguished

18-2

Often, an operant is only occasionally reinforced, that is, reinforcement occurs ____.

18-3

---

aintained

18-8

We do not always win at dice. Nor do we always get an answer when we telephone a friend. Reinforcement for these responses occurs ____.

18-9

---

me
nterval)

18-14

When reinforcement becomes available only after a lapse of time, it is said to be on an interval schedule. Using a telephone is often reinforced on a(n) ____ schedule.

18-15

.) pen
   (needle,
   stylus, line)
:) slope

18-20

Experiment 1. Reinforced responses occur at the points labeled * * *.

18-21

:sponses
)er) second

18-26

Experiment 1. Flat (horizontal) portions of the record indicate periods when ____ responses occurred.

18-27

) increase
) lower

18-32

Experiment 1. A fixed-interval schedule of reinforcement results in (1) ____ responding just after reinforcement; the rate then gradually (2) ____ and reaches a maximum just before the (3) * * *.

18-33

:sponse

18-38

In a fixed-interval schedule, a response contingency (1) * * * deliberately arranged; in a "superstition" experiment, a response contingency (2) * * * deliberately arranged.

18-39

void

33-3

Since stimuli from rapidly approaching objects often precede painful stimuli, visual stimuli from a rapidly approaching object become ____ ____ reinforcers.

33-4
← To p. 224

---

einforced

33-8

Certain behaviors are labeled "sinful," and many communities scorn "sinners." ____ associated with these behaviors become conditioned negative reinforcers.

33-9
← To p. 224

---

nxiety

33-13

When we say that a man "seems to feel guilty" about doing something, we are describing a change in a pattern of behavior characteristic of ____.

33-14
← To p. 224

) aversive
   stimulus
   (negative
   reinforcer)
) escape
   (terminate)
33-18

When the holdup victim turns over his wallet, he (1) ____ a threat and (2) ____ physical injury.

33-19
← To p. 224

---

ositive

33-23

Chopping wood because of criticism is hard work, in part, because the stimuli generated in the situation are paired with the aversive stimuli of criticism. The wood-chopping situation then provides ____ ____ stimuli.

33-24
← To p. 224

)Δ

33-28

A pigeon reinforced with food for pecking a key in the presence of S^D but not during an occasional S^Δ, will peck a second key which delays the appearance of S^Δ. Pecking the second key is called ____ behavior because of the effects on S^Δ.

33-29
← To p. 224

	Behavior must be not only acquired but also maintained in strength by reinforcement. Under continuous reinforcement, after reaching a maximal rate, an operant is _____ in maximal strength only if it continues to be reinforced.
ntermittently

18-3 | 18-4 |
| ntermittently

18-9 | In throwing dice, winning is due to "chance." There is some average *ratio* of the number of throws to the number of wins. In technical terms, this is the average ratio of the number of (1) _____ (throws) to the number of (2) _____ (wins).

18-10 |
| nterval
variable-
nterval)

18-15 | The availability of reinforcement depends on the number of preceding responses on (1) _____ schedules, and on the passage of time on (2) _____ schedules.

18-16 |
| , B, E
NY ORDER)

18-21 | On the recorder in these experiments, the paper moves very slowly, and the pen makes very small steps (1000 responses move the pen the width of the paper). It is often not possible to see the record made by a single _____.

18-22 |
| (few)

18-27 | Experiment 1. The slope between B and C indicates a response rate nearly, or a little more than, _____ responses per second.

18-28 |
| o
ncreases
ext
einforcement

18-33 | Experiment 1. On a fixed-interval schedule, the cumulative response curve is fairly smoothly accelerated during part of the interval. Since the rate is increasing, it is called _____ acceleration.

18-34 |
|) is
) is not

18-39 | The "superstition" experiment * * * an example of a fixed-interval schedule of reinforcement.

18-40 |

egative einforcement 33-2	The visual stimuli generated by rapidly approaching objects often precede painful stimuli. When we dodge such objects we _____ pain. 33-3

1) avoids
2) escapes
   from
   (terminates)
33-7
	A boy who hesitates to dive from the high board may be called a sissy. When he finally jumps, he escapes being called a sissy, and his dive is _____ by the termination of conditioned aversive stimuli.
	33-8

nxiety 33-12	Stimuli generated by "sinful" behaviors may become aversive because they precede punishment. When the behavior is emitted (because of other variables), the conditioned aversive stimuli generate _____. 33-13
ncompatible 33-17	The holdup man threatens his victim. He uses a(n) (1) * * * (TT) to control his victim's behavior. The victim can (2) * * * the threat by turning over his wallet. 33-18
negative 33-22	A camper may not find chopping wood aversive. Such behavior may be reinforced when a fire is built for cooking or warmth. Wood chopping in this case is reinforced by a(n) _____ reinforcer. 33-23
(1) $(S)^D$ (2) $(S)^\Delta$ 33-27	Loss of an opportunity to gain positive reinforcement is aversive. In other words, a(n) S_____ is an aversive stimulus. 33-28

maintained

An operant at maximal strength will be _____ if reinforcement continues.

18-4

18-5
←To p. 118

---

responses
reinforcements

A schedule of reinforcement in which the number of reinforcements obtained depends on the number of responses emitted is called a *ratio schedule*. Dice throwing may be reinforced on a(n) _____ schedule.

18-10

18-11
←To p. 118

---

(1) ratio
(2) interval

READ DESCRIPTION OF EXPERIMENT 1. Experiment 1. A response is reinforced only after at least (1) _____ _____ have elapsed since the last (2) _____.

18-16

18-17
←To p. 118

---

response
(step of pen)

The *scale* at the bottom of the exhibit shows several of the _____ which result from various rates of responding.

18-22

18-23
←To p. 118

---

zero

Experiment 1. The hatch mark at B indicates that a response was (1) _____. Immediately (2) _____ B, the record indicates a period of no responding.

18-28

18-29
←To p. 118

---

positive

Experiment 1. When the pigeon was *first* exposed to this schedule, it pecked at a high rate even just after reinforcement; but the responses which occur soon after reinforcement are never _____.

18-34

18-35
←To p. 118

---

s not

End of Set

18-40

1) escapes
2) negative
   reinforcer
   (aversive
   stimulus) 33-1

A common practice is to whip a horse until it gallops. Galloping is conditioned through ____ ____.

33-2

1) reinforced
2) conditioned
   negative
   33-6

The person who runs from the dentist's office after merely hearing the drill (1) * * * the painful stimulation involved in drilling, and (2) * * * the sound of the drill.

33-7

conditioned
   33-11

The emotional predisposition called anxiety is generated by conditioned aversive stimuli. A stimulus which regularly precedes pain generates ____.

33-12

einforced
   33-16

Severe punishment of sexual behavior may also condition stimuli which elicit the respondents seen in anxiety. These respondents may be ____ with adequate sexual behavior.

33-17

1) reinforced
2) higher
   33-21

The camper is criticized for not chopping wood in an effort to increase the rate of that behavior by using a(n) ____ reinforcer.

33-22

ower
reduce,
ecrease)
   33-26

In a discriminative operant, (1) S____ is the occasion upon which a response is followed by reinforcement. (2) S____ is the occasion upon which no reinforcement follows a response.

33-27

Read only Experiment 2 now and wait until instructed to read the rest of the exhibit.

EXPERIMENT 1.

A fixed-interval schedule.

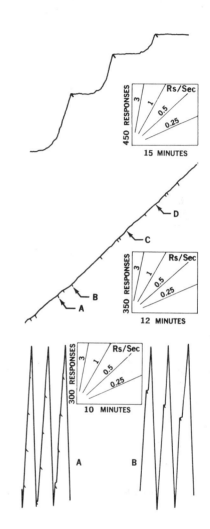

EXPERIMENT 2.

A variable-interval schedule. The experimental equipment is arranged so that a response is reinforced after an interval of time, which may vary from a few seconds to 6 minutes, measured from the previous reinforcement. The average interval is 3 minutes.

EXPERIMENT 3.

A fixed-ratio schedule. Reinforcement occurs only at the 210th (Record A) or the 900th response (Record B) after the preceding reinforcement. (Such large ratios can be reached only by beginning with smaller ratios and gradually increasing them.)

EXPERIMENT 4.

Resistance to extinction varies with the type of schedule to which the organism has been conditioned. Operants maintained by continuous reinforcement extinguish rapidly when reinforcement is discontinued (the organism seldom emits more than a few hundred unreinforced responses). Operants maintained by *intermittent reinforcement* take considerably longer to extinguish. For example, in one experiment, after the response had been maintained on a fixed ratio of 900 and reinforcement was then discontinued, the pigeon emitted 73,000 responses during the first 4½ hours of extinction.

| ▷ | A horse is whipped until it gallops. By galloping, the horse (1) _____ from the (2) _____ _____, whipping. |

33-1

---

conditioned

33-5

After experience with the sound of the dentist's drill, behavior which terminates it will be (1) _____. The sound of the drill is a(n) (2) _____ _____ reinforcer.

33-6

---

activation syndrome

33-10

"Anxiety" is a common name for the "emotional" predisposition generated by a stimulus which frequently *precedes* an unconditioned aversive stimulus. Anxiety is thus generated by a(n) _____ aversive stimulus.

33-11

---

aversive stimuli (conditioned aversive stimuli)

33-15

When, as the result of punishment, stimuli involved in sexual behavior become conditioned aversive stimuli, then sexual behavior in marriage will suffer if responses are still _____ by the termination of these stimuli.

33-16

---

activation syndrome

33-20

A camper is criticized for not doing his share of wood chopping. Either wood chopping has *not* been (1) _____ in ways appropriate to his current deprivations or some incompatible behavior has a(n) (2) _____ probability.

33-21

---

decreased (lowered)

33-25

The teacher who uses strong aversive control to get students to study may _____ the probability that the students will study after graduation.

33-26

---

negative reinforcers (aversive stimuli)

33-30

End of Set

---

1 occasionally
(may be,
a be)

19-6

Experiment 2. The shortest interval in a variable-interval schedule may be very small. One reinforcement may therefore occur * * * another reinforcement.

19-7

0.5

19-13

Compared with rates observed on some schedules, the rate in Experiment 2 is moderate. We can say that variable-interval schedules generate a relatively ____ and fairly ____ rate.

19-14

---

(1) 210
(2) 900

19-20

A pigeon could not change abruptly from continuous reinforcement (every response reinforced) to a fixed ratio of 900 because the response would be ____ before the 900th response.

19-21

---

(1) variable
(2) variable

19-27

A pause sometimes occurs after reinforcement on a(n) (1) ____-ratio schedule, but not on a(n) (2) ____-ratio schedule.

19-28

---

(1) pause
(2) positive(-ly)
    accelerated

19-34

To generate a very high rate of responding without appreciable pausing, we should use a(n) ____ - ____ schedule.

19-35

---

more

19-41

The phrase *resistance to extinction* refers to the number of responses emitted after reinforcement is discontinued. When few unreinforced responses are required for extinction, we say there is low * * *.

19-42

conditioned negative 33-4	The sound of the dentist's drill normally precedes painful stimulation of a tooth. The sound of the drill becomes a(n) _____ aversive stimulus. 33-5
Stimuli 33-9	In addition to its role as a reinforcer, an aversive stimulus is an "emotional" variable. An aversive stimulus elicits the group of respondents called the * * *. 33-10
anxiety 33-14	A child is severely punished for sexual play. The stimuli involved in sexual behavior may become * * *. 33-15
(1) escapes (terminates) (2) avoids 33-19	When threatened by a bandit, a man may engage in extensive respondent behavior (e.g., increased heart rate, sweating, pupil dilation, goose flesh, etc.). Collectively these are called the _____ _____. 33-20
conditioned aversive 33-24	The conditioned aversive stimuli accompanying "wood chopping to escape criticism" may make that activity even more aversive and the probability that it will occur in the absence of criticism will be _____ even further. 33-25
avoidance 33-29	A pigeon continues to peck a key which postpones S^Δ. This demonstrates that S^Δs also can act as * * *. 33-30

In Experiment 2, the availability of a reinforcement for a particular response depends on the passage of * * *.

19-1

---

immediately
after
(soon after)

19-7

Experiment 2. In the figure, two consecutive, relatively long periods of unreinforced responding occur at _____ and _____.

19-8

---

moderate
(and fairly)
uniform
(steady,
constant)   19-14
(EITHER ORDER)

Experiment 2. If the average interval had been shorter (density of reinforcement higher), the rate would have been higher. The longer the average interval, in a variable-interval schedule, the _____ the rate of responding.

19-15

---

extinguished

19-21

Experiment 3. In record B there is a pause after _____.

19-22

---

1) fixed
2) variable

19-28

In comparing Experiment 2 and Experiment 3, would you conclude that interval or ratio schedules produce the highest over-all rates?

19-29

---

variable (-)
ratio

19-35

Since a(n) (1) _____-ratio schedule produces no pause after reinforcement, the over-all curve is smoother than that produced by a(n) (2) _____-ratio which frequently produces a pause.

19-36

---

resistance to
extinction

19-42

When an operant is "resistant to extinction," _____ unreinforced responses are emitted before extinction is complete.

19-43

ncreases **32-4**	A synonym for "negative reinforcer" is "aversive stimulus." An electric shock is a(n) (2) _____ reinforcer or a(n) (2) _____ stimulus. **32-5** ← To p. 218
ermination (removal) **32-10**	Behavior reinforced by the termination of an aversive stimulus is called _____. **32-11** ← To p. 218
1) is (can be) 2) is not (cannot be) **32-16**	When termination of a stimulus reinforces a response, the stimulus is a(n) (1) _____ _____. It (2) * * * defined scientifically as "unpleasant." **32-17** ← To p. 218
ιvoid **32-22**	Shock elicits the activation syndrome and predisposes the organism to emit escape behavior. Because it does this even without previous conditioning, shock is a(n) _____ aversive stimulus. **32-23** ← To p. 218
loes not **32-28**	The immediate reinforcement for avoidance responses is the _____ of conditioned negative reinforcers (e.g., a light which regularly precedes shock). **32-29** ← To p. 218
›aired **32-34**	The dog which jumps from compartment to compartment as soon as a light is presented avoids a shock, a(n) (1) _____ _____ stimulus, and escapes the light, a(n) (2) _____ _____ stimulus. **32-35** ← To p. 218

(variable intervals of) time 19-1	Experiment 2. When a response has been reinforced, a variable amount of time elapses before another response is reinforced. This is called a(n) ____ - ____ schedule. 19-2
C (and) D 19-8	Experiment 2. The curve has many small "bumps" or a "grainy" appearance. This means that there are slight moment-to-moment changes in the * * *. 19-9
lower (slower, less) 19-15	Experiment 2. If we changed the average interval from 3 minutes to 1 minute, we would expect the response rate to ____. 19-16
reinforcement 19-22	Experiment 3. In record A there are few (1) ____ after reinforcement. The rate is high and (2) ____. 19-23
ratio schedules 19-29	In comparing Experiment 2 and Experiment 3, we may conclude that a(n) (1) ____ - ____ schedule generates a higher rate than a(n) (2) ____ - ____ schedule. 19-30
(1) variable (2) fixed 19-36	READ EXPERIMENT 4. Under continuous reinforcement every response is reinforced. After such a schedule, when reinforcement is no longer provided, the time required for extinction is ____. 19-37
many 19-43	It requires many ____ unreinforced responses to extinguish a response after intermittent reinforcement than after continuous reinforcement. 19-44

escape	When a rat has once escaped from shock by pressing a lever, the probability that it will press the lever when shock is again administered _____.
32-3	32-4

elicits	Escape is a form of behavior reinforced by the _____ of an aversive stimulus.
32-9	32-10

increasing	A positive reinforcer (1) * * * defined in terms of its capacity to increase the rate of a response it follows. Such a reinforcer (2) * * * defined scientifically as "pleasant" or "satisfying."
32-15	32-16

(1) avoidance (2) avoided	In a two-compartment box, when a light precedes a shock, the dog is shocked in the presence of the light for the first few trials, because it has not yet acquired behavior which will _____ the shock.
32-21	32-22

escapes (terminates, eliminates)	Avoidance behavior might appear to be unreinforced, since the unconditioned aversive stimulus (e.g., shock) * * * occur after successful avoidance responses.
32-27	32-28

unconditioned	As extinction of avoidance behavior proceeds, the animal soon waits until the unconditioned aversive stimulus is again presented; then conditioned and unconditioned aversive stimuli are _____ once more and the behavior reestablished.
32-33	32-34

reinforced	End of Set
32-39	

Experiment 2. On this schedule, the interval between reinforcements varies from (1) * * * to (2) * * *.

19-3

The rate of responding between C and D is approximately * * * the rate of responding between A and B.

19-10

Experiment 2. If we changed the average interval from 3 minutes to 4 minutes, we would expect the response rate to _____.

19-17

---

1) pauses
   (breaks)
2) constant
   (stable,
   uniform)

19-23

Experiment 3 suggests that _____ after reinforcement are more likely, the larger the fixed ratio.

19-24

A gradual positive acceleration between reinforcements is generated by a(n) _____ - _____ schedule of reinforcement.

19-31

A response which is always reinforced is said to be maintained on _____ reinforcement.

19-38

A response continuously reinforced is less _____ to extinction than one intermittently reinforced.

19-45

(1) a few seconds (2) 6 minutes 19-3	Experiment 2. On this schedule, 3 minutes is the * * * between reinforced responses. 19-4
the same as 19-10	Experiment 2. Except for the fine grain, on a variable-interval schedule the rate of responding is fairly ____, in contrast with the rate on a fixed-interval schedule. 19-11
decrease 19-17	READ EXPERIMENT 3. Experiment 3. On a fixed-ratio schedule, reinforcements follow some (1) ____ number of (2) ____. 19-18
pauses 19-24	Experiment 3. Except for pauses, is the rate of responding close to 3, 1, 0.5, 0.25, or 0 response(s) per second on these fixed-ratio schedules? 19-25
fixed(-) interval 19-31	On a fixed-ratio schedule of reinforcement, the first response on a new ratio is followed by additional responses at a(n) ____ and also ____ rate. 19-32
continuous 19-38	There is little resistance to extinction for a response which has always been reinforced (i.e., ____ reinforcement). 19-39
resistant 19-45	A mother trying to stop temper tantrums may not always give in to them. Occasionally, when she is especially tired, she may. She is reinforcing temper tantrums ____. 19-46

(1) positıve
(2) negative
  reinforcer
  (aversive
  stimulus) **32-1**
	A rat on an electric grid presses a lever which turns off an electric current strong enough to stimulate painfully. The response is ____-ly ____.
	
	32-2

reinforce **32-7**	Presenting an aversive stimulus is analogous to a sudden increase in the ____ appropriate to a positive reinforcer. **32-8**
(1) escape (terminate) (2) aversive **32-13**	When a response terminates a negative reinforcer (aversive stimulus), its rate on such occasions in the future increases. The event is termed negative ____. **32-14**
(1) avoidance (2) escape **32-19**	A dog in one of two adjacent compartments learns to jump into the other compartment when a light comes on if a shock regularly follows the light. This is *avoidance* behavior because, by jumping before the shock, the dog ____ shock. **32-20**
conditioned **32-25**	The dog which jumps from the compartment when the light comes on but before the shock comes on (1) ____ shock (the (2) ____ aversive stimulus). **32-26**
lose **32-31**	With repeated, successful avoidance behavior, the conditioned and unconditioned negative reinforcers are no longer being paired and the conditioned reinforcer becomes less effective. The avoidance behavior then begins to be ____. **32-32**
negative interfere (conflict, be incompatible) **32-37**	The "bully" uses a dangerous method of control because the aversive stimuli he administers may be ____ by his victim in a kind of counteraggression. **32-38**

erage interval ean time) 19-4	A response made immediately after reinforcement is never reinforced on a(n) (1) ____-interval schedule. A response immediately after reinforcement is sometimes reinforced on a(n) (2) ____-interval schedule. 19-5
constant (uniform, steady, even) 19-11	The record can be made smooth or "grainy" by slight changes in the particular intervals of the variable-interval schedule. The moment-to-moment rate * * * controlled by the component intervals. 19-12
(1) fixed (constant, definite) (2) responses 19-18	A *timer* or *clock* is used to program (1) fixed-____ schedules, and a *counter* to program (2) fixed-____ schedules. 19-19
3 19-25	On a fixed-ratio schedule, reinforcements occur after a fixed number of responses. A variable-ratio schedule provides reinforcement after a(n) ____ number of responses. 19-26
high (and) uniform (EITHER ORDER) 19-32	Pauses sometimes occur after reinforcement on both fixed-ratio and fixed-interval schedules. In the case of ____ - ____ schedules, responding is abruptly resumed. 19-33
continuous 19-39	Experiment 4. After behavior had been maintained on a ratio of 900:1, reinforcement was discontinued. In the first 4 1/2 hours of extinction____ responses were emitted. 19-40
ntermittently (randomly, variably) 19-46	By intermittently reinforcing temper tantrums, the mother is making them very ____ to extinction. 19-47

When presentation of a stimulus reinforces the response it follows, the stimulus is called a(n) (1) _____ reinforcer. When termination of a stimulus reinforces the response it follows, the stimulus is a(n) (2) _____ _____.

32-1

---

(1) deprivation
(2) present
(give, turn on)

32-6

Presenting an aversive stimulus is like depriving an organism of food in that they both make it possible to _____ a response.

32-7

---

(1) negative
reinforcer
(2) aversive
stimulus
(EITHER ORDER)

32-12

When we close a window facing on a noisy street, we (1) * * * noise which is a(n) (2) _____ stimulus.

32-13

---

avoidance

32-18

A dog might jump from a compartment before a shock is delivered in the case of (1) _____ behavior, or it might jump after the shock is delivered in the case of (2) _____ behavior.

32-19

---

unconditioned
aversive
conditioned
aversive

32-24

When a light is frequently followed by shock, any response which then terminates the light is reinforced. The light becomes a(n) _____ negative reinforcer (aversive stimulus).

32-25

---

conditioned
unconditioned

32-30

If the dog continues, on trial after trial, to jump as soon as the light appears, the light is no longer paired with shock; thus, the light begins to _____ its property as a conditioned negative reinforcer through extinction.

32-31

---

respondents
(reflex
responses)

32-36

It is generally not convenient to shape skillful behavior with a(n) (1) _____ reinforcer because it elicits many respondents which may (2) _____ with the behavior to be shaped.

32-37

(1) fixed (2) variable	Experiment 2. Unlike a fixed-interval schedule, on a variable-interval schedule a response made soon after an earlier reinforced response * * * reinforced.
19-5	19-6 ← To p. 125

is	Experiment 2. On this variable-interval schedule (average interval of 3 minutes) the rate of responding (in responses per second) is closest to which of these: 0.0, 0.25, 0.5, 3 ?
19-12	19-13 ← To p. 125

(1) interval (2) ratio	Experiment 3. In record A, there are (1) ____ responses between reinforcements, and in record B, there are (2) ____ responses between reinforcements.
19-19	19-20 ← To p. 125

variable	A pause after reinforcement occurs under fixed-interval schedules but not under (1) ____-interval schedules. Similarly, we expect *no* consistent pauses after reinforcement with a(n) (2) ____-ratio schedule.
19-26	19-27 ← To p. 125

fixed (-) ratio	On a fixed-interval schedule of reinforcement, there is a(n) (1) ____ after reinforcement, responding then resumes and is (2) ____-ly ____ until it reaches a terminal steady rate before the next reinforcement.
19-33	19-34 ← To p. 125

73,000	Responses maintained by intermittent reinforcement are ____ resistant to extinction than responses maintained by continuous reinforcement.
19-40	19-41 ← To p. 125

resistant	End of Set
19-47	

(1) negative (2) aversive 32-5	Before a positive reinforcer, such as food, can be used effectively, we must arrange an appropriate state of (1) ____. Similarly, before termination of a shock can reinforce a response, we must first (2) ____ the shock. 32-6
escape 32-11	A stimulus which reinforces behavior which terminates it, is called a(n) (1) ____ ____ or a(n) (2) ____ ____ . 32-12
(1) negative reinforcer (aversive stimulus) (2) is not (cannot be) 32-17	In avoidance behavior, a response is emitted before the aversive stimulus occurs and the response delays or prevents the stimulus. A dog which learns to jump out of an experimental compartment before shock is presented, shows ____ behavior. 32-18
unconditioned 32-23	Shock is a(n) (1) ____ ____ stimulus. When a light is paired several times with shock, the light becomes a(n) (2) ____ ____ stimulus. 32-24
termination (elimination) 32-29	The reinforcement for an *avoidance* response is the termination of a(n) (1) ____ aversive stimulus. In successful avoidance, the (2) ____ aversive stimulus is not presented. 32-30
unconditioned aversive conditioned aversive 32-35	Presentation of an aversive stimulus not only provides an opportunity to reinforce by removing it but elicits the many ____ of the activation syndrome. 32-36

Set 20

Schedules of Reinforcement: Summary and Review

Estimated time: 11 minutes

Turn to next page and begin ▶

---

ratio

20-4

Generally, interval schedules generate a(n) ____ rate than ratio schedules.

20-5

---

resistant to extinction

20-9

Once a response has been conditioned, it can be made very * * * by intermittent reinforcement.

20-10

---

slowly

20-14

A salesman may make a sale to one out of every 30 contacts *on the average.* Sales occur on a(n)____ -ratio schedule.

20-15

(variable–ratio)

20-19

A moderate rate of responding *without* long pauses is produced by ____ -interval schedules.

20-20

---

pause

20-24

The student who finishes one term paper may find it difficult to start another assignment. "Difficulty in starting" seems analogous to the ____ after re-inforcement when reinforcements are never close together.

20-25

---

resistance to extinction (persistence)

20-29

When a husband who has *always* been responsive to his wife's affectionate advances suddenly grows indifferent, his wife's efforts to be affectionate may____ more quickly than if he had occasionally been indifferent in the past.

20-30

(1) reinforced (2) reinforced **31-3**	Deprivation of food ____ the probability of emission of a whole class of operants which have in the past been reinforced with food. ← To p. 213 **31-4**
incompatible **31-8**	The reflexes comprising the activation syndrome occur together in many different emotions, such as anger, fear, or rage. Therefore we * * * define any one specific emotion by listing the reflexes involved. ← To p. 213 **31-9**
are not **31-13**	In most cases of fear and anger, any response which terminates the exciting condition will increase in frequency. Reinforcement by terminating a stimulus is called ____ ____ . ← To p. 213 **31-14**
elicits **31-18**	Physical restraint, an unconditioned emotional stimulus for an infant, elicits the ____ behavior of the activation syndrome, and provides for the reinforcement for any operant behavior which removes the restraint. ← To p. 213 **31-19**
adaptation **31-23**	When a neutral stimulus is paired with an unconditioned emotional stimulus, the neutral stimulus becomes a(n) ____ ____ capable of eliciting the respondents. ← To p. 213 **31-24**
emotional **31-28**	When we fail to receive an accustomed reinforcement, we say that we are *frustrated*. We are reporting an emotional state produced by * * * a usual reinforcement. ← To p. 213 **31-29**

A response is maintained by continuous reinforcement when _____ response is reinforced.

20-1

---

ower
(slower,
lesser)

20-5

The most rapid extinction occurs after _____ reinforcement.

20-6

---

esistant to
extinction
(persistent)

20-10

Affection, attention, and approval sometimes serve as generalized reinforcers. They furnish such subtle stimuli that they sometimes go unnoticed. When they are unnoticed, they * * * likely to serve as reinforcers.

20-11

---

variable

20-15

Salesmen are often on a variable-ratio schedule because sales often depend on the (1) _____ of contacts made and because it (2) * * * predicta__ that any given contact will result in a sale

---

variable

20-20

A long pause after reinforcement, followed by a *gradual* acceleration, is generated by a(n) _____ - _____ schedule.

20-21

---

ause

20-25

A radar observer searching for unidentified planes must emit "looking behavior." This is reinforced by seeing a plane. Since planes appear at irregular *times,* his looking is on a(n) _____ - _____ schedule.

20-26

---

extinguish

20-30

When a cigarette lighter which has worked *very consistently* suddenly fails to light, we stop trying to light it after a few attempts. This is an example of rapid (1) _____ of a response maintained on (2) _____ reinforcement.

20-31

| class (group, set of) | A *hungry* animal can be (1) ____ with food; a *frightened* animal can be (2) ____ by termination of the threatening condition. |
| 31-2 | 31-3 |

| reinforced | Even when deprived of food, an *anxious* person may not eat. The responses which increase in probability during *anxiety* are ____ with eating. |
| 31-7 | 31-8 |

| operant | The scientist must, in each case, discover the operations which change the frequency of a class of responses. The emotions, fear, anger, etc., * * * in themselves causes of behavior. |
| 31-12 | 31-13 |

| adaptation | Physical restraint is an unconditioned emotional stimulus for infants; thus it ____ the reflex responses of the activation syndrome. |
| 31-17 | 31-18 |

| adaptation | When a manufacturer designs an elevator to descend at a rate of acceleration which is not disturbing to most adults but frightens children or inexperienced adults, he is counting on the process of ____ to an unconditioned stimulus. |
| 31-22 | 31-23 |

| activation syndrome | Some conditions defined by their effects on operant behavior also have emotional effects. Taking candy, a reinforcer, from a baby has a(n) ____ effect (anger, rage, etc.). |
| 31-27 | 31-28 |

| emotional | **End of Set** |
| 31-32 | |

every (each) 20-1	Reinforcement continues to be important after behavior has been acquired. Certain schedules of reinforcement continue to have an effect in _____ behavior in strength. 20-2
continuous 20-6	To generate persistent and stable behavior, we shift from continuous to _____ reinforcement by gradually increasing the size of interval or ratio. 20-7
are not 20-11	Because affection, attention, and approval are often unnoticed by the recipient, behavior reinforced by them tends to be _____-ly reinforced. 20-12
1) number 2) is not 20-16	The legendary perseverance of salesmen may illustrate the resistance to extinction created by _____ _____ schedules. 20-17
ixed(-)interval 20-21	Industrial piecework pay is an example of a(n) _____ - _____ schedule. 20-22
ariable(-) nterval 20-26	The radar observer may stop "looking" if the average time between planes is too great, that is, his looking behavior * * * if not occasionally reinforced. 20-27
1) extinction 2) continuous 20-31	When an unreliable cigarette lighter lights after five tries *on the average*, the behavior of trying to light it is reinforced on a(n) _____ - _____ schedule. 20-32

predisposed 31-1	Deprivational conditions alter the probability of a whole class of responses. Similarly, emotional conditions alter the probability of a whole * * * of responses. 31-2
(1) more (2) less 31-6	We ourselves are ____ by reinforcing a person we are "in love with." 31-7
predisposed (more likely) 31-11	The layman can fairly accurately identify states of fear, anger, etc., not from reflex behavior but from changes which act upon the environment. Individual emotions are identified by ____ behavior. 31-12
unconditioned 31-16	A pigeon placed in an experimental box for the first time shows much conditioned or unconditioned emotional behavior. Before attempting to condition a response, we allow time for ____. 31-17
unconditioned stimulus 31-21	A jet pilot eventually reacts unemotionally to zero g. This illustrates that an *un*conditioned emotional reflex eventually undergoes ____. 31-22
conditioning 31-26	After words like "bad" and "wrong" have frequently accompanied punishment, they will elicit the group of respondents comprising the ____ ____. 31-27
(1) emotional (2) reinforced 31-31	When a response has been consistently reinforced in the past and reinforcement is then suddenly discontinued, *emotion* may result. Rapid pulling of the lever on a candy machine which is out of order may have one such ____ effect. 31-32

maintaining 20-2	Availability of reinforcement depends on the passage of time in ____ schedules. 20-3
intermittent 20-7	In the early conditioning of a response, reinforcement must be rather frequent (preferably continuous); if this is not the case, the response may be ____ before the next reinforcement is due. 20-8
intermittent(-ly) 20-12	Very persistent behavior is produced by intermittent reinforcement, i.e., considerable ____ to extinction is generated. 20-13
variable-ratio 20-17	Pathological gambling illustrates the high rate of responding produced by ____ ____ schedules. 20-18
fixed(-)ratio 20-22	Unless complicated by other working conditions, industrial piecework pay generates a ____ and uniform rate of working except perhaps for some pausing after completing a unit. 20-23
s extinguished 20-27	On a variable-interval schedule, the longer the average interval, the lower the rate. Thus, the radar observer in an area with many planes will show a(n) ____ rate of "looking" than one in an area with few planes. 20-28
variable(-)ratio 20-32	Which cigarette lighter do we stop trying to light after fewer trials: (a) one which has always worked to date, or (b) one which has generally worked after a few trials? 20-33

▷

An animal deprived of food is predisposed to emit behavior previously reinforced with food. A *frightened* animal is ____ to emit behavior previously reinforced by terminating the *frightening* situation.

31-1

---

increases

31-5

When *angry*, we are (1)____ likely to strike a person and (2)____ likely to reinforce him positively.

31-6

---

can (do)

31-10

Predispositions characterize a particular emotion. An *angry* man may pound the table, slam the door, or pick a fight. The angry man is ____ to emit certain operants rather than others.

31-11

---

reinforced
(reinforcing)

31-15

Since "unfamiliar" implies no previous conditioning, we treat the resulting reflexes as ____ reflexes.

31-16

---

adapted

31-20

"Falling" is an emotional stimulus for the very young infant. A marked "reduction in gravity" (i.e., the value of *g*) is a(n) ____ ____ which elicits many reflex responses of the activation syndrome.

31-21

---

conditioning

31-25

Words like "bad" and "wrong" frequently accompany punishment. Therefore, through ____, the words came to elicit the respondents of the activation syndrome.

31-26

---

emotional

31-30

Finding no cigarettes in the house when the stores are closed can result in a(n) (1)____ state because responses such as looking in pockets, cigarette boxes, etc., are not (2)____ by the discovery of cigarettes.

31-31

interval	Availability of reinforcement depends on the number of responses in ____ schedules.
20-3	20-4 ← To p. 132
extinguished	Intermittent reinforcement can make behavior very persistent, i.e., very ____ to ____. (TT)
20-8	20-9 ← To p. 132
resistance	Responses reinforced by the generalized reinforcers of affection, approval, etc., often are extinguished very ____ because the subtlety of the stimuli has made the schedule intermittent.
20-13	20-14 ← To p. 132
variable-ratio	The highest rate of responding is generated by which class of schedules? (a) variable-interval; (b) fixed-interval; (c) variable-ratio; (d) continuous reinforcement.
20-18	20-19 ← To p. 132
high (rapid)	If the unit of work paid for on piece rate is large, there may be a(n) ____ after completing a unit.
20-23	20-24 ← To p. 132
higher	When a husband is sometimes responsive but sometimes indifferent, his wife may continue to make affectionate advances during a long period when he is indifferent. Her behavior shows strong * * * because it is maintained by intermittent reinforcement.
20-28	20-29 ← To p. 132
(a)	**End of Set**
20-33	

Set 31

Predispositions in Emotion

Estimated time: 15 minutes   **Turn to next page and begin** ▶

---

increases

31-4

Presenting a painful stimulus _____ the probability of emission of a whole class of operants which have been reinforced in the past by reduction of painful stimulation.

31-5

---

cannot
(do not)

31-9

Under different emotional conditions, different events serve as reinforcers, and different groups of operants increase in probability of emission. By these *predispositions* we * * * define a specific emotion.

31-10

---

negative
reinforcement

31-14

Highly unfamiliar surroundings may function as an emotional situation. Escape from these surroundings will be _____. (TT)

31-15

---

reflex
(respondent)

31-19

With time, the Indian papoose becomes _____ (TT) to physical restraint and no longer shows the unconditioned emotional behavior in response to it.

31-20

---

conditioned
stimulus

31-24

An unlimited range of stimuli can become "emotional" through the process of _____.

31-25

---

not receiving
(lacking, loss of)

31-29

Emotional states may occur when an accustomed reinforcer is not received. In the early stages of extinction after continuous reinforcement, we expect to find a(n) _____ effect.

31-30

PHASE 1.

A hungry pigeon was conditioned to peck the key in the usual way. The behavior was maintained in short daily sessions for four weeks by reinforcing every 25th response. During this time, the key was illuminated by a red or a green light. The key changed color after each reinforcement. Figure 1 is the cumulative record for the last session on the procedure. Hatch marks indicate reinforcement.

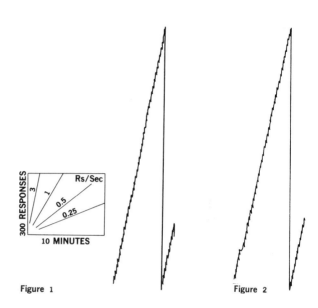

Figure 1

Figure 2

PHASE 2.

When the key was red, a reinforcement followed every 25th response as before. However, after each reinforcement the key turned green for 2 minutes during which *no* response was reinforced. After 2 minutes the key again turned red, and the 25th response was reinforced. The key then turned green, etc.

The behavior was recorded for alternate periods of red and green lights on two cumulative recorders. Figure 2 is the cumulative record of responses made to the red key. The paper moved only while the key was red. Hatch marks indicate reinforcements.

Figure 3 is the cumulative record of responses to the green key only during 2-minute periods alternating with the red periods of Figure 2. Responses to the green light were not reinforced; the hatch marks on this record indicate when the key was red (this recorder being stopped until the pigeon emitted 25 responses recorded in Figure 2).

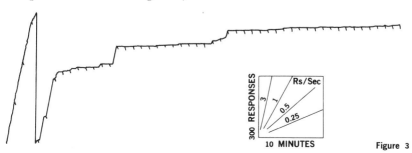

Figure 3

Part of the activation syndrome supplies needed
oxygen. Inhalation quickens, and the bronchioles
in the lungs dilate. These reflexes * * * involved
in the emotions of fear or anger.

← To p. 208 30-4

In the activation syndrome, certain reflexes increase the flow of oxygen and sugar to striate
muscles. The heart rate _____ .

← To p. 208 30-9

One way to detect the activation syndrome is to
record the GSR. One of the reflexes in the activation syndrome (sweating) (1) _____ the electrical
resistance of the skin. This response is called
the (2) _____ _____ response.

← To p. 208 30-14

In the activation syndrome, electrical skin resist-
ances (1) _____ , blood-sugar level (2) _____ , oxygen
in the blood (3) _____ , and pupils (4) _____ .

30-19
← To p. 208

The activation syndrome occurs in certain emotions, but it also occurs when there is great _____
without emotion.

30-24
← To p. 208

Doctors often advise patients with heart trouble,
high blood pressure, or stomach ulcers to avoid
exertion and emotional situations. The visceral
effects would be especially _____ in such cases.

30-29
← To p. 208

Set 21

Stimulus Discrimination

Estimated time: 35 minutes

See exhibit on preceding page

Turn to next page and begin ▶

---

1) red
2) reinforced

21-10

In Phase 2, after a response has been reinforced, the key turns green and _____ responses are reinforced.

21-11

---

as (is)

21-21

Figure 3. After the first three S^Δ periods (6 minutes of S^Δ), responding became more irregular and, by the eighth period in S^Δ, the rate was much _____ than before.

21-22

---

xtinguished

21-32

A conditioned operant may continue to be reinforced in the presence of a certain tone. Responding in the presence of that tone * * * maintained by the continued reinforcement.

21-33

---

ultiple

21-43

Behavior comes under _____ _____ in a multiple schedule.

21-44

---

iree

21-54

In conditioning a respondent, a response occurs but nothing is contingent upon it. One need only _____ a neutral stimulus with an unconditioned stimulus.

21-55

) $(S)^D$
:) $(S)^\Delta$

21-65

When an employee wishes to leave work early, his employer, if smiling, is more likely to say "yes." The smile functions as a(n) (1) _____ since it is then that the response of asking to leave early may be (2) _____. (TT)

21-66

The term *activation syndrome* describes the effect of a large group of responses which are elicited together by certain stimuli (e.g., painful stimuli). The _____ _____ is characteristic of the emotions of fear and anger.

30-3

---

1) activation
   syndrome
2) respondents
   (reflex
   responses)

30-7

In the activation syndrome, inhalation (1) _____, bronchioles (2) _____, and adrenalin is (3) _____.

30-8

---

1) cease
   (decrease)
2) cease
   (decrease)

30-12

As part of the activation syndrome, a painful stimulus elicits perspiration which_____ the electrical resistance of the skin (the galvanic skin response or GSR).

30-13

---

ctivation
yndrome

30-17

In "emotional states," (1) _____ respondents occur together in what is technically called the (2) * * *.

30-18

---

ctivation
yndrome

30-22

While the activation syndrome always occurs in fear, anger, anxiety, etc., it also occurs as the result of heavy work in the absence of emotion. Hence, the activation syndrome * * * necessarily imply emotion.

30-23

---

1) useful
2) useless
   (even
   harmful)

30-27

Psychosomatic disorders are, in part, attributable to the activation syndrome in prolonged anxiety. The activation syndrome is not only often useless; in the case of psychosomatic disorders it is_____.

30-28

During Phase 1, the behavior was maintained by a(n) * * * schedule of reinforcement.

21-1

---

no

21-11

When a certain stimulus is the occasion upon which responses are followed by reinforcement, the stimulus is called a *discriminative stimulus* (S^D). In Phase 2, the red light is a(n) * * * for pecking the key.

21-12

---

lower
(slower)

21-22

Responses are never reinforced in the presence of S^Δ. Withholding reinforcement results in _____ of a response.

21-23

---

is (will be)

21-33

If a response is reinforced when a tone has a high pitch but not when the tone has a low pitch, the high pitch becomes an (1) S_____ and the low pitch an (2) S_____.

21-34

---

stimulus
control

21-44

In a "multiple variable-interval extinction schedule," responses are reinforced on a variable-interval schedule during one stimulus and * * * during another stimulus.

21-45

---

pair

21-55

In contrast with the development of stimulus control in respondent behavior, a discriminative operant requires a(n) _____ - _____ contingency.

21-56

---

(1) S^D
(2) reinforced

21-66

The girl whose facial expressions make her look "approachable" instead of "aloof" is more likely to be asked for a date. She may assume an "approachable" expression to exert stimulus _____ (TT) over a young man's behavior.

21-67

Page 139

elicits 30-1	Most of the responses elicited in fear and anger activate the organism in the sense that they increase its capacity for physical exertion. This "activation syndrome" is important for an organism's ____ in a highly primitive environment. 30-2
adrenalin 30-6	In the so-called (1) ____ ____, the blood is richly supplied with both sugar and oxygen. The mechanisms responsible are members of a group of (2) ____ characteristic of some emotions. 30-7
cease (stop, decrease) 30-11	In the activation syndrome, activity of the smooth muscles of the intestines (1) ____; similarly, salivation and other gastric secretions (2) ____. 30-12
dilation 30-16	In certain emotions, many respondents are active together in what is called the * * *. 30-17
is not 30-21	A prominent characteristic of organisms in situations we call "emotional" is the presence of the ____ ____. 30-22
lacks (has no, is not of, has lost its) 30-26	For a person about to run a race, the activation syndrome would be biologically (1) ____ while for the executive working at a desk, the activation syndrome would be biologically (2) ____. 30-27
together (at once) 30-31	Many different emotions involve the activation syndrome. For this reason, early attempts to distinguish between emotions on the basis of the reflexes involved * * * successful. 30-32

fixed-ratio 21-1	Figure 1. Twenty-five responses per reinforcement is a relatively small ratio. Figure 1 shows a(n) (1) ____ (and relatively constant) rate of responding and few, if any, (2) ____ after reinforcement. 21-2
S^D (discriminative stimulus) 21-12	An S^Δ (S-delta) is a stimulus which is consistently present when responses are *not* reinforced.　In Phase 2, the (1) ____ light is the S^Δ, and the (2) ____ light is the S^D. 21-13
extinction 21-23	In Figure 3, responding in the presence of the (1) ____ undergoes nearly complete (2) ____ before the end of the session under discrimination procedure. 21-24
(1) $(S)^D$ (2) $(S)^\Delta$ 21-34	If a response is frequently reinforced when a high-pitched tone is present but not when a low-pitched tone is present, a(n) ____ -tion develops (in any organism capable of distinguishing pitches). 21-35
not reinforced (extinguished) 21-45	Discrimination is a special case of stimulus control.　When a response has been extinguished in the presence of one stimulus and maintained in the presence of another, a(n) ____ has been developed. 21-46
three(-)term [three(-)number] 21-56	In operant discrimination, a response (1) ____ in the presence of (2) S____ is likely to be reinforced, while a response (3) ____ in the presence of (4) S____ will not be reinforced. 21-57
control 21-67	When an infant says "da-da," the response may be especially well-reinforced when the father is present. The visual pattern provided by the father becomes a(n) (1) ____; all other visual patterns become (2) S____ for emitting "da-da." 21-68

A painful or *frightening* stimulus _____ many responses as part of the respondent behavior seen in the emotions of fear or anger.

30-1

---

adrenalin

30-5

In fear or anger, the quantity of sugar in the blood increases because_____is secreted by the adrenal gland, which in turn acts upon the liver.

30-6

---

(1) sugar (and)
    oxygen
(2) higher
    (increased)

30-10

In the activation syndrome, there is cessation of activity of the smooth muscles of the viscera. Stomach contractions _____.

30-11

---

more

30-15

The activation syndrome includes _____ of the pupil.

30-16

---

is

30-20

The activation syndrome * * * biologically useful when no unusual activity is required.

30-21

---

activation
syndrome

30-25

In civilized cultures, persons seldom engage in physical attack when angry, or run when afraid. Although the activation syndrome is present, it probably * * * biological usefulness.

30-26

---

cease

30-30

The activation syndrome consists of a large number of reflex responses which are all elicited _____ in a single pattern.

30-31

(1) high (2) pauses 21-2	The experimental conditions in effect when the data in Figure 1 were collected differ from the ordinary fixed ratio in one respect, the color of the key (1) _____ after (2) _____ reinforcement. 21-3
(1) green (2) red 21-13	In Phase 2, two recorders were used. The recorder producing Figure 2 operated only under S^D, and the other (producing Figure 3) only under S^Δ. While one recorder was running, the other * * *. 21-14
(1) S^Δ (green light) (2) extinction 21-24	Phase 2. After each 2-minute period of S^Δ, there is a period of (1) S_____ during which the pigeon emits 25 responses, and the 25th response is (2) _____. 21-25
:rimina(-tion) 21-35	When an operant response is emitted in the presence of an S^D and not in the presence of an S^Δ, a(n) _____ has developed. 21-36
discrimination 21-46	When responses occur in the presence of one stimulus and not in the presence of another, a(n) (1) _____ has been formed; the response is under (2) _____ _____. 21-47
(1) emitted (2) $(S)^D$ (3) emitted (4) $(S)^\Delta$ 21-57	The stimulus control of an operant differs from that of a respondent. The action of a stimulus in producing a response is called "elicitation" only in the case of _____ behavior. 21-58
(1) S^D (2) $(S)^\Delta s$ 21-68	In a discriminative operant, the S^D sets the occasion upon which a response may be _____ if emitted. 21-69

are

30-4

In the activation syndrome, the hormone called *adrenalin* releases sugar into the blood from the liver. In fear or anger, secretion of _____ is elicited from the adrenal gland.

30-5

---

increases

30-9

In the activation syndrome, the blood is richly supplied with (1) _____ and _____ which are carried to muscle tissue more quickly by the (2) _____ pulse rate.

30-10

---

(1) decrease
   (lowers)
(2) galvanic
   skin

30-14

In strong emotion the eyes bulge slightly, and the pupils dilate (enlarge). These respondents allow _____ light to enter the eye.

30-15

---

(1) decrease
(2) increases
(3) increases
(4) dilate

30-19

The activation syndrome * * * biologically useful if great physical exertion is required (as in running or fighting).

30-20

---

exertion
(work, energy
expended)

30-24

In moments of crisis, people have been known to do herculean feats such as lifting the front of an automobile. Such extreme effort is possible, in part, because of the _____ _____.

30-25

---

harmful
(dangerous)

30-29

Strong emotional responses after a heavy meal may be harmful because, in the activation syndrome, gastric secretions cease, and contractions of the stomach and intestines _____.

30-30

(1) changed (changes) (2) each (every) 21-3	In Phase 1 of the experiment, the color of the key alternated between (1) _____ and _____, changing after (2) * * *. 21-4
was not 21-14	In Phase 2, Figure 2 shows responses which occurred during those parts of the session in which the fixed ratio was in effect. Responses in the presence of S^D were recorded in Figure _____. 21-15
(1) $(S)^D$ (2) reinforced 21-25	Phase 2. Toward the end of the session, stimulus control has been established since responding during S^Δ occurs at a(n) (1) _____ rate while responding in S^D occurs at a(n) (2) _____ rate. 21-26
discrimination 21-36	Discrimination is a special case of stimulus control. When two different response rates occur in the presence of different stimuli, the response is under * * *. 21-37
discrimination stimulus control 21-47	Stimulus control is developed when some _____ schedule is in effect. 21-48
respondent 21-58	A respondent is (1) _____-ed by its stimulus, but in a discriminative operant the S^D is simply the occasion upon which a response will be reinforced if (2) _____-ed. 21-59
reinforced 21-69	The presence of the father, as a discriminative stimulus or S^D, is the (1) _____ upon which the child's saying "da-da" is (2) _____ if emitted. 21-70

(1) interval (2) ratio Set 18 **29-3**	The frequency with which a normal organism eats, given free access to food, changes in ____. **29-4** ← To p. 203
(1) lower (2) higher Set 22 **29-8**	A response occurring immediately after a reinforcement is never reinforced on a(n) (1) ____-interval schedule. A response immediately after reinforcement is sometimes reinforced on a(n) (2) ____-interval schedule. **29-9** ← To p. 203
cyclic (periodic, cyclical) Set 28 **29-13**	Objects at two adjacent points in space usually control reaching responses of only slightly different ____. **29-14** ← To p. 203

(1) reinforce
(2) extinguish
  (do not
  reinforce)
Set 24   **29-18**
	When a response is under the control of a single property of a stimulus (which cannot exist alone), we call it a(n) * * *.
	
	29-19
	← To p. 203

less probable (less frequent) Set 26 **29-23**	In drawing a copy of a picture, only those movements which produce a likeness are reinforced; thus reinforcement is ____. **29-24** ← To p. 203
reinforced (maintained) not reinforced (extinguished) (EITHER ORDER) Set 21 **29-28**	**End of Set**

red (and) green
each
reinforcement
(25 responses)

21-4

In Figure 1, the hatch marks, or pips, indicate responses which were _____.

21-5

2

21-15

The rates of responding are nearly the same in Figure 1 and Figure 2. Responding continues to be maintained at full strength in the presence of the _____ stimulus. (TT)

21-16

---

(1) low (perhaps zero)
(2) high

21-26

By the end of the first session in Phase 2, key pecking is under stimulus control since changing the key-color from green (S^Δ) to red (S^D) immediately _____ the rate of responding.

21-27

---

stimulus control

21-37

A key is illuminated by a yellow light during fixed-interval reinforcement and a blue light during variable-interval reinforcement, and a pigeon performs appropriately under each schedule. This is an example of * * *.

21-38

---

multiple

21-48

A discrimination procedure is essentially a(n) _____ _____ in which one schedule is extinction.

21-49

---

(1) elicit(-ed)
(2) emitt(-ed)

21-59

An S^D is the *occasion* upon which a given operant may be reinforced. The dinner bell, as an S^D, is the _____ upon which going to the table will be reinforced.

21-60

---

(1) occasion
(2) reinforced

21-70

When we read aloud, our vocalizations are under the control of a series of visual stimuli on the page. The printed characters are discriminative (1) _____, whereas the vocalizations are discriminative (2) _____.

21-71

Availability of reinforcement depends on the passage of time in (1) _____ schedules, and on the number of responses in (2) _____ schedules.

29-3

If a bright white light is often present when a response is reinforced, a light of medium intensity should produce a rate of responding (1) _____ than that of the bright light and (2) _____ than that of a very faint light.

29-8

Eating, drinking, sexual behavior, sleeping, and general activity all show _____ changes when the various conditions of deprivation are not manipulated experimentally.

29-13

In teaching a child to copy a line, we do not wait for a perfect drawing. We (1) * * * movements which produce lines fairly similar to the copy, but (2) * * * movements which produce lines very different from the copy.

29-18

The more food an animal has just eaten, the _____ _____ its ingestive behavior.

29-23

In establishing a discrimination, a response is * * * in the presence of one stimulus and * * * in the presence of another stimulus.

29-28

---

einforced

21-5

If the red and green key-colors controlled different rates of responding, the _____ of the record would change after each reinforcement.

21-6

---

liscriminative

21-16

Phase 2, Figure 3 shows responses which occurred while the key was green and no responses were reinforced. Responses in the presence of S_____ are recorded in Figure 3.

21-17

---

ncreases
raises)
acceptable:
;hanges)

21-27

At the end of the period shown in Figures 2 and 3, response rates are quite different for S^D and S^Δ. This is a form of stimulus _____ called discrimination.

21-28

---

stimulus
control

21-38

Immediately after reinforcement, a yellow key-light is turned on for 10 minutes, and a 10-minute fixed-interval schedule is then in effect. A pigeon so reinforced will first (1) _____, then emit responses at a(n) (2) _____ _____ rate.

21-39

---

multiple
schedule

21-49

A very common case of discrimination is continuous reinforcement in the presence of one stimulus, and no reinforcement in the presence of another. The two components of this multiple schedule are (1) _____ reinforcement and (2) _____.

21-50

---

occasion

21-60

A whispered word of warning may be the occasion on which a man will run vigorously. In operant discrimination, the magnitude of a response is *not* necessarily dependent upon the _____ of the S^D.

21-61

---

(1) stimuli
(2) responses
(operants)

21-71

A child learning to read is told he is "right" when the correct vocal pattern occurs in the presence of a certain visual pattern. In describing the development of his (1) _____-tive response, we must specify (2) _____ terms. (HOW MANY?)

21-72

◗ discriminations ◗ generalization Set 22 **29-1**	Properly steering an automobile requires that the organism have a(n) _____ repertoire. **29-2**
◗ class (set, group, category, range) ◗ class (set, group, category, range) Set 26 **29-6**	Each stimulus in a chain has the dual function of (1) _____ the response it follows and being a(n) (2) _____ for the response it precedes. **29-7**
is not Set 27 **29-11**	Responses reinforced by the generalized reinforcers of affection, approval, etc., are often extinguished very (1) _____ because reinforcement has occurred (2) _____ due to the subtlety of the stimuli. **29-12**
generalization (stimulus generalization) Set 22 **29-16**	When paired with several unconditioned reinforcers appropriate to various deprivations, a conditioned reinforcer will be effective under several types of (1) _____. Such a reinforcer is called a(n) (2) _____ reinforcer. **29-17**
resistant Set 20 **29-21**	(1) _____ fixed-interval (2) _____ variable-interval (3) _____ fixed-ratio (4) _____ variable-ratio a b c d **29-22**
food deprivation Set 28 **29-26**	Skill in "drawing from copy" will continue to be shaped without help from other persons once "likeness" has become a reinforcer, since this will automatically provide the _____ reinforcement needed for shaping. **29-27**

slope 21-6	When the rate or form of a response is different under different stimuli, the behavior is said to be under stimulus control. Figure 1 presents *no* evidence for ____ ____ by either the red or green light. 21-7
$(S)^\Delta$ [(S) delta] 21-17	Figure 3 uses hatch marks to indicate when the S____ ended and the recorder stopped. 21-18
control 21-28	An organism is said to have developed a discrimination when responding is maintained in the presence of (1) ____ (TT), and has undergone some degree of extinction in the presence of (2) ____. (TT) 21-29
(1) pause (2) positively accelerated 21-39	Immediately after reinforcement, the key-light changes to blue and a *short* fixed ratio is in effect. The experienced pigeon will respond at a(n) ____ rate (perhaps without an initial pause). 21-40
(1) continuous (2) extinction 21-50	An operant discrimination is established with a *three-term* contingency. Reinforcement is arranged in this order: (a) present an S^D, (b) wait for the response to be emitted, and (c) provide ____. 21-51
intensity (magnitude) 21-61	Response magnitude depends upon the stimulus intensity in the case of (1) ____ behavior, but much less so in the case of (2) ____ behavior. 21-62
discrimina(-tive) three 21-72	In operant discrimination, a response is likely to be reinforced when the (1) ____ is present, but not when the (2) ____ is present. 21-73

Page 145

▷

The professional winetaster can make very fine (1) _____. He shows little (2) _____ among various wines.

29-1

---

generalized

Set 27   29-5

For most states of deprivation, there are alternative procedures which belong to the same (1) _____ since they have similar effects on a whole (2) _____ of responses.

29-6

---

chain

Set 23   29-10

A high rate of responding * * * in itself evidence for inferring a high level of deprivation without knowledge of other factors such as the reinforcement schedule.

29-11

---

(1) respondent
    (reflex)
(2) operant

Set 21   29-15

An organism may emit the same response to two fairly similar stimuli when only one of them has been present during reinforcement. The term for this phenomenon is * * *.

29-16

---

(1) water
    deprivation
(2) reinforced

Set 26   29-20

Intermittently reinforcing temper tantrums makes them very _____ to extinction.

29-21

---

(1) S^D (stimulus)
(2) response
(3) reinforce

Set 21   29-25

In the laboratory, an animal's weight expressed as a percentage of its normal weight is used as a measure of its history of _____ _____.

29-26

---

stimulus control 21-7	In Phase 1, Figure 1, there is no evidence for stimulus control because the rate of responding is * * * for the red and green key-colors. 21-8
$(S)^\Delta$ 21-18	Responses in the presence of S^Δ are never (1) ____. The responses recorded in Figure 3 (2) * * * reinforced. 21-19
(1) S^D (2) S^Δ 21-29	The exhibit experiment demonstrates a procedure for creating a form of *stimulus control* called ____-tion. 21-30
high 21-40	When the key-light is sometimes yellow and sometimes blue (and the schedule sometimes fixed-interval and sometimes fixed-ratio respectively), responding by an experienced pigeon * * * appropriate to the schedule in effect at any moment. 21-41
reinforcement 21-51	The S^D is the occasion upon which a response, if ____, is likely to be reinforced. 21-52
(1) respondent (2) operant 21-62	A whispered warning may be quickly followed by running. In operant discrimination, the time between stimulus and response is not necessarily dependent upon the ____ of the S^D. 21-63
(1) S^D (2) S^Δ 21-73	Bringing an operant under stimulus control involves three events: a(n) (1) ____ which is the occasion upon which a(n) (2) ____ will be followed by (3) ____. 21-74

cycles

Set 28   **29-4**

Independent of the specific deprivation state present at the moment, a(n) _____ reinforcer can be used to condition a new response.

29-5

---

(1) fixed
    (-interval)
(2) variable
    (-interval)
Set 19   **29-9**

The operant called "pressing a lever for food" is composed of many stages or parts integrated as a(n) _____ of stimuli and responses.

29-10

---

forms
(topographies)

Set 25   **29-14**

Response magnitude varies closely with stimulus intensity in the case of (1) _____ behavior, but much less so in the case of (2) _____ behavior.

29-15

---

abstraction

Set 22   **29-19**

Excessive sweating due to heavy work or emotion is similar to (1) _____ _____ in its effect on the class of responses which have been (2) _____ by water.

29-20

---

differential

Set 24   **29-24**

In operant discrimination we speak of a *three-term* contingency. Events are arranged in this order: (a) present the (1) _____, (b) wait for the (2) _____, and (c) (3) _____.

29-25

In Phase 2, a response is no longer reinforced when the key-light is (1) _____, but continues to be reinforced on a fixed ratio of 25 when the key-light is (2) _____.

21-9

In Figure 3, each hatch mark occurs _____ minutes apart.

21-20

In establishing a discrimination, a response is (1) * * * in the presence of one stimulus and (2) * * * in the presence of another stimulus.

21-31

When a performance is appropriate to one schedule during one stimulus and another schedule during a second stimulus, it is an example of _____ _____.

21-42

In operant discrimination, a(n) (1) _____ stimulus must precede the response, and a reinforcing stimulus must (2) _____ the response at least occasionally.

21-53

Latency varies as a function of stimulus intensity in (1) _____ behavior but only slightly so, if at all, in (2) _____ behavior.

21-64

In respondent behavior, the conditioned stimulus is said to (1) _____ the conditioned response. But in a discriminative operant, the S^D is merely the (2) _____ upon which a response may be reinforced.

21-75

← To p. 198

; (and) E EITHER ORDER) 28-3	The two mice (C and E) taking the longest times to obtain 720 pellets * * * normal in weight. 28-4 ← To p. 198
l) 1 2) slower (less) 28-8	The normal mice's repetitive pattern of high and low rates of eating is called a *feeding* cycle. Each ____ lasts 24 hours. 28-9 ← To p. 198
ycles 28-13	If an experimenter were not careful to control deprivation, the results of experiments on operant conditioning using a food reinforcer * * * confused by cyclical changes in rate as shown in C. 28-14 ← To p. 198
l) increase 2) cycles 28-18	The female of many species shows an oestrous cycle affecting sexual behavior. The probability of sexual behavior is ____ in some parts and ____ in other parts of the cycle. 28-19 ← To p. 198
) C :) A 28-23	Records A and B reach the 720 pellet level in much (1) ____ time than Records C and E although the rates at **a** and **b** are slightly (2) ____ than those found in Records A and B. 28-24 ← To p. 198
) A (and) B :) D 28-28	Of the three obese mice (A, B, and D), the one(s) providing Record(s) (1) * * * eat(s) rather steadily while the one(s) providing Record(s) (2) * * * eat(s) very frequent "meals" with short pauses between. 28-29 ← To p. 198

(1) green
(2) red

21-9

In Phase 2, the green and red lights still alternate; when the key turns (1) _____, the 25th response thereafter will be (2) _____.

21-10
← To p. 138

2

21-20

Figure 3. During the first 6 minutes of Phase 2, responding during S$^\Delta$ occurred at a rate which * * * close to the rate shown on the previous day in Figure 1.

21-21
← To p. 138

---

not reinforced
(extinguished)
reinforced
(conditioned,
maintained)
THER ORDER)21-31

If responses are not reinforced when a tone of a certain pitch is presented, responding in the presence of that tone is _____.

21-32
← To p. 138

---

stimulus
control

21-42

In a *multiple* schedule, two or more schedules are in effect and a different stimulus is present during each. A fixed-interval during a yellow light and a fixed-ratio during a blue light is a(n) _____ fixed-interval fixed-ratio schedule.

21-43
← To p. 138

---

discriminative
follow

21-53

The necessary conditions for establishing an operant discrimination are: a discriminative stimulus, a response, and a reinforcing stimulus. The contingency contains _____ (HOW MANY?) terms.

21-54
← To p. 138

---

(1) respondent
(2) operant

21-64

Nature provides many S^{D}s. In an orchard where only red apples are sweet, the "redness" of a ripe apple is an (1) S____; the color of an unripe apple is an (2) S____ for the response of picking and eating.

21-65
← To p. 138

---

(1) elicit
(2) occasion

21-75

End of Set

25	The mice taking the longest times to obtain 720 pellets are shown in Records ____ and ____.
28-2	28-3

5	Each day the mice of normal weight have (1) ____ period(s) of rapid continuous eating followed by a period of sporadic and, in general, much (2) * * * eating.
28-7	28-8

(1) less (2) fewer (3) increases	We conclude that when an organism is always able to obtain food, its frequency of eating goes through ____.
28-12	28-13

constant (stable, level)	Passage of time since the last period of sleep serves to (1) ____ the probability that the organism will sleep. Sleeping, like eating, goes through (2) ____.
28-17	28-18

deprivation (acceptable: satiation)	Records A and C differ. (1) ____ shows large-scale cycles whereas (2) ____ shows a nearly constant, high rate of responding for food.
28-22	28-23

(1) D (2) obese (overweight)	Of the three obese mice, Records (1) ____ and ____ look alike. A different kind of record for an obese mouse is shown in (2) ____.
28-27	28-28

Read exhibit now and refer to it as needed.

A stimulus present when a response is emitted and reinforced becomes a *discriminative stimulus* (S^D). In the future, the response is relatively likely to be emitted when this stimulus is present. Other stimuli having something in common with S^D are also effective, but produce a lower response frequency. The spread of controlling power to other stimuli is called stimulus *generalization*.

EXPERIMENT

Phase 1. A pigeon is placed in a standard experimental box. A yellowish-green light with a wavelength of 550 millimicrons is constantly projected on the key. The key-pecking response, shaped in the usual way, is reinforced on a variable-interval schedule, the average interval between reinforcements being 1 minute. This schedule generates a steady rate of responding and, more important here, a considerable resistance to extinction.

Phase 2. Reinforcement is discontinued, and during extinction the color of the light projected on the key is changed at short, regular intervals. Each of sixteen colors, 10 millimicrons apart, is presented many times in random order and for the same total time per color. The responses emitted by the pigeon in the presence of each wavelength (color) are counted and plotted in the figure on the right. The resulting function is called *stimulus generalization gradient*.

(1) 25 (2) fixed-ratio 28-1	The vertical scale gives the number of pellets obtained. If we were interested in the number of bar presses at any point on the scale, we would multiply by _____. 28-2
high (highest) 28-6	Record C covers about five days and shows _____ (HOW MANY?) periods of sustained high rate. 28-7
(1) satiated (2) lower (more gradual) 28-11	As the normal mouse becomes satiated with food, it responds (1) * * * frequently and obtains (2) * * * pellets. As additional time passes, food deprivation (3) _____. The *cycle* then repeats. 28-12
(1) deprived (2) food deprivation 28-16	In experiments which use food reinforcement for pigeons, the birds are fed at a particular time of day and fed just enough to keep weight constant (e.g., 80 per cent of normal). In this way, the deprivation level is held approximately _____. 28-17
cycles 28-21	The class of responses previously reinforced with food shows periodic changes in rate which resemble changes in the level of _____. 28-22
cycles (periods) 28-26	Extremely high rates alternating with short (1- or 2-hour) pauses are shown in Record (1) _____ which is a record made by a(n) (2) _____ mouse. 28-27

Set 22

PART VI Stimulus Control

Stimulus Generalization

See exhibit on preceding page

Estimated time: 32 minutes

Turn to next page and begin ▶

IO **22-10**	If all wavelengths had acquired equal control as a result of Phase 1, then in Phase 2 each new color would have produced approximately * * * number of responses as 550 millimicrons. **22-11**

---

1) was not 2) does (can, will) **22-21**	As the wavelength changes in either direction from the wavelength present during reinforcement, the number of responses _____. **22-22**

---

common **22-32**	The Morse code signal for the letter C (– · – ·) and the letter Y (– · – –) are often confused by the learner. The two stimulus patterns (1) * * * common elements and therefore show (2) _____. **22-33**

S^D **22-43**	In the behavioral development of a child, smiles mark occasions for reinforcement. The extent of the _____ (TT) among smiling and other facial expressions decreases as discriminations are developed. **22-44**

---

control **22-54**	Verbal discriminative stimuli are commonly established in formal education. "Columbus discovered America in . . ." is the S^D after which the response "1492" is _____ if emitted. **22-55**

---

do not occur (cannot exist) **22-65**	In developing an abstraction, we must use many different stimulus objects as "S^Ds"; each must have the property in question, but among them there must be a range of other _____. **22-66**

The mice emit (1) ____ responses for each pellet of food. This is a(n) (2) * * * schedule of reinforcement.

28-1

---

(1) less
(2) slope

28-5

The mice of normal weight (C and E) show cyclic changes in the rate of responding for (and eating) food. In the portions labeled **a** and **b** (in C), the rate is ____ and, for a time, relatively uniform.

28-6

---

cycles

28-10

In portions of Record C, as at **a** and **b**, the normal mouse obtains many pellets in a few hours. The mouse becomes (1) ____ with food, and this explains intervening portions of the curve having (2) ____ slopes.

28-11

---

deprived
(of food)

28-15

An animal loses weight when (1) ____ of food. The animal's resulting weight, expressed as a percentage of its normal weight, is a measure of its current level of (2) ____ ____.

28-16

---

cycle

28-20

The frequency of emission of food-getting responses by a normal organism which can always obtain food goes through ____.

28-21

---

ack
do not have,
ail to exhibit)

28-25

The steplike character of Record D represents relatively short ____ of eating and not eating.

28-26

---

ne

28-30

Because mice A and B have similar records, we can say that in terms of the behavioral data in the exhibit, ____ types of obesity are clearly distinguishable.

28-31

| | Phase 1. The pigeon is on a(n) (1) * * * (TT) schedule with an average interval of 1 minute. A response maintained on this schedule will be extinguished rather (2) _____ when reinforcement is discontinued. 22-1 |

| the same (an equal) 22-11 | If *all* wavelengths had acquired equal control while light of 550 millimicrons was being projected in Phase 1, the data for Phase 2 would be represented by a(n) _____ line. (diagonal, horizontal or vertical?) 22-12 |

| decreases 22-22 | The stimulus generalization cannot be said to be complete because at wavelengths different from 550 millimicrons a _____ number of responses were emitted. 22-23 |

| have (share) generalization 22-33 | A man who is afraid to curse his boss may curse his wife instead. This is sometimes called "displaced aggression." It might be interpreted as * * *. 22-34 |

| generalization 22-44 | The professional winetaster would show a very steep generalization _____ for each stimulus dimension along which wines vary. 22-45 |

| reinforced 22-55 | When faced with a new problem which has elements in common with an old one, we first try the old solution. This process is _____. 22-56 |

| properties (elements) 22-66 | Since isolated properties of objects do not occur in nature, an abstraction * * * be developed if only one object is used to provide the S^D. 22-67 |

Set 28

PART VII Deprivation

Feeding Cycles

Estimated time: 12 minutes

See exhibit on preceding page

Turn to next page and begin ▶

---

were
(are)

28-4

The fact that the obese mice ate 720 pellets in (1) _____ time than normal mice is shown by the steeper over-all (2) _____ of the records for the obese mice.

28-5

---

cycle

28-9

The rhythmic changes in ingestive behavior represented by Records C and E are called _____ of ingestive behavior.

28-10

---

would be
(might be)

28-14

When food is used as a reinforcer in the usual experiment, the organism is * * * before each experimental session.

28-15

---

high, low
(EITHER ORDER)

28-19

A rat confined in a small cage with continuous access to a running wheel alternated between active and inactive phases with considerable regularity. The rate shows an activity _____.

28-20

---

(1) less
    (shorter)
(2) higher

28-24

The mice which produced records A and B overeat. Although they do *not* eat at an especially high rate, they * * * the cycles of fast and slow eating shown by the normal mice.

28-25

---

(1) A and B
(2) D

28-29

The three obese mice look alike and cannot be distinguished by weight. Lacking the behavioral evidence, we might have concluded (erroneously) that only _____ type of obesity was involved.

28-30

(1) variable-interval (2) slowly 22-1	Phase 1. A light having a wavelength of 550 milli-microns is (1) * * * in color. During Phase 1, such a light is projected on the key at (2) _____ times. 22-2
horizontal 22-12	The wavelength which was present during conditioning was (1) _____ millimicrons. In Phase 2, the greatest number of responses was emitted when the light had a wavelength of (2) _____ millimicrons. 22-13
smaller 22-23	The gradual decline in number of responses as a function of distance from the stimulus present at reinforcement is called a *stimulus generalization gradient.* The figure shows the stimulus _____ _____ as a function of wavelengths. 22-24
generalization (stimulus generalization) 22-34	Generalization and discrimination are reciprocal processes. The professional winetaster can make very fine (1) _____. He shows little (2) _____ among various wines. 22-35
gradient 22-45	The sergeant says "Squad halt!" and all the men halt. Their behavior is under the _____ of a verbal stimulus. 22-46
generalization 22-56	The child reinforced for saying "red" when looking at a red book may call all books "red." This is an example of (1) _____. In part, it is due to the common (2) _____ of shape shared by books differing in color. 22-57
cannot 22-67	An abstract response is acquired only when some single stimulus property which cannot "stand alone" comes to control the response, and other _____ of the stimulus, which normally accompany the single property, have no control. 22-68

Page 152

A mouse was kept in a standard experimental box continuously for several days. After every 25th response (pressing a bar), a mechanism delivered a small pellet of food. (Water was continuously available.) The experiment was repeated with five different kinds of mice, as follows: (Letters refer to their cumulative records.)

(A) A mouse poisoned by goldthioglucose which damages part of the brain called the hypothalamus causing overeating and obesity.

(B) A mouse with surgical damage to the hypothalamus, with the same effects as mouse A.

(C) A normal mouse from a normal strain.

(D) An obese mouse from a strain some members of which suffer from hereditary obesity.

(E) A normal mouse from the same strain (mice E and D were litter mates).

(1) yellow- green (2) all 22-2	In Phase 2, the light with a wavelength of 550 millimicrons was not projected on the key at _____ times. 22-3
(1) 550 (2) 550 22-13	Phase 2. In the figure, the wavelength at which most responses were emitted is that which was present when the response was _____. 22-14
generalization gradient 22-24	A steeper gradient would indicate a less extensive (1) _____ _____, while a relatively flat gradient would indicate a (2) _____ extensive stimulus generalization. 22-25
discriminations generalization 22-35	When a child calls all furry animals "dog," it is a case of * * *. 22-36
control 22-46	The sergeant says "Squad halt!" and all the men halt. This verbal stimulus is a(n) _____ for halting. 22-47
generalization element 22-57	A child reinforced for saying "red" when looking at a red book might say "red" when shown a black book. This is, in part, due to the control acquired by the _____ _____ of shape. 22-58
properties (aspects, elements) 22-68	Nature seldom makes a single stimulus property the occasion for reinforcing a response; hence, an _____ is seldom developed unless a second organism arranges the appropriate contingencies for reinforcement. 22-69

chain

27-3

Pressing the bar is a part of a(n) (1) ____ of behavior which ends with ingestion of food. Food
deprivation (2) ____ the rate of emission of the
whole chain.

27-4
← To p. 192

(1) likely
    (more likely)
(2) likely
    (more likely)
27-8

After conditioning, a pigeon pecks a key and the
food magazine operates with an audible click which
is a(n) ____ ____ for pecking the key.

27-9
← To p. 192

deprivation

27-13

In the usual pigeon experiment, the click of the
food magazine has been followed only by food.
The click of the food magazine * * * a generalized
reinforcer.

27-14
← To p. 192

are

27-18

The frequency of responses conditioned by a generalized reinforcer is relatively independent of the
nature of the deprivation at the moment. The frequency of responses reinforced by money is usually
* * * of any specific deprivation.

27-19
← To p. 192

dependent
upon (not
independent of)
27-23

A variable-ratio schedule, as in a gambling device,
produces a steady and ____ rate of responding.
This is true even when the level of deprivation is
relatively low.

27-24
← To p. 192

satiating
(decreasing the
deprivation of)
27-28

The widespread existence of waterfront brothels
catering to sailors is a result of ____ ____ involved in life at sea.

27-29
← To p. 192

deprivation

27-33

End of Set

all 22-3	In Phase 2, reinforcement _____ occurs. 22-4
reinforced (conditioned) 22-14	At wavelengths other than 550 millimicrons, the number of responses in a constant period of time is _____ than at 550 millimicrons. 22-15
stimulus generalization more 22-25	The control exerted by a continuous series of stimuli, similar in some respect to a stimulus present during reinforcement, is shown by a stimulus _____ _____, such as that in the figure. 22-26
ıeralization imulus ıeralization) 22-36	When a child emits the word "dog" only in response to dogs, a(n) _____ has been formed. 22-37
s^D 22-47	The verbal stimulus "9 times 9" is a(n) _____ controlling the verbal response "81." 22-48
common element 22-58	The child who first calls all books "red" soon calls only red books "red." When he is not reinforced for saying "red" to books of other colors, books of other colors come to provide S_____ for the response of saying "red." 22-59
abstraction 22-69	The verbal community * * * which single stimulus property will be the occasion for reinforcing a child's abstract verbal response. 22-70

1) conditioned (secondary) 2) deprived (of) food **27-2**	A food-deprived rat presses a bar, a feeding mechanism clicks, the rat bends down, seizes food, and eats it. This sequence of stimuli and responses forms a(n) _____ from pressing to eating. **27-3**
chain **27-7**	When we have gone without water for some time, we are (1) * * * to drink water, and we are (2) * * * to walk to a water fountain. **27-8**
generalized (conditioned generalized) **27-12**	When paired with several unconditioned reinforcers appropriate to various deprivations, a conditioned reinforcer will be effective under several types of _____. **27-13**
more than one (several, many) **27-17**	There are not many cases of primary reinforcers which are effective under more than one state of deprivation. Therefore, most generalized reinforcers * * * conditioned reinforcers. **27-18**
independent of (unaffected by) **27-22**	When a response has been reinforced by a stimulus previously paired only with a single unconditioned reinforcer, the response is * * * a particular deprivation. **27-23**
deprivation **27-27**	In order to serve small portions without complaint, a table d'hôte restaurant may serve a large supply of delicious bread while the meal is being prepared. The restaurant is * * * the customers inexpensively. **27-28**
water deprivation **27-32**	"You can lead a horse to water, but you can't make him drink." This saying overlooks the possibility of controlling behavior through _____. **27-33**

never (no longer) 22-4	In Phase 2, since reinforcement no longer occurs, if the key-color were not changed, responses would be emitted at a gradually ____ rate for many hours because the response had been maintained on a variable-interval schedule. 22-5
smaller (lower, less) 22-15	The experiment demonstrates that colors which are not actually present when the response is reinforced nevertheless acquire some ____ over the response. 22-16
generalization gradient 22-26	If a high-pitched tone is often present when a response is reinforced, a tone of medium pitch should exert some ____ over the response. 22-27
discrimination 22-37	A young child may be reinforced when approaching a smiling parent but not reinforced when approaching a frowning parent. Under these conditions a(n) ____ will develop. 22-38
S^D 22-48	The patient may come to love or hate his psychoanalyst in ways which resemble his emotional reaction to one of his parents. The analyst might call this "transference." It involves ____. 22-49
$(S)\Delta_s$ 22-59	The child who calls only red books "red" may show some likelihood of saying "red" on seeing a red car. This is (1) ____ (TT); but the probability may be (2) ____ because red books and red cars are very different. 22-60
determines (sets, decides) 22-70	In the laboratory, when the experimenter arranges contingencies under which a single stimulus property is the occasion upon which a response is to be reinforced, even animals develop ____. 22-71

conditioned (secondary) unconditioned (primary) 27-1	A stimulus which is frequently paired with food becomes a(n) (1) ____ reinforcer. Such a stimulus will be effective in conditioning a response only if the animal is (2) ____ of ____. 27-2
unconditioned reinforcer (primary reinforcer) 27-6	Satiating a rat with food lowers the probability of pressing a bar if this behavior is a part of a(n) ____ of behavior which ends with ingestion of food. 27-7
is not 27-11	A stimulus which has been paired with unconditioned reinforcers appropriate to *many different* deprivations becomes a(n) ____ reinforcer. 27-12
unconditioned generalized 27-16	Although generalized reinforcers are usually conditioned reinforcers, there are cases (e.g., a thin soup or a malted milk) of unconditioned reinforcers appropriate to * * * condition(s) of deprivation. 27-17
without 27-21	The probability of a response previously reinforced by the phrase "that's correct" is largely * * * food deprivation. 27-22
(1) rate (frequency) (2) are not 27-26	When we make a child more likely to drink milk by restricting his water intake, we employ ____ in the control of behavior. 27-27
conditioned generalized 27-31	Cocktail lounges often serve free pretzels or potato chips. Since they are salty, they have an effect similar to ____ ____ and increase the sale of drinks.

declining (decreasing)	At regular intervals in Phase 2, the color, or wavelength, of the light projected on the key is _____.
22-5	**22-6**

control	Stimuli not present at reinforcement may acquire control over a response due to the _____ of the response in the presence of a similar stimulus.
22-16	**22-17**

control	If a high-pitched tone is often present when a response is reinforced, a tone of medium pitch should produce a rate of responding (1) _____ than that of a high-pitched tone and (2) _____ than that of a very low-pitched tone.
22-27	**22-28**

discrimination	A very young child may approach his parents in more or less the same way regardless of whether they are frowning or smiling. A smile has not yet become an (1) S_____ nor a frown an (2) S_____.
22-38	**22-39**

generalization stimulus (stimulus generalization)	A young child may pick up and listen to a telephone receiver at any time, but eventually the ring becomes a(n) (1) _____ (TT) for this response, and no ring a(n) (2) _____. (TT)
22-49	**22-50**

generalization low (small, decreased)	To bring the response "red" under control of redness, a single property, we reinforce the response in the presence of red objects of different shapes, sizes, etc. The *single* property, redness, acquires _____ over the response.
22-60	**22-61**

▷	In the usual experiment, pressing the bar is im mediately reinforced by the click of the feeding mechanism, a(n) (1) _____ reinforcer. Pressing the bar for food is part of a *chain* of behavior ending, as the food is eaten, in a(n) (2) _____ reinforcer. **27-1**
(1) will not (doesn't) (2) will not be (is not often) **27-5**	Bar pressing is immediately reinforced by the magazine click, a conditioned reinforcer. Behavior reinforced by a conditioned reinforcer varies with the deprivation appropriate to the _____ _____ used to establish the conditioned reinforcer. **27-6**
deprivation **27-10**	A generalized reinforcer * * * dependent upon one particular condition of deprivation. **27-11**
unconditioned **27-15**	A thin soup or a malted milk may reinforce either a food-deprived or a water-deprived organism, therefore, they are to some extent _____ _____ reinforcers. **27-16**
generalized reinforcer **27-20**	A generalized reinforcer can be used to condition a new response _____ (with or without?) many restrictions on which specific deprivation is present at the moment. **27-21**
is not **27-25**	Popular explanations of behavior frequently employ words like "want," "desire," or "need." The observable referent for these words is usually a high (1) _____ of responding. In such cases they (2) * * * really causes of the response rate. **27-26**
(1) decrease (prevent) (2) satiation **27-30**	A government which gives money as a bonus to a family each time a baby is born is using a(n) _____ _____ reinforcer to increase procreation instead of relying on a single deprivation. **27-31**

changed
(varied)

22-6

Phase 2. Lights of many different (1) * * * are projected on the (2) ____.

22-7

---

reinforcement

22-17

In *stimulus generalization*, a stimulus acquires control of a response due to reinforcement in the presence of a similar but different stimulus. The control exerted in Phase 2 by a 570-millimicron light demonstrates ____ ____. (TT)

22-18

---

(1) lower
(2) higher

22-28

The numbers of responses made to two monochromatic lights only 10 millimicrons apart are shown to be nearly the same on the ____ ____.

22-29

---

(1) $(S)^D$
(2) $(S)^\Delta$

22-39

The traveler who says "all the inhabitants of this country look alike" is essentially reporting the flatness of his own ____ ____.

22-40

---

(1) S^D
(2) S^Δ

22-50

The linguist distinguishes between two speech sounds which seem identical to many people. The two sounds normally control a single response in what is called (1) ____, but the linguist has acquired a(n) (2) ____.

22-51

---

control

22-61

When a single property of an object controls a response, we call the relation an *abstraction*. "Redness" is such a property. It never occurs alone. When a response is controlled by the isolated property of redness, we call it a(n) ____.

22-62

---

(1) chain
(acceptable:
unit)
(2) increases

27-4

A rat thoroughly satiated with food (1) * * * ingest food. A lever which in the past has operated only a feeding mechanism (2) * * * pressed by a rat satiated with food.

27-5

---

conditioned
reinforcer

27-9

Although the immediate reinforcement for pecking the key is a conditioned reinforcer (the click), the rate of pecking is higher for greater degrees of food _____.

27-10

---

is not

27-14

A thin soup or a malted milk is a(n) _____ reinforcer because its capacity to reinforce is largely independent of previous conditioning.

27-15

---

independent

27-19

Depriving an organism of food or water does not greatly change the rate of a response conditioned by a(n) _____ _____.

27-20

---

high

27-24

A high response rate * * * sufficient evidence for inferring a high level of deprivation because rate is influenced by other variables, such as the schedule of reinforcement.

27-25

---

sexual
deprivation

27-29

Legalized prostitution is sometimes recommended on the grounds that it may (1) _____ sexual attacks on innocent women by providing another means of (2) _____.

27-30

wavelengths (colors) key	Plotted in the figure are the average (1) _____ of _____ during comparable periods of time at each (2) _____ used.
22-7	22-8

stimulus generalization	With a minor exception, the greater the difference in wavelength, the _____ the difference in number of responses emitted during equal intervals of time.
22-18	22-19

generalization gradient	Two stimuli which we describe as "similar" are likely to show _____ (TT) in their control over behavior.
22-29	22-30

generalization gradient	The traveler who says "all the inhabitants look alike" has had too little contact to develop adequate _____ among the inhabitants.
22-40	22-41

generalization discrimination (acceptable: S^D)	When a distant doorbell rings, you may "make a mistake" and go to the phone. The doorbell exerts some (1) _____ over going to the phone. This phenomenon is called (2) _____.
22-51	22-52

abstraction	When a response is under the control of a single stimulus property which cannot occur or exist alone, we call it a(n) * * *.
22-62	22-63

low (reduced)	In general, after the ingestion of a considerable amount of food, the probability of all operant behavior previously reinforced with food is _____.
26-8	26-9 ← To p. 182

higher rate (higher frequency)	Vigorous activity on a hot day causes sweating. The resulting loss of water increases the frequency of behavior previously reinforced by _____.
26-18	26-19 ← To p. 182

probability	When we see an individual drinking a large quantity of water, we usually infer a recent history of _____.
26-28	26-29 ← To p. 182

decreases (declines)	The experiment demonstrates that as deprivation (1) _____, the rate of an operant reinforced with food (2) _____.
26-38	26-39 ← To p. 182

(1) class (set, group) (2) water deprivation	If several different operants have been previously reinforced with water, then water *satiation* will (1) _____ the frequency of this whole (2) _____ of responses.
26-48	26-49 ← To p. 182

similar (the same)	Administration of salt, induction of sweating, and deprivation of water are members of a class of procedures. Responses reinforced by water are increased by _____ of these.
26-58	26-59 ← To p. 182

class (set, group)	End of Set
26-68	

(1) number (of) responses (2) wavelength **22-8**	The only wavelength which had ever been present when the response was reinforced was * * * milli-microns. **22-9**
greater **22-19**	Phase 2. The stimulus control exhibited by any given color is measured by the * * * which occur when that color is projected on the key. **22-20**
generalization **22-30**	When an abstract sculpture generates emotional responses resembling those generated by the human body, the effect is sometimes attributed to "symbolism." It is an example of ____ ____. **22-31**
scrimination(s) **22-41**	An organism may emit the same response to two similar stimuli when only one of them has been present during reinforcement. The term for this phenomenon is ____ ____. **22-42**
control generalization **22-52**	Bells, whistles, and traffic signals, as S^Ds, are all occasions upon which appropriate responses will be ____ if emitted. **22-53**
abstraction **22-63**	In an abstraction, a response is under the control of a ____ property of a stimulus (or set of stimuli). **22-64**

is not 26-7	After a heavy meal, the probability of immediately ingesting more food is ____. 26-8
increases 26-17	A soldier who is both incapacitated by wounds and dehydrated by loss of blood emits the verbal operant "Water!" at a(n)____ ____ than normally. 26-18
satiation 26-27	The common phrase "an animal gradually grows more thirsty" crudely describes an increased ____ of drinking behavior caused by water deprivation. 26-28
decreases (declines) 26-37	As the session progresses, the total amount eaten gradually increases so that the rat's deprivation gradually ____. 26-38
ood 26-47	Reaching for a water pitcher, asking for a glass of water, and walking to a drinking fountain, are all responses belonging to the (1) ____ of responses whose probability increases with (2) ____ ____. 26-48
s 26-57	Water deprivation, salt ingestion, and sweating are a class of operations or processes which increase the rate of emission of responses reinforced by water. Several procedures may have * * * effects on behavior reinforced by water. 26-58
ctivity atiation 26-67	For each state of deprivation, there are usually many alternative procedures which have the same effect on a whole ____ of responses. 26-68

← To p. 150

550

22-9

If the 550 millimicron light were the only one which acquired control as a result of Phase 1, then _____ responses would have been emitted to the other lights presented in Phase 2.

22-10
← To p. 150

---

number of
responses
[rate (since
time is
constant)] 22-20

Light of 560 millimicrons (1) * * * present when the response was reinforced; but the figure reveals that light of this wavelength (2) * * * exert considerable control over the rate of responding.

22-21
← To p. 150

---

stimulus
generalization

22-31

Generalization often depends on common elements in two or more stimuli. The control exercised by a black triangular form generalizes to a white triangular form because they have a given shape in _____ .

22-32
← To p. 150

---

stimulus
generalization

22-42

A stimulus which closely *precedes* or accompanies a reinforced response acquires control over that response. The stimulus becomes a(n) _____ for the response.

22-43
← To p. 150

---

reinforced

22-53

"Red, white, and . . ." If you tend to say "blue," you show the _____ which this chain of verbal stimuli exerts over the verbal response "blue."

22-54
← To p. 150

---

single
(isolated)

22-64

Every red object has a specific shape, size, etc. Isolated properties of stimuli * * * alone in nature.

22-65
← To p. 150

---

necessary (essential, vital) 26-6	Ingestive behavior * * * biologically useful to a man with a *full* stomach. 26-7
depriv(-ing) 26-16	An excessive amount of salt taken in food must be excreted in solution. Salty food therefore ____ the frequency of the operant behavior called "getting a drink of water." 26-17
deprivation 26-26	Saying "a man is *not* hungry" refers to a level of probability of his ingestive behavior which is most commonly brought about by the procedure termed ____. 26-27
58 26-36	The figure shows that, as the session progresses, the rate of responding gradually ____. 26-37
all (each of) 26-46	When a response is reinforced with *food*, it becomes a member of a class of responses whose rate increases with deprivation of ____. 26-47
(1) increase (2) class (3) water 26-56	Excessive sweating due to heavy work or emotion * * * similar to water deprivation in its effect on the class of responses previously reinforced by water. 26-57
deprivation 26-66	Drugs which decrease activity are similar in effect to ____ ____. 26-67

scriminative
nulus)

23-5

At the same time that sight of food is an S^D for seizing food, it is a(n) * * * for bending down to the food magazine and looking in.

23-6

precedes
(produces)

23-11

A reinforcing stimulus (1) _____ a response which it reinforces. A discriminative stimulus (2) _____ a response which it controls. (TEMPORAL ANSWERS)

23-12

chain

23-17

Each stimulus in a chain has the dual function of reinforcing the response it (1) _____ and being an S^D for the response it (2) _____. (TEMPORAL ANSWERS)

23-18

chain

23-23

When the red key-light, as an S^D, is controlling the key-pecking response, any response which "produces" the red key-light is _____.

23-24

S^D

23-29

When the pigeon "looks at" a key, which is sometimes red (S^D for pecking), the behavior of orienting its eyes toward the key is (1) _____ by the red key, and the behavior of looking is added to the beginning of the (2) _____.

23-30

does not
(should not)

23-35

A billboard which "catches our attention" is one at which we are likely to look. We look at other billboards if earlier ones contained stimuli which _____ "looking" behavior.

23-36

(1) respondent (reflex) (2) conditioned operant 26-5	Behavior reinforced by intake of water is * * * to the survival of the organism. 26-6
more probable (more frequent) 26-15	Causing an animal to lose water through the excretion of sweat or urine has the same effect on drinking as ____-ing it of water. 26-16
has (is of) 26-25	A parent who complains that a child is a "fussy" eater is advised to forbid between-meal snacks. The operation appealed to in such a case is ____. 26-26
continuous 26-35	During the first 30 minutes, the rat pressed the bar 58 times and received (and ingested) ____ pellets. 26-36
increases the probability (increases the rate) 26-45	In most animals, many different responses have been reinforced with food. Food deprivation will increase the probability of ____ these responses. 26-46
decline (fall, drop) 26-55	Eating heavily salted food and being deprived of water both (1) ____ the probability of the entire (2) ____ of responses which have been reinforced with (3) ____. 26-56
satiation 26-65	Drugs (such as benzedrine) which increase activity are similar in effect to activity ____. 26-66

| | In the usual pigeon experiment, the sight of food sets the occasion upon which seizing food is ____ (TT) by food in the mouth.

23-1 |

| reinforcing stimulus (reinforcer)

23-6 | This sequence forms a chain: bending down, seeing food, seizing food. Sight of food is a(n) (1) * * * for bending down to food and a(n) (2) * * * for seizing food.

23-7 |

| 1) follows
2) precedes

23-12 | In the usual experiment, when closure of a key operates a feeding mechanism, the noise of the feeding mechanism follows and ____ (TT) the response of pecking the key.

23-13 |

| 1) follows
2) precedes

23-18 | The sequence of stimuli and responses between pecking the key and food in the mouth is called a(n) ____.

23-19 |

| reinforced

23-24 | If the apparatus is so designed that a red key-light flashes on automatically when the pigeon stretches its neck, neck stretching is (1) ____ by the red light (the S^D for pecking), and neck stretching is added to the (2) ____.

23-25 |

| 1) reinforced
2) chain

23-30 | The pigeon is more likely to "see" the key turn red if it orients its eyes toward ("looks at") the key. This behavior of orienting the eyes is intermittently reinforced by the view of a(n) ____. (TT)

23-31 |

| reinforced

23-36 | The radar operator searches the radarscope for small luminous blips; if none appear, the behavior of scanning the scope with eye and head movements is ____.

23-37 |

unconditioned respondent 26-4	Swallowing water which is already in the mouth is mainly unconditioned (1) _____ (TT) behavior. Finding water and putting it into the mouth is mainly (2) _____ _____ behavior. 26-5
less probable (less frequent) 26-14	The longer an organism goes without water, the _____ _____ becomes any behavior previously reinforced by water. 26-15
would 26-24	Animals which do not eat or drink sufficient quantities when severely deprived of food or water will die. Increased ingestive behavior in deprived animals * * * survival value. 26-25
24 hours 26-34	In this experiment every response is reinforced. Thereby, bar pressing is said to be under _____ reinforcement. 26-35
seven (all these) 26-44	When many different responses have successfully produced food, then food deprivation * * * of all these responses. 26-45
satiating 26-54	On some intermittent schedules, the animal may receive very little food as reinforcement. Thus, level of deprivation does not _____ as quickly under intermittent reinforcement as under continuous reinforcement. 26-55
deprivation 26-64	Forcing an animal to keep moving, as on a motor-driven treadmill, produces a reduction in activity when the animal is released. Forced activity is a form of _____ since it reduces subsequent activity. 26-65

reinforced	The sight of food is a(n) _____ stimulus for seizing food.
23-1	23-2

(1) reinforcing stimulus (reinforcer) (2) S^D	In the simple chain (bending down, seeing food, seizing food), the two responses are "linked together" in that bending down produces (and is reinforced by) a stimulus which is the S^D for * * *.
23-7	23-8

reinforces	In the usual experiment, when a key operates the feeding mechanism which makes a noise, the pigeon bends down to the feeding mechanism. The noise is a(n) _____ for bending down.
23-13	23-14

chain	If the chain of behavior is seldom broken, all of it is treated as a unit. The phrase "the operant behavior of pecking a key for food" describes a well-integrated chain as though it were a(n) _____ of behavior.
23-19	23-20

(1) reinforced (2) chain	A key was raised and shielded so that the pigeon had to raise its head to see it. Raising the head was (1) _____ by any color on the key which served as a(n) (2) _____ for pecking the key.
23-25	23-26

S^D	Responses described as "looking," "searching," "attending," etc., which generally produce stimuli, frequently occur early in a(n) _____.
23-31	23-32

extinguished	End of Set
23-37	

water (liquids) 26-3	Ingestive behavior (e.g., eating) which is important for survival may involve respondent, conditioned or unconditioned, and operant behavior. Swallowing water which is already in the mouth is mainly ____ ____ behavior. 26-4
decreases (drops) 26-13	In general, the more food an animal has just eaten, the ____ ____ its ingestive behavior. 26-14
decreases (reduces, lowers) 26-23	If satiation *did not* make food-getting and eating behavior less frequent, biologically use*less* behavior * * * occupy much of an animal's time. 26-24
immediately (rapidly) 26-33	The rat has ingested no food for * * * before being placed in the box. 26-34
decreases (lowers, reduces) 26-43	If seven different operants have been reinforced with food, then food deprivation will increase the probability of ____ operants. 26-44
(1) satiated (2) one 26-53	By using very small bits of food, the experimenter can reinforce a response many times without____ the animal. 26-54
class 26-63	Confining an animal in a limited space produces an increase in activity above the normal level when the animal is released. Confinement is a form of ____ since it increases subsequent activity. 26-64

discriminative **23-2**	Bending down to the food magazine makes the food visible. The *sight* of food (a conditioned reinforcer) ____ bending down to the magazine. **23-3**
seizing food (next response in chain) **23-8**	In a chain of behavior, the same stimulus is both a(n) (1) * * * and a(n) (2) * * *. **23-9**
S^D (occasion) **23-14**	The noise from the operation of the feeding mechanism is a(n) (1) ____ stimulus for key pecking and a(n) (2) ____ stimulus for bending down to the feeding mechanism. **23-15**
unit **23-20**	An operant is rather arbitrarily designated as "key pecking," "walking," etc. It is implied that a well-integrated chain is functioning as a(n) ____ of operant behavior. **23-21**
(1) reinforced (2) S^D **23-26**	The pigeon raises its head to the level of a shielded key and "looks at the color." Because the color is a(n) ____ for pecking, the pigeon pecks and is reinforced with food. **23-27**
chain **23-32**	When the pigeon raises its head and "looks at" or "attends to" a shielded key, the behavior *produces* or *clarifies* the S^D in that it brings the S^D clearly into view. What is colloquially called "attending" is a response which ____ an S^D. **23-33**

individual (organism, member) 26-2	Biological processes cannot go on in dry tissue. The drying out of the body of an organism (such as man) is prevented if responses are emitted which result in the intake of ____. 26-3
(1) increase (2) depriving 26-12	The probability that an animal will engage in behavior previously reinforced with food ____ as it ingests a large quantity of food. 26-13
deprivation (food deprivation) 26-22	Satiation is an operation which in general ____ the probability of responding. 26-23
conditioned (reinforced) 26-32	In the exhibit experiment, it is clear that bar pressing has already been conditioned because the rat begins responding ____. 26-33
declines 26-42	A pigeon has been reinforced with food for pecking a key, stretching its neck, and walking in a circle. Satiation with food ____ the frequency of *all* these responses. 26-43
(1) reinforces (2) deprivation 26-52	It would be inefficient to train your dog by giving it a full day's ration after a single response because the dog would be substantially (1) ____ after only (2) ____ reinforcement. 26-53
deprivation 26-62	Sexual deprivation and the use of drugs and hormones which increase the frequency of sexual behavior belong to a single ____ of procedures. 26-63

reinforces 23-3	We have been using the term "reinforcer" for "reinforcing stimulus." Since reinforcers are certain stimuli which follow responses, a synonym for reinforcer is ____ ____. 23-4
discriminative stimulus (S^D) reinforcing stimulus (reinforcer) THER ORDER) 23-9	A stimulus will become an S^D when a(n) (1) ____ which regularly follows it is reinforced. An S^D will become a conditioned reinforcer when (2) ____ regularly follows it closely in time. 23-10
reinforcing discriminative (S^D) 23-15	Bending down to the magazine makes food visible, and the pigeon seizes food with its beak. With respect to seizing food, the sight of food is a(n) (1) ____. With respect to bending down, sight of food is a(n) (2) ____. 23-16
unit 23-21	If pecking is reinforced when a red key-light is on, but not when other key-lights are on, the red key-light becomes a(n) ____ for "key pecking." 23-22
S^D 23-27	The pigeon raises its head and looks at the color of a shielded key. If the color on the key is an S^D, looking at the key is ____. 23-28
produces (clarifies) 23-33	We might say that an S^D is effective only if the organism "attends to" it. "Attending" is not a mental event; it is a general name for behavior which produces or clarifies a(n) ____. 23-34

species 26-1	Operants reinforced by food are involved in the survival of each ____ of the species. 26-2
more probable (more frequent) 26-11	We can (1) ____ the probability of drinking by depriving an organism of water. We can increase the probability that an organism will eat by (2) ____ it of food. 26-12
deprived 26-21	From a practical point of view, to get an individual to eat we may use the operation called ____. 26-22
(1) deprived (2) reinforcer 26-31	READ EXHIBIT ON PAGE 181 AND REFER TO IT AS NEEDED. Prior to the experimental session during which the record shown in the exhibit was obtained, the response (bar pressing) had already been ____. 26-32
lower 26-41	The figure shows that the rate of responding declines as the degree of deprivation ____. 26-42
(1) reinforces (2) decreases (reduces, lowers) 26-51	Ingested food (1) ____ a response which it follows; it also reduces food (2) ____. 26-52
(1) lowered (decreased) (2) increases 26-61	If the probability of sexual behavior is increased by administration of certain hormones or of "aphrodisiacs," the effect is similar to that of sexual ____. 26-62

reinforcing stimulus 23-4	The same stimulus may be both a reinforcing stimulus and an S^D. The sight of food is a(n) * * * for seizing food but a reinforcing stimulus (i.e., reinforcer) for bending and looking into the magazine. **23-5** ← To p. 161
) response) reinforcement 23-10	When a stimulus has become an S^D for one response, it is also a reinforcer for any other response which _____ it. ← To p. 161**23-11**
(1) S^D (2) reinforcer 23-16	When a response produces an S^D for another response, the two form a chain. The sequence of events, beginning with pecking the key and ending with food in the mouth, forms a(n) _____ of responses. **23-17** ← To p. 161
S^D 23-22	When a red key-light has become an S^D for pecking, the red light has been added to the beginning of a(n) _____ of responses. **23-23** ← To p. 161
reinforced 23-28	In the pigeon experiments, looking at the key is reinforced by the _____ for pecking the key. **23-29** ← To p. 161
S^D (stimulus) 23-34	"Attending" * * * imply a mental event but rather a kind of behavior. **23-35** ← To p. 161

Operant behavior often has biological significance for survival of the individual or the species. Responses reinforced by sexual contact have an obvious bearing on the survival of the _____.

26-1

---

more (highly)

26-10

When an organism has been without water for a period of time, behavior previously reinforced by water becomes _____ _____.

26-11

---

(1) increases
   (raises)
(2) deprivation

26-20

A hungry man is generally one who has been _____ of food.

26-21

---

satiation

26-30

In many experiments discussed earlier in the course, organisms were (1) _____ of food before being placed in the experimental box. This was done whenever food was to be used as a(n) (2) _____.

26-31

---

negatively

26-40

If the rat had been given some food before the session began, the initial rate of responding would have been _____.

26-41

---

(1) reinforced
   (conditioned)
(2) class of (all)

26-50

In the exhibit experiment, after each response the rat receives food which (1) _____ the response. The food also (2) _____ the deprivation level.

26-51

---

class
(set, group)

26-60

Immediately after orgasm, the probability of further sexual behavior is (1) _____; as time passes (i.e., as sexual deprivation increases), the probability of this behavior (2) _____.

26-61

Many highly skilled forms of behavior, e.g., drawing pictures, singing, etc., require a *continuous repertoire* — a set of responses differing from one another only very slightly (when the response field is said to be continuous) and under the control of discriminative stimuli also differing from one another only very slightly (when the stimulus field is said to be continuous). In *drawing* a straight line with a given slope, the response field is composed of all the movements which produce an indefinitely large family of lines:

In *copying* a straight line with a given slope, the stimuli are a similar family of lines. With an adequate repertoire, the subject can draw a line with a slope close to any slope given to him to be copied. Differences between slopes can be as small as desired. In the same way, a good singer can sing a pitch which corresponds to a pitch he hears, where both stimulus and response fields are also practically continuous.

Many such skills are shaped quite gradually during the individual's life. The contingencies may be arranged in formal training (as in art or music instruction, driver training, etc.) or left to the vicissitudes of the environment. Once a child has acquired the ability to be reinforced when the "produced stimulus" matches the "stimulus to be copied," shaping may proceed without the frequent intervention of another person. Learning includes (1) discriminating subtle differences among stimuli to be imitated (in the *continuous stimulus field*) and (2) discriminating among those stimuli produced and (3) executing movements showing subtle differences of the *continuous response field*.

low (reduced) 26-9	When an animal has been without food, its conditioned and unconditioned ingestive behavior becomes _____ probable when food is again available. 26-10
water 26-19	Deprivation is a procedure which in general (1) _____ the probability of a group of responses. The probability of food-related behavior occurring is increased by food (2) _____. 26-20
deprivation 26-29	When a horse led to water does not drink, we can infer a recent history of _____. 26-30
(1) decreases (2) decreases 26-39	Since the rate of responding is declining, the curve is _____ (positively or negatively?) accelerated. 26-40
(1) decrease (reduce) (2) class (set, group) of 26-49	Food deprivation increases the probability of the whole class of responses which have been (1) _____ with food. Water deprivation increases the probability of the (2) * * * responses which have been reinforced with water. 26-50
each (all) 26-59	Responses reinforced by a given reinforcer will be increased in probability by a whole _____ of deprivation-like procedures. 26-60

Set 24

PART VI   Stimulus Control

Shaping Continuous Repertoires

See exhibit on preceding page

Estimated time: 20 minutes

Turn to next page and begin ▶

(1) be no
(2) would not

24-6

A parent may reinforce a child for making a particular drawing movement (as by saying "Good!" or "How pretty!"). The relative frequency of such movements will then ____.

24-7

---

differential

24-13

A particular "produced" visual pattern * * * closely related to the hand movements which produced it.

24-14

---

(1) reinforce
(2) extinguish
   (do not
   reinforce,
   not)   24-20

In teaching a child to draw a more complex picture, we may show him a picture and reinforce any drawing made by the child which ____ it in some respect.

24-21

S^D (stimulus)

24-27

When the property of likeness in the child's drawing has become an S^D for showing us the drawing, the property of likeness will also ____ the drawing movements which produce the likeness.

24-28

---

is not (is no
longer, will
no longer be)

24-34

When a child cannot discriminate between a perfect reproduction of a picture and a fair reproduction, the automatic reinforcement is as great for a(n) ____ reproduction as for a perfect one.

24-35

---

sound
("s," sound
produced)

24-41

The adage "practice makes perfect" is probably true only if some product of one's behavior provides ____ ____.

24-42

Exhibit for

Set 26   Do not read exhibit yet. Wait until instructed
to do so.

A white rat is placed in a standard experimental space having a horizontal bar protruding from one wall. The rat has been deprived of food for 24 hours. Pressing the bar operates a food magazine which drops a small ($\frac{1}{15}$ grain) pellet of food into a tray.

The rat has previously been adapted to the box and to the sound of the magazine and has been reinforced many times for pressing the bar.

As an experimental session progresses, the rat ingests more and more pellets, becomes less food *deprived* or closer to being *satiated* with food. The cumulative record of bar presses is presented below.

Figure 1

In moving a pencil more or less at random across paper, a child produces lines. If those visual stimuli _____ the responses which produce them, the child will tend to "scribble."

24-1

---

increase

24-7

If the parent reinforces a movement which produces a particular pattern, eventually that produced pattern will _____ that movement itself.

24-8

---

is

24-14

When the child is reinforced by certain of the patterns he produces on paper and not by mere scribbles, his drawing responses are being _____ _____.

24-15

---

resembles

24-21

After differentially reinforcing movements which produce crude copies, we may later reinforce only movements which successively _____ a good match.

24-22

---

reinforce
(differentially
reinforce)

24-28

A parent may reinforce patterns of movements producing figures which "look a little like" a picture in a book Soon, stimuli produced which "look like" something * * * conditioned reinforcers.

24-29

---

fair

24-35

The artist who cannot discriminate the subtle properties of a model's smile cannot paint it. The painter has not developed an adequate _____.

24-36

---

differential
reinforcement

24-42

End of Set

can (might) 25-4	The positions of reachable objects constitute a continuous field in the sense that any position has adjacent positions on all sides. In other words, there * * * gaps, holes, or breaks in the field. 25-5 ← To p. 175
greater (larger) 25-10	"Reaching for an object" refers to a movement made in a particular direction which is reinforced by (1) ____ with an object which is in a particular (2) ____. ← To p. 175 25-11
topographies (forms) 25-16	All reaching movements need not be separately conditioned. After being reinforced for touching two points which are fairly close together, it is likely that a person * * * efficiently touch a point between them. 25-17 ← To p. 175
is similar to (is like, resembles) 25-22	A person who can "make a good copy of any line" must possess a repertoire consisting of a(n) ____ number of drawing responses which produce an indefinite number of possible lines. 25-23 ← To p. 175
is (requires, constitutes) 25-28	Skillfully drawing from copy requires a(n) ____ ____. 25-29 ← To p. 175
(1) can (2) cannot (may not be able to) 25-34	With a continuous repertoire, a person * * * able to respond to discrete points in a stimulus field. 25-35 ← To p. 175

reinforce 24-1	Lines drawn in scribbling **are** not wholly random. They reveal the natural lever-like movements of hand and arm. Therefore, all forms of responses * * * occur with equal frequency even prior to differential reinforcement. 24-2
reinforce 24-8	When a child has been reinforced for drawing a particular pattern, that pattern, having been paired with a reinforcer, can itself become a ____ ____. 24-9
differentially reinforced 24-15	After certain produced visual patterns have become reinforcing, in the future the patterns of movements which produce them are reinforced by the * * *. 24-16
approximate 24-22	In gradually raising our standards, first reinforcing crude copies and later better and better copies, we are shaping "drawing from copy" in ____ ____. 24-23
will be (become) 24-29	When "drawing from copy" has been well conditioned, a drawn line which resembles a line being copied ____ the movement of drawing it, even if the parent occasionally provides no reinforcement. 24-30
discrimination 24-36	An artist working without a model cannot paint the subtle properties of a smile unless he can discriminate those properties because the painting movements will not receive precise ____ ____. (TT) 24-37

movement (reaching) 25-3	The positions taken by objects within our reach comprise a continuous three-dimensional field. An object can be in any position in that field, and two positions * * * differ by as small a distance as we can specify. 25-4
(1) position (point) (2) continuous 25-9	The finer the differences in the positions of objects within reach (i.e., the greater the number of possible positions), the _____ the number of different reaching movements. 25-10
stimuli (S^{D}s) 25-15	A continuous response field is one having many responses of only slightly different _____. 25-16
discrete 25-21	To copy a line, the artist must first look at a stimulus and then respond in a manner which produces a drawing which * * * the pattern being copied. 25-22
discrete repertoire 25-27	A movement producing a specific line can differ from another movement by as small an amount as we can distinguish. Therefore, the behavior of drawing lines skillfully * * * a continuous repertoire. 25-28
(1) discrete repertoire (2) continuous repertoire 25-33	One who can copy all sorts of lines and patterns (1) * * * copy the alphabet, but one who has only the discrete repertoire of copying 26 block letters (2) * * * copy a drawing or even letters of an unfamiliar style. 25-34

do not 24-2	It is useless to ask a child to copy a picture until he has acquired a(n) _____ repertoire of drawing responses. 24-3
conditioned reinforcer 24-9	The scribbling child may produce a line which looks to him like a pattern which has already been reinforced. The scribbled line, therefore, to some extent automatically _____ the movement which produces it. 24-10
produced visual pattern (drawn copy) 24-16	When a child is learning to "draw from copy," the picture to be copied consists of visual (1) _____ which act upon the child (2) _____ (TEMPORAL ANSWER) he has made the first drawing movement. 24-17
successive approximations 24-23	If we raise our standard for reinforcing a child's drawings too rapidly, even the best of his responses will not be reinforced. His drawing behavior will * * *. 24-24
reinforces 24-30	Producing a pattern like a pattern to be copied is said to be _____ reinforced because only successful movements are reinforced while movements producing unlike patterns are not. 24-31
differential reinforcement 24-37	A so-called tone-deaf person often has perfectly adequate sensory mechanisms. Such a person has not acquired adequate _____ of tones. 24-38

continuous field	In reaching for an object, the direction of _____ of the arm and hand is controlled by the position of the object in the field of vision.
25-2	25-3

position (object)	A man who is very skillful in reaching and touching objects has a "continuous" repertoire of reaching movements which brings him into contact with objects at any (1) _____ in a(n) (2) _____ field.
25-8	25-9

topographies	Each reaching response has its own topography and is under the control of appropriate _____ supplied by an object in a position in space.
25-14	25-15

discrete	A response which brings the hunt-and-peck typist's finger tip *between* two keys is not reinforced. Typing behavior is not continuous; rather it is a set of _____ responses.
25-20	25-21

continuous	Discrete movements under the control of stimuli forming a discrete field comprise a(n) _____ _____.
25-26	25-27

26 (discrete)	The ability to copy the alphabet in block letters involves a(n) (1) _____ _____ while the ability to copy any line involves a(n) (2) _____ _____.
25-32	25-33

continuous 24-3	A child who simply "likes to scribble" is said to be _____ by the lines he produces regardless of direction, change of direction, or length. 24-4
reinforces 24-10	Only a few of the stimuli produced by scribbling movements will resemble special reinforcing patterns. Hence, such patterns will reinforce only a few of the _____ in scribbling. 24-11
(1) stimuli (patterns) (2) before 24-17	Two visual stimuli are present when a line has been copied. The line to be copied occurred first; it was followed by the line * * *. 24-18
be extinguished 24-24	A child can be conditioned to call two visual patterns "like" or "unlike," quite apart from learning to draw. We present two patterns and reinforce "like" if they are (1) _____ and extinguish "like" if they are (2) _____. 24-25
differentially 24-31	Skill in "drawing from copy" will continue to be shaped in the parent's absence once "likeness" has been established as a(n) _____ for the drawing movements. 24-32
discrimination 24-38	A so-called tone-deaf person cannot sing because he cannot (1) _____ differences in tones he is to match. The sounds he produces do not provide automatic reinforcement which (2) _____ good as opposed to poor pitch. 24-39

continuous repertoire 25-1	An adult can usually reach for and touch either of two objects which lie very close together in the field of vision. Most adults have a(n) ____ ____ of reaching movements. 25-2
continuous field 25-7	The movements with which we touch objects within reach may also comprise a continuous field in the sense that for any movement there is another movement which will reach an adjacent ____. 25-8
topography 25-13	Differences between two movements are described as differences in the topographies of the responses. Objects at two adjacent points usually control reaching responses of only slightly different ____. 25-14
do not 25-19	Some collections of stimuli have discrete, as opposed to continuous, differences among them. The keys on a typewriter occupy ____ positions. 25-20
continuous 25-25	A repertoire of a continuous-response field under control of stimuli forming a continuous field is a(n) ____ repertoire. 25-26
discrete 25-31	If we call the behavior of printing a letter one response, then the behavior of copying the 26 letters of the alphabet in block letters comprises a repertoire of ____ responses. 25-32

reinforced 24-4	A child who "likes to scribble" gets more (1) _____ the more he (2) _____. 24-5
movements (responses) 24-11	When only certain produced patterns are reinforcing, movements which produced ordinary *scribbled* lines * * * reinforced. 24-12
drawn (copied) 24-18	In teaching a child to draw from copy, we reinforce a given movement only if it results in a(n) _____ resembling the line he was asked to copy. 24-19
(1) alike (2) unlike 24-25	If a child calls two visual patterns "like" when they are alike, the stimulus which controls this verbal response must show the "property of likeness." Since this property never occurs in isolation, the response is an example of _____. 24-26
reinforcer (conditioned differential reinforcer) 24-32	The better a child can discriminate "like" patterns, the _____ precise the automatic differential reinforcement of his drawing behavior. 24-33
(1) discriminate (2) differentiate 24-39	Many children articulate the "s" sound and yet say "Thammy Thnake" for "Sammy Snake." Usually these children cannot yet tell which of these sounds another person is saying; they cannot _____ between the "s" and the "th" sounds. 24-40

In a continuous repertoire, two responses may differ by only a very slight amount. Reaching for objects around you is a(n) _____ _____.

25-1

---

position

25-6

A continuum of stimuli comprises a continuous field when we can discriminate very fine differences between adjacent stimuli on the continuum. Points in space are in a(n) _____ _____.

25-7

---

indefinite

25-12

Two movements in a continuous field of movements may have only slightly different forms or *topographies*. Thus, another name for form of response is response _____.

25-13

---

forty

25-18

The keys on a typewriter, as "objects within reach," occupy *discrete* positions. There are in-between positions not occupied by keys. The keys * * * comprise a continuous field.

25-19

---

differs

25-24

Lines on a surface comprise a(n) _____ two-dimensional field.

25-25

---

discrete
repertoire

25-30

One letter differs from another by considerably more than a barely distinguishable amount; thus copying the alphabet requires a(n) _____ repertoire.

25-31

---

is not

25-36

Someone just learning to drive turns the wheel in large jerky movements. The novice still has a(n) _____ repertoire.

25-37

reinforcement scribbles **24-5**	If all scribbled marks were equally reinforcing, there would (1) * * * differential reinforcement of scribbling behavior (and the child's scribbling (2) * * * "improve"). **24-6** ← To p. 168
are not **24-12**	When certain drawing movements are reinforced and other drawing movements are not, reinforcement is ____. **24-13** ← To p. 168
line (mark, pattern) **24-19**	In teaching a child to copy a line, we do not wait for a perfect match. We (1) ____ all movements producing lines which are fairly similar to the copy, but (2) ____ movements producing lines which are very different from the copy. **24-20** ← To p. 168
abstraction **24-26**	If we repeatedly reinforce a child only when the picture he draws is much like the picture to be copied, the "property of likeness" becomes a(n) ____ for his behavior of showing us his successful drawings. **24-27** ← To p. 168
more **24-33**	After the property of likeness in a drawing has been established as a reinforcer, the presence of the parent * * * required for further differential reinforcement. **24-34** ← To p. 168
discriminate **24-40**	After the child has learned to discriminate between "s" and "th," his correct production of "s" will be differentially reinforced automatically by the * * *. **24-41** ← To p. 168

Set 25

---

are no

For each _____ that an object within reach may occupy in our field of vision, there corresponds a particular movement of arm and hand which will produce tactual contact with the object.

25-5   25-6

---

(1) contact
(2) position

There are an indefinite number of reaching responses and a corresponding _____ number of possible positions in a continuous field.

25-11   25-12

---

can

A hunt-and-peck typist must reach for about forty keys on the typewriter. Efficient typing requires at least _____ different discrete responses.

25-17   25-18

---

indefinite
(large)

A line can always be drawn which _____ from another line by as small an amount as we can distinguish.

25-23   25-24

---

continuous
repertoire

The behavior of typewriting requires a(n) _____ _____ .

25-29   25-30

---

is

With a discrete repertoire, the person * * * able to respond to all points of a continuous stimulus field.

25-35   25-36